3 b

D0203468

DATE DUE

Creating and Funding
Educational Foundations

RELATED TITLES OF INTEREST

CREATING AND FUNDING EDUCATIONAL FOUNDATIONS

A Guide for Local School Districts

James J. Muro
The University of North Texas

Allyn and Bacon
Boston • London • Toronto • Sydney • Tokyo • Singapore

Copyright © 1995 by Allyn and Bacon
A Division of Paramount Publishing
160 Gould Street
Needham Heights, Massachusetts 02194

Library of Congress Cataloging-in-Publication Data

Muro, James J.
    Creating and funding educational foundations : a guide for local
school districts / James J. Muro
        p.   cm.
    Includes bibliographical references and index.
    ISBN 0-205-15573-1
    1. Education—United States—Finance.   2. Public schools—
United States—Finance.   3. Endowments—United States.   4. Public
Education Fund Network (U.S.)   I. Title.
LB2825.M789   1995   94-7814
371.2′06--dc20   CIP

Printed in the United States of America

10 9 8 7 6 5 4 3 2 1   98 97 96 95 94

To Dr. Clovis Morrisson, Professor of Political Science,
The University of North Texas, Denton, Texas—
who taught me a lot about fund-raising,
and a lot about courage.

CONTENTS

PREFACE

Throughout this book are numerous references to an organization called PEFNet, the Public Education Fund Network. Although many school districts in the United States have been actively seeking community support for public education, efforts have been scattered and have lacked a national focus. It is the belief of the author that the Public Education Fund Network can provide the national leadership to assist communities to build citizen awareness of the need to support high-quality public education and assist in positive school reform.

PEFNet is a national association of local education funds (LEFs) from across the nation. It lists as its major mission that of improving public education for all children, especially the disadvantaged. The vehicle for such improvement is the creation of broad-based community organizations who in turn utilize private money to engage and educate their communities about quality education (PEFNet, no date, p. 1).

Initially a Ford Foundation initiative, PEFNet has roots in community-based efforts in school reform in San Francisco, Washington, DC, and Pittsburgh, Pennsylvania. David Bergholz, writing in the *Teachers College Record* notes that as executive director of the Public Education Fund, he and his associates were able to provide seed money to 53 local funds across the country. This was accomplished with the assistance of a six-million dollar grant from the Ford Foundation. Evolving from a community-based public information advisory committee to a group called the Allegheny Conference Education Fund, Bergholz's organization was successful in bringing together school officials and other community leaders. The group also articulated the needs of the schools to the business, civic, and philanthropic communities. Programs included the minigrants to teachers programs that were developed at grass-roots levels to assist board development at higher levels.

In 1982, the Ford Foundation made a grant of $35,000 to the Allegheny Conference to plan a national enterprise that would seed the development of organizations similar to the Allegheny Conference Fund in other communities. The planning grant led to the founding of the Public Education Fund in 1983. The fund was chaired by Fletcher Byrom, a retired Pittsburgh-based executive of the Kippers Company, with Michael Timpane, president of Teachers College, Columbia, as its vice chairman. Bergholz, on loan from the Allegheny Conference, served as president. Although the Public Education Fund had intended to go out of business at the end of five years (1983–1987), a continued need for assistance led to the creation of PEFNet in 1990. The organization is now an independent enterprise located at 601 Thirteenth Street, NW, Suite 370 South, Washington, DC 20005 (Bergholz, 1992).

Today PEFNet operates under six guiding principles:

- Public education is fundamental to a democratic and civil society.
- Public schools are critical institutions for breaking the cycle of poverty.
- To be effective, education reform must be systematic.
- Parents must be involved in any attempt to improve public schools.
- Community support and adequate resources are essential to the success of public education.
- Independent, community-based organizations must play a central role in building and sustaining broad support for high-quality public education and for achieving significant reform in the nation's public schools (PEFNet, no date, p. 1).

Currently, PEFNet provides consultation ranging from start-up assistance to work in programmatic and policy issues. The Network also conducts workshops, conferences, and institutes. It is important to note that the Public Education Fund Network began as a grantor and then emerged as a provider of technical assistance. In 1991, it began to establish itself as an interactive network involved in school reform. To accomplish this, PEFNet has shifted its focus from school improvement to systematic reform with an emphasis on building community knowledge about critical school issues. PEFNet has identified five areas critical to school reform: finance, governance, leadership, curriculum, and assessment.

The author believes that this vision expressed by PEFNet is essentially correct, and that their leadership is needed in these areas if reform is to take place. This book does not address the emerging and important issues that will guide PEFNet in the years ahead. Rather, it is directed to the provision of technical assistance to new and emerging LEF organizations. As a former vice president for development at a major university, and as a current chair of an academic center created to assist nonprofit organizations, the author, through this book, has attempted to respond to the pragmatic questions that school districts pose about private foundations. There are guidelines for local school districts that are considering the creation of a local education fund and outlines of fundamental approaches for securing private funds. This book should be a useful guide to both new and established LEF groups.

ABOUT THE AUTHOR

James J. Muro received his bachelor's degree in 1956 from Lock Haven University. He received his master's degree in counseling from Rutgers University in 1961 and his doctorate in counseling from the University of Georgia in 1965.

Dr. Muro has been a public school educator, counselor, and a college professor. He also has served as a college dean at two major universities. As Vice President for Development at the University of North Texas, he was instrumental in chairing the university's first capital campaign, which raised more than $47 million on a $35 million goal.

Currently, he is a professor of Higher Education and Counseling Education and director of the Center for Private Support of Nonprofit Organizations at the University of North Texas. Dr. Muro is a polished speaker and is very much in demand for presentations on counseling, fund-raising, and public education. He has written 12 books and more than 150 journal articles.

He is married and the father of two sons.

1

PRIVATE FOUNDATIONS IN PUBLIC SCHOOLS

INTRODUCTION

This book is a resource for schools and communities who wish to expand or create a private foundation in a public-school setting. As increasing numbers of school districts seek innovative ways to finance excellence in public education, many have turned to the concept of private foundations as a source of increased support.

Public education, often criticized and increasingly forced to do more with reduced budgets, have now learned what colleges and universities have known for decades—private support is available for school districts who demonstrate that they can produce positive results for the children in their charge. To obtain significant private support, however, requires careful planning, solid community involvement, the willingness to create a special entity for systematic solicitation of additional funds—and friends for their schools.

The first two chapters of this book focus on the mechanical aspects of creating private foundations in public schools. The concepts advanced by the Public Education Fund Network (PEFNet) are reviewed, not only because they have been the major force in the United States for the creation of local education fund units (LEFs), but they have also assumed leadership in developing the most comprehensive and usable materials in the LEF movement. The remaining chapters provide specific and rather detailed information on tested approaches to raising private funds. Whenever possible specific checklists are presented to aid the neophyte to organize a fund-raising program. Readers may use the entire book as a guide to organizing or enhancing a private foundation or may refer to specific chapters for discussions of particular issues in fund-raising.

This discussion introduces what is perhaps the newest educational entry into the field. Public schools, for the most part, have traditionally relied on tax support to meet educational objectives. Because public support of schools varies from state to state and even from community to community, the quality of education, at least as that quality is related to funding, varies widely. In fact, a number of states are faced with the difficult challenge of finding ways to equalize the funding among districts. In Texas, for example, the state government is wrestling with attempting to find new funds to help support poorer school districts who have been denied equal funding in the past. A controversial plan to require wealthier districts to help support poorer ones has, as one might expect, drawn more than minimal opposition from individuals in the "wealthier" districts.

Regardless of whether a district is wealthy or poor, many schools are now turning to the creation of private foundations to support excellence in their schools. In Oklahoma, for example, there are numerous private foundations in both rural and urban school districts. The movement has gained momentum, not from the fact that tax support in terms of meeting actual costs has dwindled, but rather from the realization that tax dollars will generally support only a fraction of what schools want to do. To be excellent requires additional funds, and it is the spirit of the pursuit of excellence that has been a strong motivating factor in the creation of private foundations for support of public education. Public-school foundations, once a rarity, can now be found in states from the West Coast to the East Coast. In fact, a 1991 article in *The New York Times* quotes Kenneth A. Grounds of the Educational Foundation Consultants in Williamston, Michigan, as stating that more than 1,000 new foundations in public schools will be created by 1993. Many of these will appear in the South and the Northeast, the last areas of the country to move toward the creation of these foundations.

The national leader in the effort to help organize school districts to seek private funding is the Public Education Fund Network (PEFNet), a national nonprofit association that seeks to support, develop, and strengthen local districts and provide a national voice for their efforts. This organization was initiated on January 1, 1988, as a follow-up to the Public Education Fund, which ceased operation in 1987 after a successful five-year operation as a grantmaking and technical assistance program. The mission of the Network is "to improve public education, particularly for low-income students, through the development of local education funds. PEFNet provides information and technical assistance to those interested in exploring and pursuing the local education approach" (Public Education Fund Network, no date).

The Network has indicated that events in recent years in the nation's public schools have isolated them from the communities they serve. Political and financial pressures, as well as demographic changes and declining support from business and industry, cultural agencies, institutions of higher education, and parents, have created new and difficult challenges. In addition, the Network points out that many of the nation's urban schools are experiencing difficulty securing the necessary resources to enhance their abilities to educate the young. In many cases teachers are not rewarded for their efforts, and principals lack the basic resources for innovative school projects because of the lack of unencumbered funds. One approach to the problem is the creation of community-based organizations called *local education funds.* Described as a new model, they have developed innovative ways and processes to support public education (Public Education Fund Network, no date).

Although some of their literature suggests that their existence stems from difficulties faced by the schools, particularly urban ones, my experience with local education fund efforts leads me to believe that the long-range impact of the organization will go beyond remedial efforts to help schools become adequate to new directions based on excellence. For example, two school systems in Texas, Lewisville and Irving, are in relatively well-funded suburban districts. Yet they have employed the concepts advanced by PEFNet to create activities of excellence. In other words, they are using funds to create situations that are not, and probably will not be, supported by tax dollars. In this sense, they are following the lead set by the best of our nation's private and public universities. What private funding has done for Harvard University and The University of Texas, it can also accomplish for local public schools. The movement is new, but the direction is firm. Local education fund organizations are the wave of the future.

WHAT IS A LOCAL EDUCATION FUND?

As defined by PEFNet, "a local education fund is a third-party, nonprofit entity whose agenda, at least in part, consists of developing supportive community and private sector relationships with a public school system. It provides limited private sector support, and it launches initiatives and broker relationships leading toward school improvement" (PEFNet, p. 2). This general definition serves as a guide to local mission statements of various local education funds around the country. For example, the Boston Plan for

Excellence in the Public Schools describes itself as a unique endowment that provides the city's school students with inspiration and incentives for academic and personal success. In Denver, the Public Education Coalition is an independent nonprofit organization that works to improve the quality of education in the Denver metropolitan area, and in Indiana, the Gary Educational Development Foundation seeks to enhance learning within the Gary schools and, with external resources, to help insure that students of every level acquire the skills, knowledge, values, motivation, and vision needed for success in careers as citizens. The private foundation in Lewisville, Texas, describes its mission as "an independent nonprofit corporation that is a coalition of the private, business, industrial, and civic sectors created to promote quality education by establishing, supporting, and enhancing programs not otherwise funded by the Lewisville Independent School District." PEFNet has summarized key elements of local education funds around the country. Some common goals and objectives are to:

- *broaden the constituency support for public education*
- *better inform the community about the strengths and challenges of the local public schools*
- *break down the isolation of public schools from the general community*
- *restore and build confidence in public schools*
- *catalyze initiatives that support and enhance school improvement strategies*
- *leverage community financial and nonfinancial resources on behalf of local public-school districts*
- *serve as an independent, third-party intermediary on behalf of local public education*
- *be a liaison between public schools and their many publics, encouraging community and business involvement in a positive and supportive base.*

                                                              (PEFNet, no date, p. 2)

Note a similar theme in these objectives gathered from across the country. They seek to enhance and support public education, and, in places where support has eroded, they seek to restore public confidence. They also seek a closer relationship between community and school.

In many areas of the United States the initiation of a local education fund has been in response to the erosion of support, but in others, the emphasis has been one of seeking excellence as well as helping meet challenges.

Typically, local education funds focus on an entire district. Their efforts are independent from local school districts, hence they serve as natural channels of support. Since there are generally other groups and organizations that also support schools, LEFs do not duplicate the work of PTAs or other education-related groups. Nor do they seek to broker, convene, or initiate programs in all areas of education. Rather they strive to develop broad community interest as they work with institutions of higher education, civic, and other governmental groups (PEFNet, no date, p. 3).

Through such broadened support and the generation of funds that are not provided by tax dollars, the LEF is able to meet objectives that would otherwise not be possible.

WHAT DO LOCAL EDUCATION FUNDS DO?

LEFs are engaged in a wide range of programs and services, many of which are detailed later in this book. In general the work of an LEF is determined by the specific mission and goals of a local unit. PEFNet suggests that brokering, convening, and program implementation are three fundamental aspects of locally created organizations (PEFNet, no date, p. 15).

Brokering activities are those that attempt to match a need of a local school district with available resources. For example, in an effort to help students improve their PSAT and SAT scores, the Irving Schools Foundation contracted with an education center in Dallas, Texas, to provide help for juniors in the district's three high schools. Each student received 44 hours of instruction, and part of the cost was borne by the Foundation. In Massachusetts, the Boston Plan for Education in The Public Schools is supporting a program to develop literacy in the very young called Support for Early Educational Development (SEED), which has a $1 million endowment from the law firm of Goodwin, Procter, & Soar (Boston Plan, 1990). In Santa Fe, New Mexico, Santa Fe Partners in Education lists their basic role "as one of broker and matchmaker, linking what people are willing to give (time, money, services, expertise) with what schools need" (Personal Communication, September, 1991; Lorraine Goldman, Director). During 1991, Santa Fe partners managed to link 75 citizens as tutors with individual students or as teacher's aides. In addition they collected and distributed used children's books and provided additional school transportation with their own bus, purchased through a grant from City of Santa Fe Children and Youth Commission (Lorraine Goldman, 1991, personal communication). In other parts of the nation the familiar "adopt-a-school" programs, use of executives in the classrooms, and a wide range of programs for training teachers and administrators have been brokered.

A second major function of LEFs is that of convening. In order for a new ideas or new programs to move forward, it is often necessary for some agency or individual to arrange for people to meet, discuss issues, and take appropriate actions. While convening and brokering are evolving roles for individuals in LEFs, they can and do provide a forum for important topics such as school finance, desegregation, and at-risk youth (PEFNet, no date, pp. 15, 16). A major goal of LEFs is to increase the knowledge and information base of the local community about the school system. Unless a school district is fortunate enough to have a public relations staff, the knowledge level of most members of a community can be minimal. In times of crises or emotionally charged issues such as budgets or an increase in the tax base, lack of information can disrupt attempts to reach well-thought-out solutions. "The LEF can play an important role by bringing together and expanding the awareness, interest, and ultimately, school support and involvement of realtors, who need accurate, up-to-date information about the schools; the elderly, who may vote but have little or no information about the schools; and youth-serving social service agencies, whose only contact with the schools is through the youngsters they see as clients" (PEFNet, no date, p. 17).

It has often been noted that we, as Americans, are problem oriented. We document our failings and shortcomintgs perhaps more than any other nation in the world. Our print media, hungry for stories that sell, dwell on the negatives, and our broadcast journalists fill the airwaves with story after story of what can, has, or will go wrong. If schools are to receive positive publicity for the good that they do, they will have to provide the information to the public by themselves. The LEFs can play a large role in these efforts.

Close to the heart of almost any LEF is the concept of program implementation. These programs are not considered ends or goals in themselves, but rather strategies that help establish the credibility, visibility, and track record of the LEF (PEFNet, no date, p. 18). These programs should further the LEFs mission, enhance and complement the educational mission of the school district, improve classroom education, quality, and school leverage into the community. All programs should be fundable and should have good potential to encourage the professional school staff and elicit positive community regard (PEFNet, no date, p. 18).

In almost every public-school district that has an LEF, the very core of the effort seems to be the small grants program. The range of these programs is limited only by the imagination of the individuals involved in the LEF and the creativity of the teaching and administrative staff. In Denver, minigrants of $500 are provided to teachers for innovative projects on a competitive basis—projects that from 1985 to 1988 ranged from programs to help prevent teenaged pregnancy to drug abuse prevention training for high-school peer counselors. In 1989 in Irving, Texas, sample programs included projects in kiln design and construction, the learning of math skills through lifelike experiences, and the use of enrichment literature to unite past and present aspects of United States history. These are only samples of what can be done. In each case, the LEF was able to support these projects because of its ability to raise funds from the private sector.

Similar programs are also held for administrators. In Chattanooga, Tennessee, in 1990, the Public Education Foundation provided $6,000 toward a staff development grant for school administrators. Based on the belief that sensitivity to others is a key element in successful management, Foundation support provided administrators in the system opportunities for personal growth. These illustrations represent but a few of the countless ways that private funds enhance public education (Report to Foundation, 1990–91).

POTENTIAL PROBLEMS

The fact that LEFs have the potential for providing excellent support for school districts does not mean that the concept of seeking local funds does not have its detractors. Many states are concerned with the problems associated with the equalization of funding, and there is some concern that the differences between tax-poor school districts and tax-rich districts will become even more pronounced if tax-rich districts are able to raise more private funding because of the likelihood of a wealthier populace and the presence of more businesses, industries, and private foundations in their communities. In fact, equalization of funding is now a legal issue in 22 states.

In California, the State Department of Education is taking a close look at the concept of private foundations for public schools. Joseph Remcho, a lawyer in San Francisco, has noted that private foundations could undermine the concept of equal funding for all districts. "It raises questions. If foundation contributions become exaggerated, they would have the potential to undermine the principle of equal educational opportunity" (Cellis, 1991). While many public school foundations will not have the capability of raising the kind of dollars that will alter the budget discrepancies between rich and poor districts, there are some districts capable of raising enough funds to make some colleges and universities envious. For example, the Beverly Hills Unified School District in California raises about $350,000 of the district's annual budget (Cellis, 1991).

Other than equity issues, some districts and some educational leaders frown on the concept of raising dollars in addition to what is raised through taxes because they fear an adverse community reaction or a backlash on the regular budget. One superintendent in Texas has indicated that it is the responsibility of the state and the community to fund education, and his district would not engage in the process while he was serving as the chief educational officer.

Other concerns include the paucity of individuals with training in fundraising, and the relative lack of information about the process. In addition, statewide networks are uneven, and it may be difficult for professionals in one district to get assistance from peers in more established programs. With public-school foundations growing as rapidly as they are, the concerns noted here will probably continue for the immediate future.

GETTING STARTED

School districts wishing to create LEF groups or nonprofit foundations should carefully consider the various elements in the process prior to taking concrete action. In the history of public education in the United States, numerous excellent ideas never came to fruition because of errors in presentation and implementation. No matter how sound an idea may be, one must assume that even the best of ideas will be doomed to failure if attempts at implementation are too hasty. For example, a college obtained a sizable grant to help improve education in a rural Maine community. The college dean immediately targeted a local school, met with the superintendent, and together they sold the concept to the school board. However, the project was designed to improve *classroom* behavior and the teachers targeted to be helped were not consulted! It was akin to the well-meaning boy scout attempting to help the little old lady across the street and wondering why she was resistant. She did not, in fact, want to cross that particular street!

Individuals familiar with the dynamics of groups will be quick to relate that individuals who have little or no say in determining the goals of a given group or organization will have little incentive to work toward those goals. In the case of launching a private foundation it is not sufficient for one individual or even the school board to decide to initiate the project. It is absolutely essential that the community involved reach a consensus, and in order to reach this consensus, one must have some organization or group that can effectively convene the leadership of the community for the purpose of focusing on the provision of school support (PEFNet, no date, p. 6). In the seeking of major gifts, most fund-raisers will suggest that the professional institutional development person use a "prime" or volunteer who has a close relationship with a potential donor. The "prime" is the individual who may actually make the "ask" for a gift. In the establishment of an LEF, the school district must find a "prime" or "primes" in the community to either launch or expand an organization and be the leader or leaders of its effort.

Prior to even considering the launching of any effort, a professional school person must do some internal networking and research. The following are some of the issues to consider:

If we are successful in starting a foundation, who will serve as its leader?

Is there anyone in the district qualified to head this effort, or must we hire a new person?

If we are to hire someone or provide released time for someone, are funds available? Do state regulations allow individuals to remain on state salary if they are not in normal teaching (certifiable) positions?

If the effort is not launched by the superintendent, what is her/his attitude toward such an effort? What kind of support will she/he provide?

What is the attitude of our school board? Will it provide support? is the concept likely to cause controversy?

Do we have the services of a school attorney to assist us with the legal work necessary to incorporate? If not will the school board provide funds to hire such assistance?

Assuming the idea to create an LEF was an internal one, then, the school district must also consider some important and immediate factors that are related to the school, but may be *external.* PEFNet (pp. 6–7) makes a number of suggestions:

What is the climate of the community? For example, if the only industry in your community has just announced that it is closing its doors, the climate for the initiation of the effort may not be good.

What community resources are available? Are there organizations capable of convening others to build consensus? Are there individuals with the interest and stature to provide leadership? Is there one or more private or corporate foundations in the community who will provide assistance and perhaps even seed money for the project? Is there fund-raising experience in the community?

Is there a community like ours in our geographical area? Will they help?

What is the perception of our school district in the community for which we will be seeking funds? Are we perceived as poor, good, or excellent? Remember private funds flow to excellence!

What will our competition be? What groups or organizations are now engaged in raising funds for our school district? Is there an athletic booster club? Does the PTA raise funds? The band? Chorus? The drama club? What will happen to their efforts if we launch a major fund-raising drive in our community?

Is it possible for our key civic leaders and our key school personnel to work together?

These are examples of internal and external questions that should guide the thinking of a district as it moves forward. Once answers to these have been attained the district is probably ready to identify and organize those who will assume responsibility for bringing together the key individuals in the community and in the school district. PEFNet notes that these could be a group of business executives, a local community foundation, a broad-based civic organization whose agenda includes education, a chamber of commerce, and perhaps the local school superintendent (PEFNet, p. 6).

Experience suggests that a superintendent is the least desirable leader because it is she or he who will benefit in the long run. Whenever possible in fund-raising, a volunteer should assume the leadership position. However, PEFNet is correct in its assumption that a superintendent *may* serve and that there is no correct agency or person, but rather a range of people and agencies. The nature of the community and the availability of volunteers play a large part in the selection of individuals.

Once a small group has been selected, the next step is the creation of a steering committee. This committee should have representation from labor, business, and other perhaps diverse aspects of the community. This committee mirrors the community! The tasks of this steering committee are critical:

- Gather information about LEFs in other communities. This will save time and energy and allow the use of experience gained elsewhere.
- Do the other feasibility planning that will test the validity of the concept and seek those who may be asked to serve on the board. (*Note:* Although not mentioned by PEFNet, this concept is closely aligned to the process used in colleges and universities planning to launch a capital campaign. It seeks to answer, Who is out there to help? What will individuals contribute in time, wealth, and support?)
- Explore initiatives that will help carry out the mission and enhance visibility.
- Propose an organizational structure that includes a board, staff, office, and credibility.
- Develop a plan of action that includes possible financial resources.
- Elicit feedback about the plan from all aspects of the community including business, parent, industry, civic groups, nonprofit organizations, and colleges and universities.

ORGANIZING

PEFNet stresses the importance of establishing a relationship between funds from the private sector and the schools' general operating budget, and rightly so. As noted, opponents of LEFs fear that private funds will upset attempts to equalize funding in many states. Funds raised by LEFs cannot and should not be considered for use to make up any shortfalls in tax dollars. The LEF concept was not designed to relieve local financial pressures, and most do not, even though systems like the Beverly Hills Unified District do raise substantial funds that do have budget implications. The success of an LEF rests, in part, on the assumption that the dollars will enhance the educational process, rather than to remediate deficiencies. Again, a basic principle of fund-raising is that individuals, corporations, and foundations are more likely to support excellence (particularly in relation to activities that promise to solve difficult problems) than they are to support a mere bail-out for deficits.

As in many private fund-raising organizations, an LEF should be governed by a board of directors. This board should be a separate entity from the locally elected school board or, as it is known in New England, a school committee. School boards are elected by individuals and are, of necessity, political bodies. Their mission is much broader than that of an LEF and their actions reflect the will of the community. While all LEFs must have community support to become a viable part of the school district and the community at large, they need to be able to set their own agenda, and make decisions that may or may not be on the agenda of elected members of the school board. Obviously, there must be a close relationship between the elected school board and the LEF. In fact, it seems improbable that an LEF could operate at all without the blessing and support of the school board and the staff and administration of the district.

Not all relationships among members of the LEF board and those of the school board will automatically be good. Someone may, for example, seek membership on an LEF board because of dissatisfaction with school board action. This can be very destructive, and every effort should be made to remove the work of the LEF from politics (PEFNet, no date, p. 9). On the other hand, cohesion or a sense of "we-ness" is a function of interaction, and care must be taken to insure that members of LEF boards and school boards are provided opportunities to interact. Minutes of meetings, projects, and other activities of the LEF board need to be communicated to school board members on a regular basis. In a sense, school board members must learn what college regents have known for many years—the raising of dollars is best done by volunteers *outside* the governing boards of colleges and universities. School board members should support the efforts of the LEFs with dollars, and perhaps service.

The Board of Directors

It is the task of the steering committee to create a new nonprofit organization (if one does not already exist). Most school districts will not have a nonprofit organization, although a group formed to enhance a given community may be available.

The selection of an LEF board is extremely important in that the members will be charged with the all-important tasks of establishing credibility, making policy, and of course raising funds. The members must also reflect the nature of the community with respect to age, ethnicity, involvement or lack of it with school, business, industry, labor, civic organizations, religious groups, and, if available, representatives from local institutions of higher education. The board should also attempt to find individuals with a wide range of expertise. Although there is no absolute figure, a survey of various boards in the United States indicates that 20 to 25 members is common, however, a few boards in smaller communities operate with 10 or 12 members (Muro, 1992).

The steering committee may develop written criteria to insure the proper diversity on the board. At times the enthusiasm to launch a new effort causes some committees to present names for consideration in a rapid fashion, and often the names submitted are of individuals who work on every other civic group in the community. This is not wrong in and of itself, since the most prominent and active individuals seem to be first to jump to mind, however the committee must reach out as much as possible in creating the board. Remember that when the board of directors initiates fund-raising campaigns, all parts of the community will probably be solicited. Thus individuals on the board should represent a diverse group.

What categories should be considered? Certainly age is important. Some members should come from the senior community of those older than 60 years of age. Representation is also needed from those between 45 and 60 years of age, as well between 30 and 45, and those under 30 years of age. The board should also have a proper balance of male and female members and should reflect the ethnicity of the community. African-American, Asian, Hispanic, Caucasian, and other ethnic groups in the community should be part of the organization. If the community is large, the committee may consider membership from the city as a whole or from the suburbs.

Expertise is very important in the selection of the board because some of the work necessary to start a group and maintain it can be donated by one or more members. Typical memberships include individuals from banking, marketing, communications, insurance, education, religion, transportation, planning, law, fund-raising, accounting and finance, and administration. Lant (1990), while not considering LEF boards per se, lists additional criteria for board membership that are appropriate for local LEF groups. He suggests that, if possible, fund-raising groups should find a member of a local private foundation, a representative of the largest corporation in the area, a small businessperson (such as a printer), a religious leader, a civic leader, and members of professional groups in the community. In crafting a board it is important to seek individuals with interests in serving a non-profit organization in the areas of business, finance, promotion, publicity, and programs and services.

There is no standard for terms of membership, however, most groups have set two- or three-year rotating terms of office so that a seasoned core is always available for ongoing activities. A board may also have several ex officio members, including the superintendent of schools or her/his representative, the president or a member of the school board, and the professional staff member who will serve as the paid director.

Officers of the Board

President of the Board

This is the most important member of a board. In many respects the success or failure of the LEF depends on whether or not it has an effective board president. The chair of the board should be able to devote rather large blocks of time to the effort. A major concern of some LEF directors is that board presidents may not be able to give enough time to the work of the organization (Muro, 1992).

This should not, however, prevent selection of individuals who may seem exceedingly busy or involved elsewhere. At the present time in the United States, numerous individuals are very much concerned with the quality of public education. For example, many corporate leaders have a personal stake in quality public education because they realize that future workers for their companies are now enrolled in public schools.

A board president should be elected by the board. Therefore, it is essential to have good board members who will select the proper leader for the effort. As in most organizations, the chairperson of the board will preside at all meetings and direct the business of the organization. In most groups that were reviewed (Muro, 1992), the president of the board also had responsibility for authorizing and signing documents and other instruments authorized by the board.

A number of other duties are part of the board president's responsibilities. She/he must oversee the planning of the board, the appointment of key committees and chairs, and the general management of launching the fundraising process. In many cases, the board director may solicit the other board members for gifts to the LEF; in other cases, the president may work with the director in the solicitation of major gifts from individuals and private and corporate foundations. In all cases, the organization will work effectively when the chemistry between the president and the director of the LEF is positive (Lant, 1990).

Clearly, the president sets the tone of the board. The president must be able to communicate to the members that it is indeed their responsibility not only to help raise money, but to be active contributors to the process. No member should be added to the board unless she/he has an understanding of the expectations and duties. Far too often in nonprofit organizations, members are added to boards and are not told in advance that a major responsibility is the raising of funds and that this process includes a personal donation. This should not be taken to mean that all board members must give equal amounts, but it does mean that all should give. In fundraising the "rock in the pond" theory holds for LEF groups. Those closest to the organization must support the cause if there is an expectation that others will do the same. In general, board members who have not given donations will not be good fund-raisers. The key point is that all members should know in advance what is expected of everyone on the board. Failure to relate these when a board member is recruited will cause ill feelings, and lack of commitment and participation at a later date.

Vice Presidents
Most LEFs have an organizational structure that includes one or more vice presidents. For example, the bylaws of the Lafayette, Louisiana, program call for a first vice president who will perform all the duties of the president should that person not be able to do so, and for a second vice president who will perform similar duties in the event both the president and first vice president are unable to do so. The Bridgeport Public Education Fund in Bridgeport, Connecticut, operates under a structure that includes a chairman and a vice chairman. In Lewisville and Irving, Texas, four vice presidents work closely with the president. In the Irving, Texas, organizational structure, there are vice presidents for administration, community relations, development, and scholarships and programs. In Lewisville, Texas, the structure includes a vice president for administration and finance, a vice president for community relations, one for development, and one for program allocations. Lewisville also utilizes each vice president to correspond to a working committee. The vice president for finance works with the corresponding finance committee to oversee the budget, deal with the allocation and investment of funds, and makes any bylaws revisions.

As the name indicates, vice presidents of community relations in both Lewisville and Irving are responsible for promoting the LEF concept to the public, engaging speakers, designing brochures and materials such as video presentations, planning awards events, and other avenues of communication with the community.

In both the Lewisville and Irving Foundations, the vice president for development has the important task of overseeing the fund-raising projects and helping in awards events. This committee, as one might expect, has a heavy responsibility because solicitations and distribution of funds is a major task of the organization.

The vice president of scholarships and programs in Irving (named the program allocations committee in Lewisville) is responsible for the programs and activities areas of the foundation. This committee oversees the selection process for grant applicants and helps in award ceremonies. Similar organizational structure can be found in other LEF groups in most states.

Secretary and Treasurer

Most organizations that were surveyed (Muro, 1992) listed a secretary and a treasurer as members of the team. In most cases the secretary is responsible for the taking of minutes and the keeping of any special books that boards require. The secretary is generally responsible for notifying members of meetings and keeping records required by law. Because of the heavy requirements of this position, many directors of foundations operate closely with the secretary to insure that minutes of meetings and other communications are sent out at the proper times.

Almost every organization surveyed listed the services of a treasurer. This key position involves the accurate keeping and supervision of all accounts, and includes assistance to the board of directors who will need to conduct routine inspections of the financial status of the organization. Most LEF groups require at least an annual report of the financial status to the board. This report is, of course, the responsibility of the treasurer. Some LEFs operate with substantial funds and so require their treasurers to be bonded.

Other Committees and Support Groups

PEFNet (no date) suggests that the bylaws of most LEFs list a number of standing committees, the most common of which are executive, finance, development, nominating, personnel, and program. Others, such as long-range planning committees, can be created on an ad hoc basis. At times these committees become the specific responsibility of a vice president as noted in the Lewisville, Texas, model; at times they are chaired by separate board members.

It is also common for LEFs to have *advisory* committees in addition to the regular board of directors. However, in some communities such as Bridgeport, Connecticut, the advisory board is the board of directors.

In Lewisville, Texas, the director created an advisory board of 100 members in addition to those serving on the regular board. This was done to provide additional support and increase the visibility of the Lewisville

Foundation. In this structure each regular board member is asked to provide or invite five individuals to be members of the advisory board. Each of the individuals selected is then assigned to serve on one of the four standing Lewisville committees (administration and finance, community relations, development, program allocations). The advisory committees usually meet once or twice a year, but play a major role in fund-raising efforts.

From the perspective of fund-raising techniques, advisory committees are a good way to move individuals closer to the school district. This is the "rock in the pond" theory that was noted earlier, that is, the fact that those closest to the organization are most likely to contribute. In this context, all who agree to serve on the advisory committee are automatically closer to the organization and as such represent potential donors.

In addition, one should not overlook the possibility of the contacts that each of these individuals may have. If a group has 100 or even 50 members on an advisory committee, the probability increases that many of these individuals will either work for corporations and business that are potential sources of funds. In professional fund-raising, a key concept is the necessity of forming close or personal relationships with as many potential donors as possible. Thus if a member of your board or your advisory committee is able to get the LEF director an appointment with the head of the giving committee of a major corporation, then the chances of receiving a gift are very much enhanced.

Additional Duties of Boards

We have noted the role of the board members on committees of the LEF and some of their responsibilities with respect to vanguard efforts in the raising of funds. Board members are at the very heart of American philanthropy. It is not enough for board members to simply manage the funds and activities of an organization; they also have a major responsibility in the raising of funds. To simply be a member of a board and not support its activities is not sufficient (Lant, 1990). Each member of an LEF board must be an energizer. By actively encouraging others to participate in the activities she/he is communicating, in a very positive way, the commitment of the board members and the importance of the organization.

In addition to making a personal contribution, an important duty of board members is to cultivate *others* to give. Obviously, those who have not given themselves will not be able to make much of a case to other donors.

Once a person has made a financial contribution, she/he will likely be able to seek out and involve others in the organization, a process labeled *cultivation* in fund-raising parlance. Board members help others see the importance of their work, get them involved in committees or special projects, invite them to events related to the organization, and help the director identify and evaluate new individuals who are both donors and potential members of the group.

Again, the "rock in the pond" theory is key. If an important individual is not close to the organization, then board members must develop ways to bring him or her close. Those closest to "the rock" are most likely to make a valuable contribution. Cargill and Associates, a professional fund-raising firm in Fort Worth, Texas, indicates that prospective board members should not only give of themselves, but should understand that they are needed to solicit others, cultivate others, and to identify and evaluate prospects. Organizations who fail to inform board members of these essential duties may encounter difficult times in meeting fund-raising goals.

LEGAL AND REGULATORY ISSUES

Those who would initiate a local foundation need to be concerned with legal and regulatory matters. The first of these is that all concerned with the LEF have a thorough knowledge and understanding of state laws and regulations that apply to school foundations. These laws vary from state to state. In many cases professionals in your state department of education can help you obtain copies of legislation.

Most local units use the services of an attorney to help them with legal and regulatory matters. It is not a difficult task for attorneys familiar with nonprofit groups to assist you with three important tasks:

1. Your organization should be incorporated in your state. This is generally done through the Office of the Secretary of State. As an example, Appendix A contains the Articles of Incorporation of Lafayette Public Education Fund, Inc.

2. You will need to file with the Internal Revenue Service to attain 501(c)(3) or tax-exempt status. In order to do this you must use form 1024, an extensive document. A three-year budget must accompany the application. If all is in order, the Internal Revenue Service will allow your organization temporary exemption from taxes. You are required to show this form is requested. When the advanced ruling period is complete, the IRS will request additional information in order for your group to obtain permanent tax-exempt status. All of this information is very important and must be retained by the organization. Complete details on filing for 501(c)(3) (tax-exempt) status are available in the Internal Revenue Publication 557, *Tax Exempt Status For Your Organization*. This publication discusses the particulars of tax-exempt groups. Also you will need form 8718, which details the cost of the filing. To obtain these forms the Internal Revenue Service prefers that you call their toll-free number 1-800-829-3676 and request the forms.

3. You will need to develop bylaws. PEFNet (no date, p. 12) notes that bylaws are required for application for 501(c)(3) status. In all cases, if your LEF is a separate organization (and it should be) then bylaws are essential. PEFNet also recommends that bylaws be as simple and as free from detail as possible. These bylaws, drawn up by an attorney and a steering committee, should be adopted during the initial meeting of the organization. As with other aspects of LEF operations, bylaws vary. The Lafayette Education Fund in Lafayette, Louisiana, has developed a set of bylaws that includes the designation of officers, annual meeting, special meetings, regular meetings, notice of meetings, quorums, action without meetings, organizational meetings, committees, officers, and indemnification. Appendix B contains a copy of this fairly typical set of bylaws.

THE DIRECTOR AND STAFF

PEFNet (no date, p. 13) notes that staff is the most critical component in the success of an LEF. In any enterprise, the administration of activities is essential. In the case of LEFs with a large volunteer base, the operation must have a designated director, or executive director. This individual is responsible to the board of directors, and has supervisory responsibility for daily operation of the organization's business. Most directors have heavy budgetary and fund-raising responsibilities in addition to normal organizational tasks. Fund-raising, as with other kinds of endeavors, requires planning and attention to detail. The director must be able to do both and more.

PEFNet (no date) recognizes that finding funds for a director's salary may be an issue, but feels that groups who are timid about asking for such support to launch an LEF are shortsighted. A director is essential for LEF groups to staff the following:

- *brokering new relationships between the schools and community*
- *implementing programs focused on school improvement*
- *developing the organizational identity and visibility*
- *necessary to success in securing resources (p. 13)*

PEFNet (no date) also points out that less than a full-time director requires increased involvement by volunteers and that the seeking of funds to support an initial effort should not be categorized as simply operating expenses. Some districts have gone to utilization of part-time staff, or have added LEF responsibilities to existing district lines in such offices as public relations and grant writing. To be successful, however, at least one full-time individual with staff support is desirable.

There are concerns to consider in addition to the funds needed to hire a director. Of course, space must be provided, and in most school districts buildings were not constructed in anticipation of specialized personnel such as fund-raisers. PEFNet suggests that directors not be housed in the school system's buildings, but rather space should be found in places like chambers of commerce, corporations, or nonprofit agencies. Off-campus office space shows that the LEF is a visible part of the total community. In actual practice, however, many LEF offices are housed in space provided by school districts. However, when funding is available or if appropriate space can be provided by a corporation or nonprofit agency, it is probably preferable to move the unit off campus.

Most districts who seek to launch an LEF will also be faced with the problem of finding and recruiting professional individuals to hold the office of director or executive director. Individuals with experience in fund-raising are in demand in colleges and universities, and can generally command rather respectable salaries. School districts who are seeking experienced fund-raising individuals may have to compete with institutions of higher education, as well as a range of other nonprofit organizations for the services of qualified professionals.

Training programs for the preparation of fund-raisers are not readily available in colleges and universities. Fund-raising literature is scattered and is not yet organized in the manner of an academic discipline. In spite of excellent efforts by the Council for Advancement and Support of Education and the National Society of Fund Raising Executives, there are relatively few places to learn the skills of professional fund-raising.

The birth of PEFNet represents the best efforts to lead the growth and development of LEFs. Several universities, among them Vanderbilt University in Tennessee and the Center for Private Support of Non Profits at the University of North Texas, have taken a very active role in preparing fund-raising professionals. In 1992 the University of North Texas Center for Private Support of Non Profits held the first conference for professionals working in LEFs in public schools.

Given these problems, it may be difficult to find and hire "the perfect director," if indeed one exists. In the Irving and Lewisville foundations in Texas, both directors hold doctoral degrees in specialized fields of education but along with most of those presently in the field, their training was "on the job" and their learning the result of their own efforts. Experience with fund-raisers at all levels of education, leads to the belief that the individual selected to direct a local education fund must:

- be deeply committed to the concept of the inherent worth of public education
- understand the importance of support from the private sector for excellence in public schools
- be able to relate well to a wide range of individuals and groups
- have a basic knowledge of fund-raising principles and techniques and a basic knowledge of the structure and operation of public schools
- be able to organize, plan, follow through, and evaluate
- be able to write and draft documents such as grants, proposals, fund-raising letters, and articles for the media
- understand boards and board development
- be able to develop budgets
- understand and organize a volunteer structure
- have a willingness to be involved in the school and community
- have a desire to continue to learn and grow in the job

There are other criteria that could be listed, although some may think this list requires a superwoman or superman. Notice that college degrees are not listed since some of the very best individuals in the field of philanthropy today do not hold college degrees. Of course, as in other fields, academic credentials will become even more important in the future.

Like colleges and universities, more and more school systems are turning to the creation of LEFs for support for excellence activities in public schools. In fact, the number of local units is growing rapidly and will continue to grow well into the next century. Much of the credit for this growth must be given to the Public Education Fund Network, an organization that has led the nation's efforts in this area since 1987.

As a third-party, nonprofit group, LEFs seek to work with communities on a wide range of projects designed to support and bring together schools and the communities that schools serve. Each LEF is engaged to some extent in brokering, convening, and program implementation in a school district.

Districts wishing to initiate LEF activities must first get broad-based community support, school district support, and support from key civic agencies in the local area. Organizational activities include the establishment of a steering committee, the organization of a board of directors, the selection of officers, and the creation of committees and other support groups. Once organized, those involved with an LEF must consider the details associated with incorporation, obtaining 501(c)(3) tax-exempt status, and the naming of a director. Issues related to the funding and housing of a local group must also be considered.

SUMMARY

Seeking private support for education programs has long been an important aspect of U.S. colleges and universities. In fact, some of the very best institutions of higher education can trace their reputations for excellence to the private support that they receive.

Public-school districts, however, have only recently begun to seek private support for programs in elementary, middle, and secondary schools. The Public Education Fund Network (PEFNet) is a national leader in promoting the development of local education fund organizations in schools from Massachusetts to California.

Local education fund organizations are third-party, nonprofit entities that seek to develop community support and private sector relationships for public-school systems. Broadened support and the generation of funds are two of the primary objectives of these local groups.

The activities of local education fund groups include brokering activities that match school needs with available community resources, covering activities that bring together segments of the community interested in education, and the support and implementation of programs of excellence for teachers, administrators, and children.

Public-school districts who have formed local education fund groups have done so by carefully marshalling community support, organizing volunteers, crafting boards, and electing skillful leaders, and creating an effective committee structure.

Also related to the organization of local education fund groups are legal and regulatory issues, the hiring of professional staff, and seeking appropriate space in which to base their operations.

2

USING PRIVATE FUNDS TO CREATE EXCELLENCE: WHAT DO LOCAL EDUCATION FUNDS SUPPORT?

The funds raised by private foundations have been utilized in a variety of ways in local school districts. Some school systems have used private funds to promote school reform, others have dedicated the majority of what they have raised for scholarships. Some have targeted funds for staff development for teachers and administrators. Numerous districts have raised private dollars to develop programs for minority students. Other districts have created "scholars-in-residence" programs wherein private funds are used to bring scholars and artists to a community to work with teachers, parents, and children. Still others have raised funds to support educational materials and the creation of specialized laboratories in computer sciences and languages. A few districts have assisted teachers and administrators with travel funds to attend national and international educational meetings.

A number of local school districts have used private funding to forge closer relationships among public schools, parents, and business and industry. Such relationships are deemed essential by many who feel that school improvement is ultimately related to involvement of parents and business people with educators.

Regardless of how funds are utilized, it is safe to note that all activities supported by private funds have a common theme—that of promoting excellence in the public school. Virtually no private foundation in any school district in the United States attempts to raise private funds to replace or restore actual or perceived budget deficits.

THE MINIGRANTS PROGRAM

Directors of LEFs around the nation are eager to relate the success of their "minigrants" for teachers and administrators. This is not surprising in light of the fact that most tax dollars allocated to education in U.S. school districts supports salaries for teachers and administrators, leaving very little funding for supplies, materials, or other projects. In fact, in a survey (Muro, 1992) of most independent school districts in Texas, the one item that teachers felt they needed most to improve their performances was that of obtaining additional teaching materials. Far too often media reports focus on teachers' salary concerns, perhaps causing many individuals in the general public to believe that this is the issue on the minds of teachers. Those familiar with public education, however, know that personal pocketbook issues are not ordinarily the greatest concern of teachers. The vast majority of teachers feel that, although they would appreciate a higher level of pay, they are very concerned with equipment and other teaching needs. It is this crucial need that LEF groups around the country are addressing, primarily through programs of grants to teachers and principals for projects of excellence. It is not surprising that these programs enjoy widespread popularity.

As noted, the small grants programs in most districts have evolved from the need to bring new resources into the classroom and the need to close the distance between the schools and their community's business and civic leaders, local government, parents, and other adults who do not have children enrolled in public school. The small grants programs operate along very similar lines in most districts. An agency in a community raises private funds to support a wide range of projects. Teachers on all educational levels submit proposals for funding for review by a committee of community leaders. The actual grant process varies from state to state and from district to district within each state. Some school systems may have more than one cycle for proposals. The minigrant program in Lafayette, Louisiana, is fairly typical of the process in most school districts in the country and is used here to illustrate the process.

The Lafayette Public Education Fund (as outlined in chapter 1, a 501(c)(3) nonprofit corporation) is guided by a board of citizens. In this community, individual teachers may apply for grants of up to $300 and a team of teachers may apply for grants of up to $600. In Lafayette, the process is generally initiated in March with a letter from the president of the fund to the principals of each school. The letter encourages the administrators to support the concept (see Appendix C). Packets of information are supplied for principals and teachers to review. The packet at Lafayette includes a sheet that describes the way a proposal will be judged and rated (Appendix D), an information sheet listing the dates for submission and grant notification

(Appendix E), and a general specifications sheet with information on eligibility, rules regarding multiple submissions, method of application, and the overall timetable (Appendix F). In addition, potential applicants receive a detailed list of the selection criteria that explains what actions the review panel will take (Appendix G). In the Lafayette application, principals are asked to write a letter of support (Appendix H) and include a summary information sheet (Appendix I).

Application forms also vary from district to district. In essence, respondents are generally asked to complete a form with seven basic information areas. The Lafayette form is used here for illustrative purposes.

1. Describe the project: Who will do the projects? What will it be? What resources are needed? Where will the project take place?
2. Determine project goals and objectives.
3. Assess the need for the project.
4. Approximately how many students will be impacted by the project?
5. What is the schedule of events?
6. Evaluation plans for each project must be included.
7. Applicants are asked to develop plans for the continuation of the project beyond the grant completion. Each applicant is asked to predict the impact of the grant on classroom instruction.

The Lafayette system also provides forms for evaluation of budgeting (see Appendix J). While the Lafayette district calls for detailed information, the Bridgeport, Connecticut, Public Education Fund provides a guideline, such as the grant limits ($500), priority and nonpriority items that will be considered (software, a low priority in 1991), how funds may be used, and details related to interviews with a member of the selection committee. In addition to personal information, applicants must describe their projects, the method or methods used to implement them, and the evaluation process. Bridgeport also asks each applicant to submit a detailed budget request. To show how different districts approach the minigrant process, the Bridgeport application plan is included in Appendix K.

It is probably wise for each district to publish its own forms and guidelines for the minigrant process; however, the Allegheny Conference on Development Fund, with the support of the Ford Foundation, published a handbook that has been republished by PEFNet (successor group to the Allegheny Conference). It provides general guidelines that are perhaps utilized in some form by most LEFs engaged in minigrant programs. They suggest the following:

1. The program coordinator should issue calls for grant proposals six to eight weeks in advance of the application deadline.

2. Teachers can submit applications in mid-November and mid-February. [Note: Some districts use mid-March.]

3. As applications are received, the program committee contacts teachers for personal interviews.

4. The review committee meets several weeks after the application deadline, enabling the coordinator to prepare summaries of each project. At this point the committee accepts, rejects, or suggests revisions. [Note: Committee members should be from outside the school district. A nine-member committee is most common.]

5. Two weeks after the review, individual responses are sent to all who applied. Lists of approved proposals are sent to the school administration and board, to every school location, and to the media.

6. The funding process should be kept simple. Once the grant is awarded, each recipient receives a personal check. All teachers are asked to keep records and receipts of expenditures for the final report.

7. Projects are to be carried out within one year of the grant award date, ideally the same year the award was made.

8. Upon completion of the project, the teacher submits a final report, which may include samples of the work completed and appropriate photographs.

9. The grant coordinator prepares a written overview of each project at the end of each grant period.

(Allegheny Conference on Community
Development, no date, pp. 14–15)

GRANTS FOR PRINCIPALS

While the minigrants program is designed to provide support for individual teachers or groups of teachers for focused small-scale projects, the grants for principals program is generally larger in scope and schoolwide in its potential impact. These projects are more extensive than those of teachers: the potential impact is greater, the audience larger, the objectives more ambitious, and planning and challenges operate on a larger scale (Allegheny Conference Education Fund, *Mimeo,* no date).

This program has grown out of the concept that the principal of the school is a special individual who is able to assess the needs of the school. By funding grants for principals, programs offer administrators the opportunity to put ideas into practice.

As with the minigrant program for teachers, a time line must be established for informing the school selection committee that planning for a proposal is under way. Proposals must be filed on a date in early spring, and grants are usually awarded in late spring. The material from the Allegheny Conference suggests a notification date of January 11, a submission date of

April 4, and an award notification date of June 1. These dates, of course, can be modified to meet the needs of a given district and to comply with the appropriate days on the calendar. For example, if a suggested notification date falls on a Sunday, the actual notification would not take place until the next day.

The original materials distributed by the Allegheny Conference suggested two prime categories: principals grants and parent involvement groups. While these types of grants are still being utilized by some LEF organizations, other districts have modified the concept. Chattanooga, for example, has a staff development focus that involves principals and teachers in a wide range of projects. The Lewisville, Texas, foundation operates under the category of school site grants wherein each campus can receive up to $1,000 for projects that identify and address needs, challenges, and concerns that may be unique to that campus.

Regardless of how they are labeled or organized in a given district, the intent of principals grants was, and is, to address special needs on a larger scale. In many cases projects are selected for funding if they have system-wide implications. Academic improvement, school unity, student behavior, school government, group relations, attendance, staff development, and classroom management are examples of grants awarded to principals. A suggested funding level is $1,500.

PARENT INVOLVEMENT GRANTS

As the name implies, parent involvement grants are those awards that target increasing parent involvement with schools. These grants are typically in the areas of outreach, parent/school meetings, and school/parent communication programs. The suggested funding level for these grants is $500 per year. However, the actual funding is contingent upon local philosophy and availability of funds (Grants for Principals: Building A School Wide Project, 1988).

These grants imply a team approach and involve considerable pregrant planning. The program could involve any or all of the school staff including support personnel. It could also involve parents. Projects such as newsletters, issue forums, workshops, and school business luncheons are examples of awards.

Parent involvement grants incorporate a team approach, with parents as key individuals in these projects. Proposals should have a clear plan of action and include evaluation.

GRANT FORMAT

Although each district will likely develop its own form for the submission of principals grants, the one developed by the Allegheny Conference Fund serves as a good example (see Appendix L). It suggests the following be included on the form:

1. *Identifying data:* principals grant, parent involvement grant, principal's name, school name, address and phone number, number of students in the building, the program manager if different from the principal, and the project title and budget request.
2. *Summary:* A one-paragraph description of the project should be on the cover page.
3. *Signature:* Provide space for all appropriate signatures. The principal's signature and that of the program manager (if different from the principal) are necessary.
4. *Need:* What school problem does the proposal address? If the grant is for parent involvement, detail the existing obstacles to parent/school interaction.
5. *Pregrant progress:* Describe the pregrant planning that led to the conclusions listed in the proposal. Include the names of all who were involved in the process.
6. *Project description:* Outline all objectives and desired or expected outcomes.
7. *Activities:* Describe all activities and who will do them.
8. *Evaluation:* State how the recipient will determine if goals have been met, and include a specific evaluation plan.
9. *Future activities:* Will the project be continued after the conclusion of the grant? How will it be funded?
10. *History:* If other projects have been attempted to address this need, how have they fared?
11. *Budget:* The budget should be detailed. Budget items should reflect project activities. Specify all necessary services, materials, and equipment.
12. *Additional assistance:* List all additional materials, grants, labor, or dollars devoted to this project.

(Allegheny Conference Education Fund, 1988)

Each grant is then reviewed according to specific criteria. Common criteria are:

*   Is the need accurately identified and defined? Were all concerned parties involved?

- Is the proposed project an innovative solution to the stated problem or issue?
- Does the project have promise of improving the school by addressing a specific schoolwide issue?
- Does the project team have the capacity to implement the proposed program?
- Are the objectives and the procedures for carrying out the project clear?
- Are the plans for evaluating the project suited to the nature of the project?
- Is the budget request reasonable and sufficiently detailed?

Once the selection committee has reviewed all proposals and selected those that will be approved, the principal should receive a check that may be deposited in a separate account such as a school activity fund (Allegheny Conference Education Fund, 1988, mimeo).

EXCELLENCE IN LEF MINIGRANT AND OTHER INNOVATIVE PROGRAMS

Business and Education Partnerships

Most districts with LEF activities have some form of minigrant program for teachers and administrators and a number have special projects that go beyond grants to individuals and schools. In many school districts private support is utilized to forge relationships between schools and various business enterprises.

The National Association of Partners in Education, a professional group with headquarters in Alexandria, Virginia, notes that the number of nationwide education partnerships in public elementary and secondary schools rose from 42,000 in 1983–1984 to 140,000 in 1987–1988 (National Center for Education Statistics). More than half of these partnerships provided goods and services.

Another program worthy of note that is not directly parent related is the MAACS (Motivation for Academic Achievement and College Study), a unique venture that involves the hiring of college students to work with selected high-school students with solid college potential.

What is most interesting about the Bridgeport effort is the wide range of activities they have been able to sponsor with relatively few dollars. The total income to the Bridgeport Fund in 1991 was only $14,638. In terms of overall expenditures of the district for their public schools, this fund would represent only a small fraction. Yet one must be impressed with the range and scope of what they are doing. Note also that their projects speak of excellence and action. In too many school districts, professional educators, parents, and community members spend too much time looking for negative aspects of the school system. In Bridgeport and in other communities with private funds, there is strong evidence of a proactive stance and a willingness to make solid progress. Such are the hopes and promises of LEF activities.

The Boston Plan for Excellence

In Boston, Massachusetts, the Boston Plan for Excellence in Public Education has successfully forged a partnership between the business community and the public schools. The project was initiated in 1984 through a $1.5 million endowment from the Bank of Boston (LEFs are capable of raising amounts far beyond five- and ten-dollar contributions. Raising major gifts is discussed in Chapter 7.) The partnership involves projects from kindergarten through high school, and seven corporations and foundations have provided the majority of the funding for their plan for excellence. A major objective of the Boston Plan is helping to fulfill the educational promise of bright and talented students by making it possible for them to complete their educations.

In their 1990 annual report, the Boston Plan managed the operations of six programs: the Action Center For Educational Services and Scholarships (ACCESS), the Charles Hayden Fund, the Hancock Endowment for Academics, Recreation, and Teaching (HEART), the Bank of Boston Initiatives Grants, the School and Its Neighborhood program, and Support for Early Educational Development (SEED). In the ACCESS program advisors spend at least one day a week in several assigned high schools helping seniors who want to attend college but lack the financial means. Since 1984 The Bank of Boston Initiatives Grants Program has distributed $620,185 to projects designed by teachers, principals, or parents to improve individual schools.

A unique venture, Project SEED addresses the needs of early childhood education by developing supportive, nurturing, and challenging classroom environments. The Hancock Endowment (HEART) provided by John hancock Financial Services provides funds for middle schools and may be the only private endowment in the country that specifically sponsors middle school programs. In 1990, $438,261 in interest from the endowment has supported 117 programs! For example, the Thompson Middle School used private support to create a "Legacies" project, an effort to increase self-esteem through writing poetry, essays, and stories, which were published in a magazine called *Legacies*. The School and Neighborhood program encourages students to identify with and care about their public school's neighborhood and to learn about the meaning of local philanthropy. The Charles Hayden Fund is an innovative approach to the prevention of school dropouts (Boston Plan, 1990).

What is worthy of note in each of these endeavors in Boston is the fact that all programs seek excellence in some way. In higher education in the United States the difference between very good colleges and universities and those considered outstanding often can be traced to the degree of private support received by those considered excellent. The same holds for public school education. In most districts tax dollars support only essentials, meaning that in some cases the programs remain mediocre. The funds to promote excellence must be obtained elsewhere. Hence, the critical role of LEF activities in public education.

The Grand Rapids, Michigan, Approach

In Grand Rapids, Michigan, the Grand Rapids Public Education Fund has created a concept similar to the Boston Plan, but stresses the heavy use of volunteers in a direct attempt to bring together business, industry, and community organizations with the school district in a wide range of initiatives. The core of the program involves "partners" working at the building level to improve student output. The founding brochure notes that more than 700 employees bring their expertise to school improvement. They target improved attendance, motivation, encouragement, and parental involvement. They also tutor students and help enhance curriculum. Of the 10 schools that showed student improvement over prior years, nine of them were "partnered schools." The projects are broad in scope and innovative. For example, the *Partnerships Newsletter* in March of 1989 highlighted the involvement of the Michigan National Bank with Central High School in an effort to help the yearbook staff improve marketing strategies, along with assisting students with long-range academic, career, and financial planning. Another company, Bissell and Stocking, provided training for school staff in computer technology, and Cascade Engineering staff provided special training for teachers in problem-solving approaches. It would be difficult to measure in dollars the energizing impact of business involvement with the Grand Rapids Schools! (Grand Rapids Public Education Fund, 1981).

The Gary, Indiana, Plan

Improvements in public education in Gary, Indiana, are enhanced through the Gary Educational Foundation, which celebrated its fifteenth year of support in 1990. Starting with funds donated by the board of directors of Gary

College, a nonprofit group that dissolved in 1950, the Gary school initiated a scholarship program of $10,000. In 1969–1970 the Gary school board initiated efforts to involve the business community of the city and in 1970 the district received a grant of $28,000 from Urban Ventures, a nonprofit group in Chicago. The foundation became an operating entity in 1977 when the board passed a resolution recognizing its existence. The Gary program has as one focus the Martin Luther King Grants which helps students help themselves. The King endowment has reached $78,327, and supports such projects as sending students to the NASA Space Camp and helping students who have opportunities to study or perform abroad. Each year students from elementary schools and older contribute to the fund.

An additional innovation from the Gary Foundation is a program to develop "economic literacy" among Gary's students. In this approach business leaders in the metropolitan area offer speakers, tours of facilities, informative handouts, and other relevant materials. The program has managed to involve The Gary Public Transportation Program, Gary Regional Airport, Gary Police Department, Gary Sanitary District, Gary Department of Weights and Measures, the Gary Commission for Women, Gary City Court, and the Gary Common Council. These are in addition to the Gainer Bank, Indiana Bell Telephone, Northern Indiana Public Service Company, NIPSCO Industries, Methodist Hospital, and the *Post Tribune*. Each of these is listed to show how broadly based support for public schools can be. This support can then be counted upon when the district faces crucial issues related to tax support for schools. There are many ways to earn community support, but initiatives involving business, industry, and government with education through LEF efforts are among the best ways to elicit support for excellence. (Facts taken from Gary Educational Development Foundation Inc. brochure.)

The Business/Education Plan of Lynn, Massachusetts

In Lynn, Massachusetts, the very name of their foundation, the Lynn Business/Education Foundation, relates some of their major objectives. While the Lynn foundation does include the usual grants to teachers, parents, principals, and parent/teacher organizations, the large portion of Lynn children wearing T-shirts with the names of local businesses and industries highlights another of their major efforts, the school/business (Adopt-A-School) program. This effort matches companies with schools in what is emphasized as a true partnership for quality education. Business "partners" in the city work directly with building principals and teachers to motivate and reward student performance, and to increase student self-esteem. Each business brings resources, personnel, and materials to support education. A major objective is to allow business to have a direct impact on public education.

Some of the business involvements are New England Telephone's support of Lynn Vocational Technical Institute's Annual Trade Expo; Mass Electric's assistance to upgrade lighting at St. Mary's school; Warner Cable's support of Earth Day activities at Cobbett school; Carr Leather's support of a Christmas Fair at Fallon school; and Eastern Bank's help to Brickeet School by the establishment of a school store in addition to helping with a read-aloud program. These are simply representative of the more than 20 school/business partnerships in the Lynn area. It is indeed exciting to see the extent of community support in that city! (Facts taken from the Lynn Business Education Foundation brochure and additional documents provided by the foundation.)

The New Orleans Metropolitan Partners in Education Plan

In New Orleans, the Metropolitan Area Committee Education Fund sponsors Partnerships in Education, with a mission similar to those of Boston, Gary, Lynn, and Grand Rapids in that they seek to join local businesses and organizations with individual schools. Their material includes an excellent brochure called *Partnerships in Education, Process Guide.* The publication outlines a six-step process in three broad areas: planning, implementation, and evaluation.

In the planning phase, a principal and business partner meet to determine the scope and commitment of the project. Next a planning committee is organized to establish the partnership responsibilities. A third step of the planning process is to establish the objectives, activities, budget, and time lines. In the final step, the principal submits the plan to the Chief Executive Officer for approval. In the implementation phase the planning committee should review all projects, allocate funds, evaluate activities, and document accomplishments. Each partnership should have a final evaluation when it is either renewed or concluded. Examples of some projects in New Orleans include those in career education such as job shadowing, site visits, and career guidance; curriculum enhancements such as math and science programs and school media projects; and motivational programs with incentives for achievement and appropriate school behavior. Other activities include personal student development and training opportunities for teachers. Efficient organization has helped make the New Orleans approach a success! (Facts taken from STEP, Partners in Education brochure and Partners in Education handbook: Metropolitan Area Committee, New Orleans.)

Business and industry cooperation is possible not only in large urban areas such as Boston, Gary, Grand Rapids, and New Orleans. Many small and relatively rural areas are involved in attempts to link business and industry together. Efforts are under way in suburban communities such as Lewisville and Irving, Texas, and in even smaller ones such as Ada, Pauls Valley, and Sand Springs, Oklahoma. No community is too small or too large to benefit from close liaison with whatever business and industry may be available in the area the school district serves.

STAFF DEVELOPMENT PROGRAMS

Reform Issues in Chattanooga, Tennessee

The Public Education Foundation of Chattanooga, Tennessee, has created a partnership between the public and private sectors of the metropolitan area with a goal of raising expectations for public education as well as becoming a force for school reform. While the foundation does include the more traditional programs such as minigrants, the major thrust of the organization focuses on reform. In their summary report issued in May of 1991, the foundation states that professional development is the key to achieving the greatest degree of effectiveness and satisfaction for educators. Using a central question, "What do educators (including both teachers and principals/administrators) need in order to achieve the greatest degree of effectiveness and satisfaction?," a steering committee determined that shared responsibility, collegial relations among principals and teachers, sensitivity and skill in dealing with diversity, and continuing intellectual development and challenges were worthy avenues for their efforts.

This innovative thinking has encouraged the development of a range of projects not commonly found in school districts. For example, in 1991 the foundation provided $8,000 for a site-based management seminar for seventy Hamilton County teachers and principals. This seminar was designed to help develop a system of educational management to promote decision making at the lowest possible level. An additional $20,000 was awarded to five Hamilton County Schools to implement site-based decision-making pilot programs. Other projects funded by the foundation include a grant to faculty and staff from Big Ridge Elementary School to study Application culture, another to the students and faculty of Brainerd High to study Afro-Hispanic poetry, and a grant to the Chattanooga City Schools to conduct a series of workshops called "A Fresh Look At Black English," to help educators understand the structure of Black English and the unique needs of black students in acquiring standard English skills (Chattanooga Educational Foundation, 1989–1991 reports).

The programs listed here are only a few of the many innovative approaches of the Chattanooga program. Most school districts have long been aware of the importance of promoting good human relationships among teachers, staff, administration, parents, and students from a range of ethnic and racial backgrounds. These goals are often expressed and promoted by state departments and politicians seeking election, yet they are not always funded. In Chattanooga, they have obtained the private funding to meet these lofty educational goals. It is intriguing to imagine the impact of improved relations in our nation if private funding were available to offer similar programs in all schools across our nation!

The Denver, Colorado, Public Education Coalition Literacy League

Hailed by educators as an excellent vehicle for promoting enormous positive change, the Literacy League Program in Denver uses "top-notch" trainers with broad experience in the writing process to work with teachers by providing demonstration lessons and conducting sessions on the problem-solving process. A trainer serves five or six teachers with a four- to six-week intensive training process with follow-up visits throughout the schoolyear. Private funds also enable Denver to bring in outstanding individuals to work with teachers. In many schools in the city, the Literacy League has helped initiate reading and writing groups for teachers to share their personal writing and discuss a variety of books. Among other benefits, teachers learn or perhaps relearn to understand the struggles and achievements that children face in writing workshops. The goal of this program, creating a "literate school environment," has captured the fancy and the financial support of the Adolph Coors Foundation, the Anschutz Family Foundation, and the Boettcher, Gannett, and Pitton foundations.

Like Chattanooga, the Denver Public Education Coalition supports programs in leadership team building for administrators, public information projects, school-based decision-making programs, and series of workshops on educational reforms. These efforts, along with the more traditional minigrant programs for teachers, help make Denver a national leader in the use of private funding for the support of public education (Denver, Colorado, Public Education Collation, Annual Report, 1990).

Public Schools of Hawaii Foundation Travel Grants

One of the reasons for the formation of public-school foundations is the desirability of decreasing the isolation of schools and the community. In a similar vein, teachers themselves are often isolated from their professional colleagues in other parts of the state and in other parts of the nation. In almost every state, there are countless workshops and conferences designed to assist teachers, administrators, and other specialized school personnel with continuing education. However, less-than-ample budgets in most districts prevent most educators from traveling to and learning from many of these conferences. There is a reluctance in many districts to spend tax dollars for perceived "frills;" hence, many districts shy away from allowing teachers to take professional days and to support travel. Teachers who wish to continue to grow must pay the costs themselves. In a recent conference in New England for school counselors, attendance was only a little over 200 participants, even though it was held on a weekend so participants would not have to miss work. During the 1970s this conference attracted in excess of 1,000 practicing school counselors. Budgetary cuts in New England have taken their toll. The sole hope for this important conference may be to seek private funds.

The Hawaii foundation initiated a program of travel grants of varying amounts to teachers, administrators, and students when exceptional performance is being recognized nationally or even internationally, or when the benefit to be gained is of significant value to the school system. In evaluating applications, the foundation asks:

1. *Will the project product results that are potentially applicable to other classes, schools, or districts?*
2. *Can the project be implemented as proposed?*
3. *Does the project supplement, rather than supplant, existing school funding?*
4. *Does the project have potential for stimulating community awareness and involvement in Hawaii's public schools?*

(Public Schools of Hawaii Foundation,
Education Is Everybody's Business,
no date, p. 6)

These general guidelines are for all projects supported by the Hawaii foundation, but are included here to illustrate how a teacher can make a case for support for professional travel. In essence, projects that may be beneficial to the individual, but more important are of benefit to the district or at least a portion of it, have a better chance of support. Unquestionably, educators and students in Hawaii have a better chance of learning and of displaying particular skills through this program. In Hawaii, staff development may extend to almost any part of the world if the criteria for support are met!

The Eclectic Approach in Los Angeles

Unlike many "school foundations" in California and in other states, The Los Angeles Educational Partnership was formed by a small group of concerned community leaders to help reform and improve school districts, not only in the city of Los Angeles but in other districts as well. It provides an example of how private support can have a positive impact on a very large urban area.

Since its inception in 1984, the Partnership has invested more than $10 million in private sector resources to help student performance in schools. The group serves as a broker and a catalyst for new ideas and for a source of venture capital for educators interested in reform. It should be pointed out that this organization works closely with professionals in the schools in designing reform initiatives (Funknouser, 1991, personal communication).

Their activities involve more than 3,000 teachers, who in turn work with more than 625,000 students in this, the second largest school district in the United States. In a manner similar to small school districts, the partnership sponsors a traditional "minigrants to teachers" program that stresses leadership, training, and collaboration among teachers and schools and the private sector. Their Humanitas program, for example, is a teacher-directed, leadership collaborative designed to organize teachers and students into a "community of scholars" wherein instruction is enhanced through an interdisciplinary thematic, writing-based approach incorporating history, English, social studies, art, math, and science. This is done through a team of three to five teachers from each grade level.

The partnership also provides support for innovative projects to improve the teaching of mathematics, science, language, art, humanities, and special education. Staff development is supported through new information on educational research, professional standards, and school reform, which is distributed to the teaching staff.

In addition to the small grants program, the partnership is involved in a new project to provide incentives and assistance to school-based management teams concerned with the restructuring of schools. The group has also provided support for a math-science council composed of educators and executives from major corporations for the purpose of developing a strategic plan to help improve instructional practices and student achievement in math and science. The popular (+ Plus +) program is a unique attempt to assist math, science, and computer science teachers through a paid six-week internship in industrial sites.

Other broad areas of interest for the partnership include providing technology in the classroom, integrating health and social sciences, school-to-work transition programs, public information, and school-to-community linkages.

The Los Angeles Unified School District, because of its size and diversity, presents a large array of challenges and opportunities. Although smaller districts may not be able to match the scope of the partnership, they can learn from the dedication of the people in that city and use that dedication to attack problems in their own localities. In a broad sense, there are opportunities to marshall private support for public education in virtually every school district in the United States.

Other Programs of Note

The New York Alliance for the Public Schools, the Mentor Program, and Public Relations Program

The New York Alliance for Public Schools is a voluntary civic organization of diverse individuals from the community, corporate world, the Board of Organization, the United Federation of Teachers and Administrators, and the United Parents Association. It includes a working consortium of deans of education from St. John's University, New York University, Columbia Teachers College and Fordham University. While the organizational structure is broader than those in other towns and cities of the country, the Alliance mission is similar in that it believes that quality public schools are essential to the social fabric and economic health of New York City (New York City Alliance for the Public Schools, Ten Year Report, 1980–1990, p. 1). The Alliance sponsors a number of projects including specialized skills development for high-school principals, a high-school principals center at Fordham University, an oral skills communications program, and a teacher awards program.

Among the most interesting of the Alliance's efforts is a wide ranging mentor program of more than 100 firms and organizations that contribute staff time and resources to Mentor programs that serve nearly 2,000 students. Such programs include the Mentor in the Law Program that brings law firms together with high-school students to expand law-related curricula; the Mentor in Engineering program sponsored by Mobil Oil that helps teachers incorporate engineering concepts into the curriculum through a program of seminars with engineering professors; and the Mentor in Education program that includes weekly seminars on education, peer tutoring, teaching small groups of children, and presentations at "spring graduation." Similar programs are available in nursing and health careers, advertising, banking, real estate and construction, retailing, and public relations.

Another innovation of the New York City Alliance is the publications guide for schools. With the assistance of a grant from the Bankers Trust Company of New York, the Alliance prepared a document entitled *Going*

Public, a 25-page booklet that assists schools in preparing printed public-relations materials, understanding the media, and telling their story through news releases, news advisories, photographs, community calendars, and press relations. The book also has sections on community relations and fund-raising, particularly for special events.

At least two important avenues for public schools are reflected in this aspect of the New York Alliance. The mentor program can assist to make school more meaningful by tying academic concepts to the real world of work, at the same time providing career information in a lively way. Second, the development of a public-relations booklet is an example of an excellent tool for schools to use in what seems an ever-present battle with some print and broadcast media. As noted, in a problem-oriented society, problem-oriented media thrive on problems and controversy. Any failure of the school or in the school will encounter little or no difficulty making the front pages of almost any newspaper. Good news, however, does not sell to newspapers, and even when schools do something exceptionally well, obtaining space in the press is difficult. The press will not operate as a public-relations tool for schools. Good public relations must be initiated by the schools themselves. The book published by the New York Alliance is an example of private funding used to help schools publicize their successes.

The Phoenix, Arizona, Educational Enrichment Foundations Advocacy Efforts

The Educational Enrichment Foundation of Phoenix is a private nonprofit group dedicated to raising and enhancing the quality of public education in Phoenix, Arizona. The foundation has a traditional minigrant program to teachers, operates a special-need fund to help needy children stay in school, and provides grants to principals and schools.

A unique aspect of what Phoenix supports is a commitment to advocacy for public education. In this context, the foundation hosts a number of forums and conferences, including a comprehensive effort called Tucson 2000. In addition, members of the Educational Enrichment Board serve on the community's Business Advisory Committee, the Drop Out Collaborative, the Education Television Committee, and BEST (Better Education Serves Tucson). Although almost all foundations advocate for public education, the Phoenix approach lists that as a specific program. Advocacy is not left to chance; it is organized and reaches into the heart of the community structure. Such effort can make an enormous difference in the way public education is perceived by the general public.

The Santa Fe, New Mexico, Partners
in Education Brokering Program
The Santa Fe Partners in Education program is an outgrowth of the Santa Fe
Communities Foundation, but became independent of that parent group in
1991. Recall that one objective for LEF organizations as specified by PEFNet
is brokering. At Santa Fe, the concept of brokering is considered a basic role.
The group attempts to match what individuals in a community will give
(time, money, services, expertise) with what the schools need. The program
director, Lorraine Goldman, notes that the program in Santa Fe is "fully
bilingual" in that it speaks both "school" and "business." That is, the very
essence of the program is to bring people together who might otherwise
have problems communicating. In this effort the group is teaching teachers
to "think corporate" through long-range planning, clear written presentations of ideas and needs, and appropriate thanking of donors. Although it
may seem that huge staffs are essential to initiate local efforts, the Santa Fe
Partners in Education has a single paid employee and two VISTA volunteers. Yet in 1990 Partners raised about $25,000 that was given to individual
projects, and linked some 70 citizens with classes or individual students as
tutors or teacher's aides. They have also collected and distributed children's
books, and helped supply special transportation to school children with a
bus purchased through a grant from the City of Santa Fe Children and Youth
Commission! Santa Fe is an excellent example of a few individuals making
a major difference in public education (Goldman, 1991).

The Irving, Texas, Public Schools
Foundation PSAT/SAT Program
Recognizing the importance students (and some colleges and universities)
place upon SAT scores, the Public Education Foundation of Irving, Texas,
has implemented a special PSAT and SAT preparation program for juniors
and seniors in the district's three high schools. Although each student who
wishes to attend is charged a fee for the 14 hours of instruction for the PSAT
and the 20 hours of instruction for the SAT, additional costs are absorbed by
the foundation. Scholarships are available for students unable to pay the
tuition. The scholarship dollars are also privately raised. While program
costs exceed $16,000 a year, the benefits to students can be seen in improved
SAT scores, which may have a direct relationship on selective admissions
and college scholarships.

SUMMARY

The projects and activities supported by private contributions to public education seem limited only by one's imagination. From school advocacy

programs in Phoenix, Arizona, to mentoring programs in New York City, private funding can and is making a significant difference in virtually all aspects of education, to include human relations, staff development, curriculum improvement, and improved community/school and school/business relationships. Truly the growth of private support for public schools must represent a very significant trend in public education.

In virtually all school districts that have private foundations or some form of LEF operations, private dollars are utilized for basic minigrants to support classroom programs and innovations. In most schools private dollars support school- and district-wide projects and provide special assistance to principals and other administrators. Most districts have developed a formal application process to apply for private funds, and while the process may be relatively simple or rather complex, funds are generally awarded on the basis of merit by a committee of the local foundation board.

In addition to the minigrants programs, many schools have utilized private dollars to forge projects for school/business partnerships, staff development, school/community, parental involvement with schools and specialized advocacy. The use of private dollars to support education seems limitless, and such specialized efforts as the public-relations endeavor in New York City, the brokering approach in Santa Fe, and the assistance to Irving students on the Scholastic Aptitude Test are examples of the range of programs that have been funded. In the years ahead, the number of private foundations for public schools will continue to grow, and the programs they support will continue to expand. As such, the movement to have an LEF in every school district represents one of the most exciting movements in public education in decades!

3

CONCEPTS OF FUND-RAISING

WHY GET INVOLVED IN FUND-RAISING FOR THE PUBLIC SCHOOLS?

If this question were put to administrators, teachers, and concerned parents in most U.S. school systems, the response would probably be something like "We really do not have enough money to do what we need to do," or "The state keeps cutting back. Each year we seem to get less money than we did the year before." Others might say "The people are fed up with high taxes. We pay more and more taxes and yet every time I turn around I read that our schools are not as good as those in European countries or in Japan. Why pour more dollars into a losing effort?"

Each of these responses has at least a ring of validity. In most schools tax dollars only support education at a level that allows them to be mediocre; hence, most districts do not have the funding to do what they would like to do. In addition, the economic conditions in many states have caused legislators to take a close look at what is being allocated for education. In some states, local districts have had to operate with no budget increases; in others, the schools have been forced to operate with budgets that are lower than in previous years.

The question of whether or not our schools are doing well is, in part at least, a matter of public perception. Such factors as declining SAT scores, high drop-out rates, and questions regarding the quality of our nation's teaching force have been covered extensively in the print and broadcast media. The public in general still supports our schools, but doubts in the corporate sections and in some governmental agencies tend to erode confidence in what our schools have done or are doing.

Political campaigns at the state and national levels have focused on the weakness of our system and politicians seem to have a plan to fix the ills that appear to plague us. A more helpful focus is on what can be done to promote excellence in schools, how schools need to go about promoting excellence, and what they need to do to finance the process. Many people criticize our schools, but there is excellence in public education, although excellence is scattered. In some schools and districts, one would be hard pressed to discover programs, teaching, or activities that could legitimately be described as excellent. In other districts, one could step into any school building, observe almost any class, or attend any cocurricular activity and be impressed with the quality of teaching.

Politicians, particularly those with conservative points of view, like to reiterate the old saw "you can't fix the problem by throwing money at it." This may be, at least in part, a fair critique. Massive infusions of dollars into many schools and districts have not produced the hoped-for results.

The fact remains, however, that excellence in education is not possible without adequate funding. Who will question the quality of a Harvard, Yale, Stanford, University of Michigan, Duke, or Vanderbilt? Most parents would proudly point to these and like schools as outstanding places for the education of their children. A close look at each of these schools will indicate the reasons that make them excellent. Each can boast a top-flight faculty, each has a wide range of significant research projects, and each can boast of the quality of public service that faculty provide. Each makes a difference in our society, and many reach beyond our shores and make a difference in the world.

The excellence of each of these schools and numerous others like them can be directly traced to financial support. A world-class scientist will seldom be found at a small rural college in the South, Northeast, or Midwest unless that institution can offer the kind of financial support that allows him or her to be excellent. Support may include a competitive salary, laboratories and equipment to conduct research, funds for professional travel, and funds for research. This is not to state that faculty and programs of high quality do not exist in less adequately funded colleges and universities. However, the best and the brightest professors tend to congregate at institutions that offer the most assistance. The best ideas, the best projects, and the leadership in many fields flow from our major educational institutions. In general this fact is recognized by our government and by private and corporate foundations. Excellence breeds excellence, and excellence garners support. This is a cardinal rule of fund-raising and holds for almost any organization seeking private dollars.

FUNDING AND EXCELLENCE
IN PUBLIC SCHOOLS

Excellence in public schools is related to how well each school district is supported. Early in my career I had the good fortune to work in a school district in New Jersey that placed a high value on education. The citizens of this community were willing (and able) to raise the tax dollars to support what at that time resembled an elite private school. For example, the district offered four years of foreign languages including Spanish, Latin, German, French, and Russian. The approximately 700 students had the services of six full- and part-time counselors to help them get into the "good" colleges. Class size was small and the range of cocurricular activities at the high school would be the envy of most.

At the same time, a neighboring district did not have the means to support its schools in a similar manner, and was unable to offer the range and scope of programs that were such a vital part of the district. It was an excellent school system for a number of reasons, but the major reason was that it had the strong financial base. School counselors were able to discuss and compare a wide range of colleges because the district provided the travel funds to visit college campuses across the nation. Is this a form of excellence in a counseling department? To the citizens of that community it was; they defined excellence and then supported it.

Not all school districts are so fortunate. Many states, faced with mandates from the courts, are grappling with the difficult task of finding ways to equalize funding for all districts so that children who go to school in "tax-poor districts" will receive the same education as those who go to school in wealthier systems. It is hard to argue against this concept. All children, of course, should have the same opportunities. The difficulty is that tax dollars never have been and never will be able to support excellence in all or even the majority of school districts in our country. Equalization formulas attempt to deal with the distribution of dollars and accordingly some districts receive additional funds. Most, however, still receive only enough dollars to be average or mediocre. How then, do we achieve excellence? All concerned with public education must constantly work to insure that our legislative leaders provide as much support as possible for public education. Beyond that, the time has come for school districts to do all that they can to enhance education at the local level. This means that local schools must become involved in the business of seeking private support for some programs.

Private support should *not* be an attempt to *replace* the budget shortfalls that plague many districts. Rather it should be a process of seeking funds for targeted programs of quality. Virtually every school district in the country is capable of raising private funding. Yes, some districts are capable of raising more than others, but *all* are capable of raising more than they are doing now. Although some skeptics and "nay-sayers" frown on the business of fund-raising in public education, almost every high school and elementary schools are involved in some form of fund-raising each year for athletics, band, class trips, various clubs, and special projects.

In recent years more than $80 billion was given by more than 300,000 charitable institutions in the United States. Of this amount, more than $10 billion was given to educational institutions. More than 85 percent of what is donated comes from gifts of individuals with foundations and corporations supplying roughly 5 to 6 percent. It is true that the bulk of this money has gone to colleges and universities, but in recent years private foundations and executives in the corporate world indicate growing interest in supporting public schools. Even some of the major donors at large universities have made significant gifts designed to have the faculties become more involved with public schools. Again, the time is now for all public-school systems to become more involved in seeking private support to promote excellence. Those who are not now planning to become involved will be at a distinct disadvantage when they find themselves competing with districts who have well-organized financial development efforts.

GUIDELINES FOR DEVELOPMENT

Differences Between Fund-raising and Development

The term *fund-raising* provides a focus for this chapter, however in the not-too-distant future it is likely that a professional *development person* (as distinguished from a fund-raiser) will be an integral part of the staff in most schools. It is essential to differentiate between a professional development person and one who may be simply serving as a fund-raising technician. A fund-raising technician organizes and implements an array of methods and techniques designed to produce revenue for a variety of projects and causes. Thus, the high-school sponsor of the cheering squad who organizes and supervises a Saturday car wash at the local gas station, could be considered a fund-raising technician. The squad needs new uniforms, and there are no funds to purchase them. The sponsor and the boys and girls on the squad organize a series of acts that they hope will produce all or part of the revenue needed to purchase the uniforms. The goals and objectives of the sponsor do not go beyond the purchase of the uniforms. Next year she may organize a similar event to provide scholarships to send her squad to cheer-leading camp at a local university.

Development professionals, however, operate at a different level. While some writers use the term *development* as synonymous with *fund-raising* (Pray, 1981), development in its broadest context implies a *process* wherein an institution seeks to develop a favorable climate to attract support from a wide range of groups, organizations, and individuals. In this context development is frequently thought of "friend-raising" as well as "fund-raising." In fact, institutions that are not successful in friend-raising will more than likely not be successful in fund-raising.

Experienced development professionals will attest to the fact that the building a favorable climate and winning institutional friends occupies 80 to 90 percent of their time. The actual process of raising funds may involve less than 20 percent of the development officer's time.

Some public-school foundation directors have made the actual fund-raising process a major part of what they do. While this may be beneficial for short-term efforts, a successful development program for a local school district must also focus on establishing and maintaining long-term relationships that will generate future support. While solicitation is obviously important, the public-school development professional must also be concerned with such factors as parent and community perceptions of the school, and public relations efforts that deal with these perceptions. Like successful individuals working at the college level, the development professionals in public schools must be concerned with the organization of the school's alumni for long-term psychological as well as financial support. In addition, development as a concept involves short- and long-range planning, cultivation efforts, and the utilization of boards and other volunteer groups. In summary, the term *development* must be considered broader than the term *fund-raising*. Development (also called *advancement*) goes beyond the act of seeking gifts and grants from individuals and groups, and concerns itself with a wide range of present and future activities designed to increase support for the school system.

Concepts to Guide Development Programs

David R. Dunlop, a development professional at Cornell University and a leading expert on obtaining major gifts, has identified a process that all major benefactors to institutions seem to go through (Dunlop, 1991). At a conference for major fund-raising executives he outlined some key aspects, which are adapted here for consideration by those who are now or are considering becoming development professionals in public schools.

1. Create Awareness

How much does your community know about your school system? How well do they understand what you do? Where do they learn about you? In many instances, what takes place in school is poorly understood by parents, let alone corporations, foundations, and other potential donors. Some individuals with an interest in marketing have noted that in fund-raising one must have something to sell, someone to sell it to, and someone to do the selling. In organizing your development philosophy, it is essential to seek ways to create awareness, which involves time and planning. One of the first tasks in creating a development program is to determine all aspects of the school that are worthwhile. In what areas do you excel? In what other areas are you approaching excellence? What efforts are being made to help individuals in the community become aware? What awareness activities are scheduled on a recurring basis? Obviously, individuals cannot support projects or concepts which they know nothing about. To leave awareness activities to local media is shortchanging the school and running the risk of allowing problem-oriented reporters to control "awareness" information.

2. Develop Means to Provide Supporters

Development professionals must work closely with the public-relations departments of their schools to insure a continuing flow of knowledge to supporters and potential supporters. It is not sufficient for individuals to be aware of your school district; they must know your school philosophy, curriculum, special projects, activities, and other important aspects. Most schools do not have public-relations departments, and in such cases printed materials such as fact sheets that outline the school's history, quality of staff, and physical plant may be the responsibility of the development professional. Individuals can learn through a variety of techniques, such as newsletters, brochures, press releases, presentations on the local radio and television, appearances at parent groups and at civic organizations. The key point is that the first task is to help others become aware of what schools do. A second task is to provide them appropriate *knowledge* of the excellence of your efforts.

3. Create Interest

If you have been successful in developing awareness and in helping individuals and groups become more knowledgeable about your school, you should next consider ways of creating interest in your institution. It is possible to determine a rough degree of interest by noting attendance at school-sponsored events and activities. Do your local businesses and industries support you in a variety of ways? Does a local filling station work with you on a car wash project? Who attends athletic events? Do personnel directors inquire about any of your programs? Are there any school/business partnerships? It is possible, of course, to create interest and fund-raising programs should assess and perhaps create interest in what schools do.

4. Stress Involvement

If an individual or group expresses an interest in your school, efforts should focus on ways to involve as many friends, parents, business-people, and civic leaders with your school as possible. This is perhaps the most important aspect of a development person's job. Rarely is support, financial or otherwise, given if an individual is not involved with a group or organization. Those closest to the institution are likely to be its best supporters. Those who lack awareness, knowledge, and interest must be brought closer to the institution if they are to become major supporters. In this sense, a major task of any development office is to determine interest and create involvement. Activities range from serving on school committees, to consulting about the curriculum; there are countless opportunities for involvement.

5. Obtain Commitment

Commitment requires more than words. It requires individuals willing to donate time, treasure, and/or talent to your school. Obtaining commitment is a *process* that should be carefully monitored by the development office. Who is involved? At what level? What needs to be done to move those who are aware and interested to a commitment? What is the extent of community-wide commitment?

Assessing commitment may be done in a number of ways, ranging from discovering who attends school events (simple counting) to the number of individuals and groups who contribute time, talent, and dollars to support your effort. For example, if the president of a local manufacturing plant agrees to serve as chairperson of your local education foundation, her/his willingness to serve, represents solid commitment. Not all individuals are able to make commitments in the same fashion, and equal commitment from all should not be expected. However, your development philosophy, which guides your day-to-day activities, should list ongoing individual and group commitment as a major goal.

6. Assess Individual and Group Commitment

In the example above, the individual who agrees to serve on your development board has shown strong commitment. The overall goal of a development professional is to gain as much commitment as possible from as many individuals and groups as possible. At times this commitment is expressed in dollars or gifts-in-kind such as a donation of computer equipment. At other times, individuals donate personal talents (music, art, fund-raising), but regardless of how a commitment is made, it is vital that efforts work toward obtaining a commitment of some kind.

In summary, your development philosophy should guide and determine your activities. Development is not simply fund-raising, which is often a single event that is repeated annually. Rather, it is a continuous process and involves effort to "friend-raise" as well as "fund-raise" by creating awareness, providing knowledge, assessing interest, creating involvement, and obtaining commitment for your school and its programs from a wide range of individuals, groups, and organizations. In this sense, development is as much a point of view as it is a series of tasks designed to elicit support.

PRINCIPLES OF FUND-RAISING

Regardless of the organization seeking support, all must be able to respond to some basic questions, that is, "make a case" for the institution. Thus a public school, in a manner similar to that of colleges and universities or even The United Way, must be able to respond to the following questions:

1. Why is my school district important?
2. In what ways does my school district serve our community, and what individuals in the community does it serve?
3. What does our school do and why?
4. Why does our school district deserve support?

Establish Goals and Objectives

Prior to seeking funds, the goals and objectives of the school district must be established. No school district should attempt to raise funds simply because "It seems like the right thing to do." Each school district has (or should have) both long- and short-range objectives. Obviously, many of these objectives are met and are supported with tax dollars. Some of the school's objectives, however, may include those that are not supported by taxes. It is in this context that most school districts involved in fund-raising operate. In essence, school districts seek private funding to expand and enhance normal operations. Private funding is used to meet those objectives deemed important and deserving of support but not provided for in local and state appropriations.

For example, one general objective of a given school district could be ensuring that all children who wish to attend a college or a university are fully prepared to meet the admission standards of most universities. This objective is met, in part, by the development of an outstanding academic curriculum in math, science, English, history, and other subjects commonly required for college admission. These subjects are supported through taxes. Such items as teachers' salaries, supplies, and transportation are tax supported. Suppose, however, the school district feels that students who want to meet competitive admission standards would benefit from a specialized course offered after school hours to prepare them for such college admission tests as the Scholastic Aptitude Test. If funding is not available or if state law or school board policy prohibit the use of tax dollars for such an activity, then the objective could be met by soliciting private funds for the project. Of course, funding must follow and reinforce institutional planning. It is basic that school priorities determine fund-raising goals.

Organizations Have No Needs

In the context of fund-raising a school district has no needs (Lord, 1985). Attempting to raise funds on the basis of what is *needed* is similar to asking a car dealer to let you use one of her/his vehicles because you need to get to work. Just about everybody has received a letter or a phone call from someone who asks for support because the situation with a certain group is desperate. "Unless you help, we will lose our building. We can't meet the rent demands beyond January." School districts have used this approach to seek public support for a bond issue or for a tax increase for salaries. "Unless we get a significant increase, we will lose a substantial percentage of our best teachers." Does this sound familiar? If so, your first task as a fund-raiser is to *forget the need approach* to soliciting private funds. Your school district is not a problem, and you are not seeking funds to shore up a sagging curriculum or poor athletic field. Your school, and you as a fund-raiser, are the *ones who provide solutions to society's problems.*

Remember that unless adults have children in school, their knowledge about schools may come from articles and stories in the print and broadcast media. More often than educators would like, these stories deal with the negative aspects of the educational process. People who provide support, however, *do not want* to contribute to programs and activities that are perceived as problems. In a larger sense, the request for support for a project should be addressed in terms of an opportunity. "We invite you to share with us this unique opportunity to insure that our school system remains among the highest ranked districts in the state and in our region." This statement demands attention.

Volunteer Involvement

Effective fund-raising relies heavily on volunteers, but no volunteer development officer can meet fund-raising goals by herself/himself. It is important to involve volunteers in the school's fund-raising efforts from the very beginning. Recall from chapter 1 the importance PEFNet placed on involving community leaders at the start of creating a LEF organization. There is good reason for this. Volunteers who support your schools, who work actively on their behalf, and who serve as effective spokespersons, are not only absolutely essential for fund-raising operations, but they also represent a major segment of the potential donor pool. Rarely are major gifts given to an institution by a donor who is not somehow involved with that institution. It is also essential that volunteers have a sense of ownership of the fund-raising process. Human beings encounter difficulty mustering up enthusiasm for ideas that someone else has developed. It would be a serious mistake for a development professional to create a fund-raising plan for a school district and then attempt to "sell" that plan to a hastily recruited group of volunteers.

In addition, an individual who accepts an offer to volunteer may be an excellent prospect for a major gift, either in the near future or as part of an estate. One of the best ways to cultivate a donor is to have her/him volunteer to be part of your fund-raising effort.

Initiate Fund-raising Projects

Schools should initiate fund-raising projects with those closest to the school. Who are the natural partners of the school? Identification of these partners is fundamental to all fund-raising efforts. In some organizations the term *natural constituency* describes those who are closest to the school. In colleges and universities, the obvious natural constituency is composed of the graduates of that institution. This is why one of the first tasks of a newly created development office is to compile an accurate list of the school's graduates, and why colleges and universities go to great lengths to work closely with their alumni associations. Public schools have generally not done so well with alumni associations, but there is no reason to believe that they cannot do so. Even if 50 percent of the senior class in a school system goes on to college and becomes a loyal supporter there, the other 50 percent may still live in or near the school district. These graduates are natural partners. Other natural partners include businesses and industries in the school district, private and corporate foundations nearby, members of the school board, parents of the students, the general public, and individuals who have moved into the district at a later stage of their lives.

Effective Fund-raising

Cultivation is essential to effective fund-raising. Dunlop (1991) differentiates between speculative fund-raising and relationship fund-raising. In speculative fund-raising, an organization seeks help in a speculative way; that is, it asks for support for a worthy cause and counts on good will for contributions. Most people have probably received letters that read "Dear Friends of The Association to Save the Swamp Maple," or something to that effect. Most organizations who solicit in this manner are *hoping* for your support. As one might expect, such letters do not produce a high rate of return. Rather, as Dunlop suggests, a major approach to all fund-raising is building relationships with individuals and with corporate and private foundations. This is why all good fund-raising efforts start with natural partners, because a relationship has at least in part been established.

Cultivation does not simply mean sending out letters. It means carefully planning activities for current givers and for those who may give in the future. Cultivation, both of individuals and of groups, takes many forms. Recall the use of volunteers in school as a form of cultivation. Other forms include placing individuals on school committees, in booster clubs, as classroom volunteers, and as consultants with special skills beneficial to the school program. The actual nature of the involvement, however, is secondary to the principle that in the long run an institution's major supporters are those who participate in some way in the school's program. Cultivation is the process that insures this involvement.

Know and Understand Your School

It is virtually impossible to motivate others to support a product (your school district) unless you know it well. Be aware of your faculty and their strengths, the success of your graduates, the relative position of your school compared to others of its size, and the overall aims and objectives. Someone who is not excited about the school can not expect potential donors to become either excited or generous.

Seek Funds from Past Supporters

Initiate all fund-raising drives with those who have supported past efforts. This concept is related to the notion of seeking funds from natural partners. Most organizations start each fund-raising effort by seeking assistance from those who have been supportive in the past. Individuals and groups who have donated to the school at least twice are excellent candidates for continued giving. When properly thanked, continually involved and well-informed individuals and groups can be counted on not only for annual support, but they may also be a source of new gifts.

Marketing Principles

Fund-raising is based on marketing as opposed to selling principles. Marketing professionals have taught us to take the viewpoint of the consumer rather than of the "seller". Recall that "organizations have no needs," although many fund-raising documents still base their cases on what the *institution* needs. A good fund-raiser asks "What do my potential donors want to support?" Fund-raising programs are then created to meet the wishes of the donor group. This does not mean that a school can not seek funds for projects that it does want and perhaps need. In preparing a case for such "asks" however, it is always beneficial to keep the "consumer's" (donor's) wishes in mind.

Solicit Peers

The best solicitors are peers. Some organizations hire individuals to raise funds with the thought that the individual hired will do most of the asking for donations. Observations indicate that the director of the LEF is generally active in the solicitation of gifts, particularly those that require proposals, and in the fund-raising associated with special events. In most cases, however, the best results from fund-raising are obtained when a volunteer solicits a peer who has the same or similar financial status. For example, the best person to solicit the chief executive of a local bank may well be the volunteer member of the board who is the chief executive of another bank. One of the oldest tenets in fund-raising is that the best solicitation occurs when the right person asks the right person for the right amount, for the right purpose, at the right time. In the majority of instances, the right person is a volunteer peer who is active in the school district. In fact, the paid professional person may be only the second- or third-best person to solicit a prospective donor!

Do Not Ask for the Average

Fund-raising goals are seldom achieved by dividing the needed total by the number of prospective donors and asking for the average from everyone. In most campaigns, the majority of the money raised comes from a minority of the names on the prospect list. Another tenet of fund-raising is the so-called 80/20 rule—that is, 80 percent of the goal will come from 20 percent of the people solicited. In recent years, some fund-raisers report that as much as 90 percent of the goal will come from 10 percent of the donors. In some public-school campaigns, especially among those who have little or no experience raising funds, there can be a tendency to approach goals by dividing up the donors and hoping each will contribute the average amount needed to meet the objectives. In general, this approach is not effective!

Advance Work

It is beneficial to secure at least 30 percent of the goal, preferably 50 percent, prior to publicly announcing the campaign. This rule is frequently used in capital campaigns for colleges and universities, but the principle applies to public-school activities as well. For example, if an LEF has an annual sustaining goal of $100,000, then the director of the group is well advised to secure gifts that total $30,000 or even $50,000 *prior to announcing the fund drive.* No one wants to be associated with a losing effort, and securing gifts that reach one third to one half of the total needed will help insure success.

Contributors as Volunteers

Volunteers who solicit must make their contributions first. If a volunteer or a member of the board of directors is unwilling to make a financial commitment to the cause, he or she will probably not become an effective solicitor of others. Individuals and foundations frequently ask the question, "What have your board members given?" It is not sufficient for board members to contribute time and talent, although these are certainly valuable. Each board member and each volunteer should be expected to make a contribution. While some are able to contribute more than others, all who are involved are expected to participate.

Rule of Fives

Set up the fund-raising structure by the rule of fives. In developing the approach to donors, consider a structure that has one captain or leader for every five committee members, and one solicitor for every five prospects. This structure has frequently been used in a variety of setting and has been effective in establishing and maintaining control of the process (Brackley, 1980).

Seek Investments, Not Charity

Your school is not entitled to charity (Lord, 1985, p. 4). Although it may seem harsh, individuals who give expect to receive something in return. In the case of giving to public schools, individuals are being asked to invest in the process of producing competent, well-educated young men and women.

In raising funds, as in providing services, the most effective terms are achievement, accomplishment, performance, and success (Lord, p. 6).

Face-to-Face Solicitation

This is always the most effective approach. Regardless of the nature of the organization, nothing can substitute for face-to-face solicitation. The higher the giving potential, the wider the spread between results from personal solicitation and any other approach. In general, a personal call produces $50 to every $10 raised by phone and to every $1 raised by direct mail. In addition, if letters or telephones are used, solicitors should write letters and make calls in the same way that they would speak to an individual in a one-to-one meeting (Brackley, 1980, pp. 164–166).

Careful Planning

Basic to all fund-raising efforts is planning. The concepts presented here are all aspects of a process that requires careful planning. If a school district does not have a well thought-out plan, the results are likely to be less than spectacular.

PREPARING A CASE
FOR YOUR SCHOOL DISTRICT

A case for any fund-raising organization is the combination of reasons that justifies its worthiness for support. A good case emphasizes the past and present services of the group and may include material on the group's potential. Lord (1985, p. 40) has described it as similar to an investment prospectus for a business. The major purpose of a case is to attract donors.

In a fund-raising program, a case can take many forms. For example, a case may appear in a brochure, it may be part of a proposal to a foundation, or it may be discussed in face-to-face meetings with donors. It is essential that the case "tells the story" of your school and indicates how a donor's investment in the organization will make a positive difference.

Perhaps the most commonly used statement related to the development of the case is that "it must be bigger than the institution." This statement is related to the basic principle of fund-raising that a school as an organization has no needs. Rather it is an instrument serving society and humanity, and on *this* basis it deserves support. Thus, to make the case "bigger than the institution," it should present a vision of the future that donors will find attractive, achievable, and worth working toward. The best cases are often those that can be summed up in relatively few powerful sentences and perhaps a memorable phrase or two. While a case should include pertinent facts, it should not drown the prospective donor in material. Your donors may want to know how well scholarship recipients are doing in college and how other innovative attempts at excellence are progressing, but these are best presented as examples with additional facts contained in supplementary materials (Lord, 1985, pp. 18, 19). For example, a case statement prepared for the University of North Texas's Centennial Capital Campaign, with the assistance of campaign counsel, was reduced from a document of more 45 pages to one of fewer than 30. Colored pictures and examples replaced excessive verbiage and quotes from well-known individuals expressing the quality of the institution were liberally used. The result was a striking booklet that helped the school exceed its first capital campaign goal by more than $8 million!

Most public schools do not have the funding to produce four-color case statements (or the need to, for that matter), however, they do need to consider elements that might be necessary to include in a case. Some or all of these may appear in brochures, proposals, and guidelines for one-on-one solicitations. There is no standard format for the elements in a case statement, but the following considerations seem fairly standard.

The Mission of Your Public School

In preparing your case, you must consider the role of your school in society. What is the purpose of your school? What are its mission(s), goals, and key programs? What is its history? Do not assume that groups or even parents in your school district will be fully aware of what the school does. Remember, your statement must reflect a stance that reflects a "bigger-than-the institution" point of view.

List Your Successes

Lant (1990, p. 21) suggests that brochures and proposals include a section that lists successes. Because many schools present the case statement in a brochure, listing successes is essential, in statements such as "Last year, three teachers in our district won county teaching awards," or "Of the 100 students who applied for admission to premedical programs over the past three years, 97 were accepted." The point is that you need a list of accomplishments, stated in succinct "bullets" to use in written and verbal presentations of your case.

Increase Public Awareness

Remember to develop your case by "looking in the window" rather than by "looking out the window." Keep in mind individual donors, foundations and targeted civic groups, as well as the community at large as you develop your case. Again, mention high standards, realistic goals, and widespread community support. Your case should never contain statements about survival or saving a program that is going down the drain.

Outline the Problems
Propose Solutions,
and Qualify Your School

Donors want to know how you will solve problems, not how their dollars will help your institution. Your case statement must identify the problems, provide solutions, and indicate why your district is capable of solutions. For example, suppose your local foundation determined, as did the Public Education Foundation in Chattanooga, Tennessee, that professional development is a key to the greatest degree of effectiveness for educators. The plan, therefore, would be to attack the "problem" of increasing and expanding opportunities for professional development.

In the case statement, that foundation would show how the system would attack that problem, perhaps by providing additional seminars and programs in such areas as shared decision-making, collegial relationships among principals and teachers, and continued intellectual development. The statement could then focus on the successes of the program, and show how teacher satisfaction and student learning have been enhanced. Stated another way, indicate that private funds are being sought in order to assist a highly qualified staff become even better, and consequently improving student learning! If your district has been noted by the media as uniquely good in any area or in other publications, include this data.

List Future Plans

Indicate in your case statement the features of your program that will have "carry-over" value. Note all of the present and future beneficiaries. For example, in the Chattanooga school system, it would be useful to state that private funding will enable 98 percent (or some achievable percentage) of the educators in that school system to participate in some professional development activity by the year 2000.

Include Priorities and Costs

Fund-raisers for public schools must always be aware that they seek funds to supplement and enhance local budgets, not to replace them. Thus, a good case statement includes the priorities of the district in targeted fund-raising activities. How will dollars be used? For what purposes? Is seeking scholarship funds the highest priority? Are you seeking endowments? If so, for what purpose? Are you attempting to raise funds for an expanded program of fieldtrips? What is the cost of each of these efforts? Is this our second priority?

Include Plans for Accomplishments

How will you meet your goals? What actions will be initiated? By whom? What is the time frame for meeting these goals? What kinds of gifts are needed? Both individual donors and especially private foundations will be keenly interested in specific plans to meet the goals.

Recall that a case statement needs to include material on the problems the school district addresses. Do not assume that potential donors know the schools well. In addition to listing successes, keep in mind your objective, and the programs and processes you will use to meet your objective and solve problems. Some case statements (and proposals) also indicate past and present support by key organizations and foundations. It is not necessary to include long financial data in the case statement, however, there must be records of audited financial statements.

A case and any form of case statement should not be created in isolation. It is essential that your board, and the public school-system you represent, be part of what you develop. Teachers and principals, for example, should be provided opportunities to contribute to the case and the case statement. They should share their dreams for excellence and these dreams should be transmitted to the director and the board to find ways to meet these dreams. Remember, high goals and excellence is what fund-raising from the private sector is all about. (An example of a case statement is in Appendix M).

CREATING INVOLVEMENT
WITH YOUR SCHOOL

Fund-raisers relate that significant gifts to an institution almost always follow an individual's *involvement* with that institution. Most LEF organizations probably combine involvement activities and speculation (asking for funds "coed") activities in seeking funds for their school districts. There are individuals who are naturally involved in some way with a school district—members of the PTA, booster clubs, band parents, drama club supporters, and others. This involvement is likely to continue at least as long as parents have children attending school. Additional involvement activities include those that are specially created to fulfill certain functions or provide services for the school. If your school has an LEF organization, the members of the board and those whom they solicit to help in fund-raising campaigns are generally those who already have invested their efforts in the district. Remember that involvement is a basic and fundamental aspect of fund-raising.

The concept that involvement is a *process* is most important in creating involvement. School districts that seek leadership and support only when seeking funds are ignoring this basic fund-raising principle. The process of securing leadership and commitment of individuals must begin early in the planning of each LEF. Remember that most individuals do not work well toward goals developed by others. For an individual to work toward goals, he or she must feel an *ownership* of the plan. Prior to asking for gifts for your school, outline your plans for involving all individuals and groups. This is especially important in solicitation of major gifts.

To foster involvement, the school development officer must create plans that are meaningful, important, and continuous. One common mistake is creating advisory boards for academic departments, centers, schools, and colleges of universities. A major problem with these boards has been asking busy people for advice, and then never using it. It is essential that your school district not fall into this trap. A poorly used and ignored advisory board is worse than no board at all. Use of individuals must focus on activities and tasks that are meaningful. If not, members will almost always lose interest and place their energies with organizations that make effective use of their talents and advice.

WHO ARE YOUR POTENTIAL DONORS?

As mentioned, involvement and cultivation are very important in the solicitation process, and those closest to the institution are the most likely donors. Another consideration in planning a fund-raising project is that the development officer in a school district should carefully target potential donors for both short- and long-term fund-raising efforts. For example, the Temple Education Foundation in Temple, Texas, is soliciting planned and differed gifts. Special materials are prepared for those individuals who may be willing to provide support through wills, trusts, and other planned-gift instruments. This has been described as "planting orchards, rather than picking fruit," meaning that they are looking for funds in the near future and also at a later date.

Most LEF organizations, however, are more concerned with solicitation of annual support, and as such must identify people most likely to support them. Although most school districts typically look for support from agencies of the state and local government, or from private and corporate foundations, the chief source of funds of most nonprofit agencies in the United States is the individual. Approximately 85 percent of the funds raised in the United States come from individuals. Private and corporate foundations provide only about five percent each of the charitable dollars given each year. These figures provide an important direction for the development professional. The focus of fund-raising must be the individual. Although corporations and foundations are appropriate sources for funds, they should not constitute the major focus for your organization. The following "types" of donors should be considered in fund-raising plans.

Individuals Close to the School District

As noted, individuals will, in the long run, constitute the major source of funding for your LEF. If the national figures hold true for your local organization, then one can reasonably expect that 85 percent of your funding will come from individuals. Roughly five percent may come from corporate foundations, and an additional five percent may be generated through proposals to private foundations.

In planning solicitation of individuals, remember to plan according to the "rock in the pond" theory, in that those closest to the institution should be solicited first. It does little good to ask members of the community for gifts if board members, faculty, and others have not made a contribution. It is not unreasonable to expect 20 percent of the operating expenses, and 20 percent of the overall goal to come from the members of the LEF board (Lant, 1990, p. 78). Members of the school board, though they are usually elected, should also be solicited.

All faculty and all members of the school staff are also potential donors. It is these individuals, as well as children they teach, who will ultimately benefit from the funds collected. Some directors of LEFs have indicated a hesitancy to solicit faculty because of low teacher salaries. However, a majority of teachers contribute to a number of causes. It is appropriate that they at least be asked to contribute to a cause that may benefit them. There is another important reason for soliciting teachers, administrators, and board members. The question, "How much did your faculty and/or board contribute?" is frequently asked by individuals, corporations, and foundations.

They want to know that those closest to the institution believe in it and are willing to support it before they, too, are willing to contribute to the campaign.

Parents in the Community

Most parents are interested in the quality of the education their children are receiving, which makes parents logical candidates for contributions to the school. Statements like, "Your help will enable our school district to provide the best possible education for your children" go a long way in convincing parents to support your cause, especially if the cause speaks to excellence and the creation of educational opportunities that are not possible with tax-supported budgets.

Alumni

Colleges and universities focus major efforts on the solicitation of alumni. This is not surprising because the alumni represent a large part of the institutional family. In fact, most broadly based campaigns have the alumni as a major focal point, both for short- and long-term giving. Alumni represent a major source of large personal gifts.

Some directors have indicated that a large percentage of alumni are more loyal to their college or university or to their church than they are to their school district. While this may be true, remember that a significant percentage of high-school graduates in many communities do not attend college, and high school was their last formal educational experience. In an educational context they "belong" to your school district; they are not likely to support a college or a university. Second, it is important to remember that individuals support more than one cause. Thus, even alumni who do support a college or a university or who support their local churches may be willing to support the school district also, particularly for projects of excellence. Even individuals who did not attend local schools but who now reside in the district are candidates for gifts.

Major Donors

Major donors are individuals capable of making gifts in the range of $10,000 to $100,000 or more. In general, colleges and universities consider a gift of $100,000 to be a major gift, but the actual dollar figure is arbitrary. It is not uncommon for institutions to consider a gift of $10,000 to be a major gift. In defining a major gift to your institution, a rule of thumb is that it should be based on the size of the gift, rather than its source or whether or not the gift is given now or is deferred. Thus $10,000 is a major gift whether it comes from an individual or a foundation. In fund-raising, it is desirable to develop a list of potential major donors by studying the annual giving patterns of some of your donors. Suppose, for example, you were seeking gifts of $100 for a special project and a donor has given you $200 or even $300 toward the project. This individual's name should be placed on a special list for possible future cultivation. Most major donors initiate giving patterns through smaller annual gifts, however, a major donor program should be very much a part of your fund-raising plans.

Contributors from the Business World

In the development of fund-raising plans, it is important to develop a list of the businesses, industries, and corporations in the area. Corporations like to be considered good citizens and they like to contribute to causes that enhance the image of that corporation. Corporate foundation officials frequently ask if their gift for the year would in any way provide a "photo opportunity" for their corporation. In other words, how will their gift make the corporation look good? How will their gift make the chief executive officer of the corporation look good?

If possible, it is a good idea to have at least one executive member of a large local corporation on the LEF board. Not only will this individual assist with the process of soliciting gifts from her/his corporation, she/he may also provide entries to other corporations. Do not overlook large corporations whose physical plants may not be in your area, but who do business there. Examples of such corporations are utility and communications companies. Many corporations, of course, have corporate foundations for the purpose of distributing financial gifts.

In addition, do not ignore small local businesses, local establishments of national chains (fast food franchises) and all of those with whom the school district does business (called *vendors*). For example, a company that supplies fresh vegetables to the school lunch program is a good candidate for a gift because a significant part of that company's income may come from business with a local school. A word of caution is appropriate here. It is legitimate to ask vendors for gifts; however, to imply that the business the school does with them is contingent upon the size and frequency of their gifts is unethical and in some states illegal.

Many smaller businesses who do not do contractual work with the district also benefit from the presence of the school. So-called "mom and pop" stores where children buy soda and candy, and stores that sell clothing imprinted with the school logo or mascot are the kinds of businesses that should be on your solicitation list.

Private Foundations

In the decade ahead, more and more private foundations will in all probability increase their gifts to public schools. Once the "private domain" of the colleges and universities, the private foundations will turn their attention to helping revive a system of public education that has been labeled "at risk." Therefore, the school district that is not becoming poised to solicit the private foundations may find itself missing out on significant opportunities in the decade ahead. Private foundations can and will contribute to public schools with increasing frequency. However, the basic tenet that private foundations will not give to lost causes holds for public schools. The job of the development director is to indicate how her/his school district is providing solutions to educational problems. Give foundations an opportunity to participate in a process of excellence, not provide Band Aid dollars to a sinking ship. (Solicitation of private foundations is discussed in chapter 8.)

Organizations

Local civic and service organizations have long been a source of a wide range of community endeavors. As such they represent a solid potential for solicitation by LEFs. Some of these groups are national (Rotary, Kiwanis, Lion's) and in some communities there may be local lodges or civic groups that will also support education. The development professional needs to make a list of these and determine how they will be approached. Many organizations have members of local civic groups on their LEF boards and these individuals provide entrance to the civic groups.

SUMMARY

LEF organizations exist in large part to support projects of excellence in a school district. They form to enhance tax-supported budgets, not replace them. They exist to make public education as good as it can be. They do not exist to make up real or perceived budget shortfalls.

A number of public-school districts now employ full-time directors of LEFs. With the help of volunteers, they strive to create awareness, provide information, create interest, and help assess and obtain commitment for school districts.

LEFs operate with the same principles of fund-raising that other nonprofit groups use. They must determine educational goals prior to developing fund-raising goals. They provide opportunities to give, rather than solicit for inadequacies. They rely heavily on volunteer support, and initiate and cultivate individuals and groups for continued assistance. Solicitation and cultivation start with those closest to the organization, and fund-raising plans must consider marketing concepts, effective peer solicitation, and tested solicitation strategies to produce the best results.

The development professional, other educational staff, and volunteers must prepare a "case" for the reasons that a group should give to their school district. A case statement tells the district's "story" and focuses on excellence. It is one aspect of the careful planning that must be a part of all fund-raising efforts.

A good fund-raising strategy includes identifying and targeting potential donors, including individuals within and outside the school district, corporations and corporate foundations, small local businesses, vendors, and regional and national corporations.

4

ORGANIZATIONAL ISSUES
IN FUND-RAISING

A number of issues in fund-raising require the close attention of the director of the board and of the board members. Most fund-raisers would probably agree that successful results are significantly enhanced through board involvement in budgeting and accounting, creation of gift policies, work with volunteers, board development, work with the chief executive officer of the organization, and issues related to professional staff.

BUDGETING AND ACCOUNTING

One of the chief concerns about some nonprofit agencies voiced by major foundation officials, is the relative lack of sophistication with budgeting and accounting procedures. Some foundations have even funded the creation of local agencies that provide consulting assistance to local nonprofit groups. Budgeting is, of course, a key consideration for any LEF. If at all possible, an accounting system needs the expertise of a professional accountant. In fact, it is wise to get an accountant on the steering committee when the LEF is being formed and to include that person (or another with similar expertise) on the LEF board. A publication entitled *Oklahoma Schools Foundations* recommends the following steps in the creation of an accounting system:

   1.   An accountant should draft a chart of accounts, develop a general ledger and journals and draft a format of a set of financial statements for the LEF.

2. A budget and allocations should be established to include the expected contributions and expenditures for the initial year. A determination of amounts that are expendable and those that will be used for endowment purposes, if any, should be developed.

3. An accountant should help the director establish controls over donor records from the point of donation through financial statements and tax preparation. Included should be consideration of whether or not the organization will accept restricted contributions and a system to track them, whether or not the foundation will accept noncash contributions (commonly called *gifts-in-kind*) and how they will be valued, and how the organization will deal with negotiable instruments such as gifts of stocks and bonds. An additional control issue is that of a consideration of the level of accounting knowledge and the time available for the individuals who will be receiving gifts. The issues related to restricted gifts, noncash contributions, and negotiable instruments should be part of a gift policy approved by the board. (Gift policies are discussed later in this chapter.)

4. If possible, the director, perhaps with the assistance of the board, should find an individual in the community who is knowledgeable in accounting procedures and regulations for nonprofit organizations to implement the controls and perform the routine bookkeeping and financial reporting to the board (*Note:* This could be the accountant noted above if she/ he is willing to serve.)

5. An accountant should be named to audit the financial statement of the foundation and prepare the tax return. All plans for implementation should be approved in advance of the initiation of any projects. (Adapted from Oklahoma State Department of Education, *Oklahoma School Foundations*, no date.)

Taking these steps, though it may seem complex and cumbersome, can in the long run save time and alleviate problems. For example, the Internal Revenue Service will annually ask for the details of significant contributions to include the name, address, date, method of evaluation, and amount (IRS Service Form 990). Other potential problems include poor control over noncash contributions, inaccurate reporting of fund-raising events, inadequate minutes of meetings of the board of trustees, and inadequate documentation of the expenses paid (Oklahoma State Department of Education, no date). At some time your organization *may* be examined by the Internal Revenue Service, and the document used is a checksheet (Form 9215) that requires the charitable organization being examined to respond in great detail to some of the issues noted here. As is true in most fund-raising, good planning combined with good professional advice will eliminate errors and insure a smooth-working organization.

There is no single form for budget planning and preparation, however, most nonprofit groups need to consider several budget categories and analyze them with respect to what has been budgeted, the actual expenses for the current year, and projected expenses for the year ahead. At least four broad categories—*administration, office materials, public relations,* and *general consideration*—should be aspects of the budget.

Administrative expenses include the salary of the director (and assistants and support staff) and any benefits to individuals paid by the LEF.

The printed forms the LEF uses constitute a second category for consideration. Budgeted items, for example, include cards, forms, letterhead, and typing, copying, and printing costs.

The third category includes funds budgeted for items related to public relations. All brochures, materials for special presentations, pictures, videos, slides, and anticipated costs for special meetings are in this category.

The fourth category includes items not covered in the other three, but almost all organizations must budget for travel, costs of luncheons and dinners, general office supplies (paper clips, scotch tape, etc.), fax and telephone costs, mailing costs, and any equipment rental.

As noted, these budgets should be prepared in advance and approved by the board.

The cost of operating an office is part of the total fund-raising effort, and needs to be among the first items considered. Beyond this basic budget, the director and the board must decide what funds are to be raised for what purpose, how they will be disbursed, and what portion will become part of an endowment, which retains it corpus while only the interest earnings are spent. In essence, budgets reflect three broad categories: those of operating expenses, those that support programs, and funds for capital purposes (construction, equipment). Of these categories, operating funds tend to be the most difficult to raise, and funds for capital purposes may or may not be solicited annually. In most cases LEF organizations concentrate on annual campaigns designed to secure funds to support programs (i.e., teacher and minigrants) and perhaps endowments. As LEF groups mature, they will become more sophisticated in their fund-raising approaches and include more effort in such areas as specialized capital campaigns and sophisticated planned-gift programs

GIFT POLICIES

Issues related to the acceptance of restricted gifts, noncash contributions, and gifts of negotiable instruments should be outlined in the organization's gift policy. These written policies should be part of every foundation's documentation, and should be available on request, especially by potential donors.

Gift solicitation policies can and should be tailored to fit an existing school district, and so the format may vary. A key aspect of gift solicitation policy should be a determination of what kinds of gifts the school district will accept and what kinds may not be acceptable. For example, the LEF may agree to accept gifts of land, but may not want to accept land with an environmental hazard associated with it. Another example of a questionable gift is land with conditions. Suppose, for example, that a donor wants to give your foundation a house in a town that is some distance from your school district, but a condition of the gift stipulates that the property never be sold and only be used by the district for conferences, retreats, and other such functions. Most districts would not want to accept such gifts. This is why gift policy should clearly state the kinds of gifts you are willing to receive.

The gift policy should also discuss appraisals of potential gifts. Suppose that a donor wishes to give your foundation a painting and indicates that she believes the painting is worth $20,000 or more. Once she has given the painting that she evaluates at that amount, she is eligible for a substantial tax deduction. From the standpoint of the donor, the gift may well be worth that much, but when your organization wants to report the total dollar value of gifts received, they may want an independent appraisal. The painting in fact could be worthless, and although such instances do not occur often, they can happen. Your organization could become an unwitting partner in a tax fraud!

Additional sections of the gift policy should contain information on which individuals in the school district are authorized to accept gifts on behalf of the organization, and when and how the institution will refuse a gift.

Coordination of the solicitation of individuals and of corporations is usually not a problem for public-school districts, especially those that have a single-person office. However, as development activities increase, there is a high probability that more than one person in the school district will want to solicit donations from an individual or a private foundation. Directors of LEF organizations should develop guidelines in the gift policy that stipulates who can solicit whom and for what purpose. Many foundations, for example, do not want to consider two proposals for funding from a single educational entity at the same time. Well-organized gift policies prevent embarrassing situations by clearly indicating how the solicitation of donors is to take place.

Other areas to include in a written gift policy are discussions of how gifts are to be liquidated (sold), how tangible personal property will be recorded and reported, how to handle gifts of life insurance, securities, real estate, wills, annuities, trusts, and gift procession through the school system.

Many school districts do not have written gift policies because of the relative newness of LEF organizations and the fact that some aspect of gift policies may be covered in some sections of the group's bylaws. As your organization grows and becomes more complex, however, it will need to develop a well thought-out gift policy. (Examples of gift policies are in Appendix N.)

WORKING WITH VOLUNTEERS

Barbara Snelling (1985) of Snelling, Kolb, and Kuhnle, a professional fund-raising firm with offices in Vermont, Philadelphia, and Washington, DC, defines a *volunteer* as "someone who believes in a cause and gives freely of his or her time without compensation; someone who is involved because she/he has an interest in, rather than professional training in, the field of activity." This probably describes the majority of individuals who do volunteer work for LEF groups.

Volunteerism in the United States involves large numbers of individuals from all segments of society. In recent years, in excess of 92 million individuals volunteered in a wide range of activities. Of those who do volunteer, more than half are women, although more than 40 percent are men. They volunteer for many reasons, but almost all indicate a sincere desire to help others, and the nature of the work they perform is interesting to them.

To be effective, a volunteer must have a sincere belief in the worthiness of what he/she is doing. In fact, this belief forms the basis of all unspoken volunteer contracts. A volunteer's time must be treated as important and valuable, and assurances must be given that he/she will never be asked to do anything in the name of any cause that will compromise any beliefs or detract from the best interests of the cause (Snelling, 1985).

In establishing the volunteer program for an LEF group, it is important that the director first establish the need for volunteers. In local school districts this will be relatively easy because the objectives of the program will likely be beyond what can be accomplished by a paid staff. Districts who have only a half-time director will find that dependence on volunteers will increase if objectives are to be met. In addition, in major gift fund-raising, the director of the LEF is possibly the second or third best person to solicit individual donors. The most effective is, of course, a peer soliciting a peer.

When the need has been established, the objectives of the program should be carefully analyzed to determine the ways in which the volunteers will function. With those objectives in mind, develop in writing the purpose of the board, committee, or group. It is also important to consider at this juncture their responsibilities, their governance role if any, their reporting lines, their staffing, and their decision-making powers. Other areas to consider are relationships with other volunteer groups, how their efforts will be coordinated, and how long each will serve (Will there be terms of office?).

Once this has been done, the director can develop a job description and assess the kinds of talents and skills that are desirable. Then the director can initiate the process of developing a pool of prospects. If possible, create a list of first, second, and third choices for each position (Snelling, 1985). For example, in LEF organizations, the director will probably recruit individuals with a wide range of skills, such as public speaking, communication, accounting or financial skills, grant writing, marketing, and direct solicitation skills. In small rural districts, this may be difficult, but the categories represent desirable goals. Recall that in the most common structure of LEF organizations, there is a volunteer board and an additional group of volunteers who are sometimes called an advisory committee. For example, in the Lewisville, Texas, Educational Foundation, each member of the twenty-one-person board is asked to help recruit and invite five members to serve on an advisory committee for the purpose of creating additional support, generating enthusiasm, and increasing visibility. This means that the director of that foundation has the responsibility of working with a minimum of 121 volunteers!

All volunteers want to know what the group expects of them, some assessment of whether or not they will be able to complete the task, and the kinds of assistance that will be available to help them with their work. This is the purpose of a simple form with the title of each position, the general purpose of the position, the qualifications, and the responsibilities that the job entails. In the Lewisville program, a major function of the advisory board, in addition to providing advice, is assistance in raising funds. It is vital that this expectation be communicated to each volunteer at the time of recruitment.

TRAINING VOLUNTEERS

Members of the volunteer pool who have been selected to be interviewed need an introduction to the organization. Directors who assume that volunteers and lay parents are familiar with how schools operate and how nonprofits operate are overlooking the fact that some individuals have not been associated with the public schools since the time of their own graduations.

Orientation programs can be done in groups or individually, but each individual who is new to your *board* should have an individual orientation session if at all possible. They (as well as all other volunteers and advisory committee members) need to be made aware of all policies related to their work, of expenses, if any, that each must bear (meals on meeting day?

mileage?) and any expected use of personal funds. The structure of your organization, its officers, and reasons for existence also need to be covered in detail to acquaint the volunteer with the group. If the group has a handbook, then an orientation session is a good place to review this document containing important details of the group. If there are to be training sessions for volunteers, dates and topics should be presented at this time. Remember that some volunteers probably give their time to other groups, and they need to know in advance the time or times you expect them to be at a certain place or involved in a certain activity. Also remember that orientation is a process, not a one-act play. It is something that is ongoing in a planned and organized way. In some cases, an activity may have to be scheduled for more than one day to insure that all who will be involved know and understand the overall process. For example, if a volunteer is to solicit funds, the director is flirting with disaster if that individual is allowed to go out "on his/her own" to seek funds without a clear understanding of what should and should not be a part of the solicitation process.

The director will schedule the inservice training of volunteers. Inservice training can involve almost all aspects of advancement, but some common topics include sessions of why and how individuals give, tax benefits of giving, the solicitation process, the information contained in the documents printed by the LEF (brochures, case statements, forms, annual reports, donor lists, and planned giving materials).

It is also important that volunteers receive training for special campaigns, or any aspect of the annual campaign. They should also become familiar with the common tools that the LEF uses, such as pledge cards, thank-you notes, and scheduling and solicitation forms. (*Note:* The material in the major donor section of this book is useful in helping train volunteers in the solicitation process.)

In all of this the director must decide on methods of control. Even the best-intentioned volunteers can find themselves in situations they have difficulty handling, and in spite of very careful selection procedures, some individuals will not function well as volunteers in fund-raising efforts. The director must keep in mind the individual's goals as well as the goals of the organization. Problems must be dealt with immediately, and if a volunteer is not functioning well in one aspect of the program it is sometimes possible for him/her to function in another. For example, a person who does not feel comfortable soliciting funds may provide excellent support to the director in arranging a special event or coordinating a campaign kick-off luncheon or dinner (material in this section adapted from Biles, 1987).

Finally, do not forget to find a host of ways to thank your volunteers. An axiom in fund-raising says that one cannot thank donors enough. This should be extended to those who volunteer for your LEF. Volunteers thrive on praise and appreciate birthday and holiday cards. When possible invite them to important meetings, and listen to their advice. Give them recognition through award dinners and luncheons; work to have their names and pictures in newspaper stories about your group; create awards for a range of service contributions; and allow volunteers to represent your group at various community functions. Find ways that the individual and collective identities of your volunteers are enhanced through their work with you. In truth, local educational fund groups will not be able to exist without volunteers!

ROLE OF THE BOARD
IN FUND-RAISING

Chapter 1 discussed the importance of the board of directors of a fund-raising organization. Recall PEGNet's suggestions that the steering committee used to create the organization needs to help recruit the members, and the information on a suggested structure for a board.

Board members are volunteers, of course, but they are very special volunteers. A board must be an active, dedicated, and responsible body whose members serve without compensation. If an LEF is to make progress, then everyone involved, especially the members of the board, must have a strong conviction that fund-raising is not the sole responsibility of the director, but is a total broad effort. The material of some LEFs give the impression that the development committee of some LEF boards had been designated as *the* committee to do the actual fund-raising. If this is accurate, then it can be considered an error in terms of good fund-raising technique. Although there is nothing wrong in having a committee with a specific charge such as fund-raising, the principle that *everyone* must be involved is essential for long-term success of the operation.

All boards provide the LEF public accountability, governance, and fund-raising assistance, and serve as spokespersons for the cause at hand. In essence, the chair of the board and all members must assume ownership of the program, and set an example for the school and the community that she/he serves.

One of the most difficult tasks that plagues directors is seeking funds from the members of the board. In many cases, members are not properly informed when they are asked to be members, and may have been given only vague directions about what is expected of them. Statements such as, "We need your help" or "We need your advice" are common. It is not too difficult to guess what one will get from members recruited in this fashion—lots of advice and few dollars. It is not unreasonable, as Lant (1990) suggests, for board members to contribute 20 percent of the operating expenses of the organization. Regardless of how much each member contributes, it is absolutely essential that *each* member contribute something. Most prospective donors would find it unreasonable to donate to a group whose board members have not given first. One can not ask others to do what those closest to the group have not done.

The actual solicitation of each board member should fall to the chairperson as one of his or her major duties. An effective technique is for the board chair to open an initial meeting of the campaign with a statement like: "As you knew when you agreed to serve on the board, each of us will need to provide personal support for the cause. Here is my contribution of (amount) that I am turning over to the director now. I will be discussing your personal contribution with you in the next week or so. As you know, it is vital that we present a united front to the community in terms of how we as members support this cause." If the board chair is sophisticated and understands nonprofit boards, she/he will probably know exactly how to approach this task. With individuals new in the position of chair or with unsophisticated members, the director must be responsible for making certain that all expectations of members, including personal contributions, be made clear prior to any member actually joining the group. Remember, 100 percent participation by board members is a powerful signal of support to the community.

Cargill Associates, a professional fund-raising firm in Fort Worth, Texas, notes that every board member can do something useful to assist in the fund-raising program. In addition to financial contributions, board members:

1. Should be solicitors: *Members are expected to be involved in the direct solicitation of gifts.*

2. Should help cultivate major donors. *Board members are likely to have relationships with a variety of people in the community and perhaps have relationships in corporate and private foundations. One of their tasks is that of telling others of the worthiness of your LEF, and perhaps setting up special events such as luncheons and appointments for the director. If the director calls a corporate office, chances are this is a "cold call." If a board member makes a call to a personal or professional peer, then this is friend-to-friend interaction. Again, peers soliciting peers is the most effective way to reach fund-raising goals.*

3. Should help identify prospects and other volunteers. *Members may not want to serve on your board for more than a single term. They must be replaced and the board should assist the director in finding new members. In addition, board members should use their community contacts to identify individuals who are seeking a worthy cause in which to make an investment.*

4. Need to assist with evaluating prospects. *This is a role that some board members may resist in that they may be uncomfortable with discussing giving capabilities of others. Nonetheless, this is an important board function, and with the help*

of the chair, it should be considered a vital aspect of membership. If fresh information about prior donors and new information about prospective donors is to be obtained, then board members are the key individuals to provide it.

(Cargill & Associates, 1992)

In planning an annual campaign, Lant (1990) suggests that the chair work with the board membership to set up specific committees to concentrate on different target groups for solicitation. These committees include a board committee (with the board chair as the key member), a committee of friends of the board, one of users (those who "use" the school district), a civic group committee, special events committee, a small business committee, a corporations committee, and a foundations committee. Although this structure may seem overwhelming to a director and chair of most LEFs at present, the use of such subcommittees with specific fund-raising goals has proven very effective.

Again, the creation and development of an LEF board is one of the most crucial things to do. As you follow the process suggested by PEFNet and begin to organize your LEF by forming a steering committee, you should also be thinking of potential board members at this time.

THE SUPERINTENDENT OF SCHOOLS AS A FUND-RAISER

The majority of the superintendents of schools in the United States do not consider fund-raising a part of their jobs. At present, most do little, if any, but fund-raising certainly will become a significant part of the superintendent's job in the next two or three decades.

The reasoning behind this prediction stems from knowledge gained at the college and university levels. At many conferences of professional fundraisers, the president of the university is described as the chief development officer. In private institutions, this has long been the case, but in the past 10 years more and more college presidents of state-assisted institutions are expected to raise a significant part of the institutional budget from private sources. Many, of course, dislike this role, but in a sense it is inescapable.

The president of a college or university is the institution's leader. She/he is the top person in the institution just as the superintendent is in a local school district. When there are matters of critical importance in the school district, the individual whom others wish to see is the superintendent. At present, many LEF groups are involved in speculative annual fund approaches to find-raising and may not have paid much attention to such areas as major gift solicitation and planned gifts. However, as LEFs become more sophisticated in their fund-raising approaches, they will be seeking more five- and six-figure gifts. It is in this area that the superintendent will become important. For example, if an individual in a community is considering a six-figure gift to a school district, none but the superintendent can adequately represent the district to that donor. In addition, many superintendents are personally persuasive; that is why they are superintendents! They believe in the school district and generally they are good communicators. They also tend to be highly knowledgeable about specific projects in the district. If they have good listening skills and the ability to relate to others, then they have excellent potential for securing major gifts.

In almost all research on gift solicitation at the college and university levels, the head of an organization plays a significant role in obtaining gifts. The very best solicitation team that could be sent to approach a major donor is the combination of the chair of the board of directors and the superintendent of schools. The development professional provides support information and helps this team outline strategies for making the "ask" for a major gift.

Some may smile at the thought of the superintendent of schools as a fund-raiser. In the 1950s, 1960s, 1970s, 1980s and even into the early 1990s, the smile may be appropriate. Few superintendents are now major gift solicitors, but that will change. As state dollars become less and less a percentage of what is needed for excellence, funds must be discovered elsewhere. The "elsewhere" for many schools will be the private sector.

USEFUL DOCUMENTS FOR FUND-RAISING

A number of occasions require the director of development to have specific information about the school district readily available for use in fund-raising activities. Information about the school district is especially useful in the development of grant proposals, the solicitation of major donors and to back up material for presentations to civic groups and other organizations. The following have proven especially useful:

Fact Sheets

The development professional, if she/he does not have detailed information, will discover that a special effort to compile it will be useful at a later date. A fact sheet can contain as many categories as needed, and typically include the following areas:

1. When was the district established? What is the size and scope of the physical plant? Are there any special features (science lab, planetarium)?
2. What is the annual budget?
3. What is the history of the school district? What significant changes took place in its development?
4. Who are the leaders in the district? List the members of the school board, the superintendent, principals, and department heads. Generate material on your LEF board, with special emphasis on the board chair.
5. What is the size and nature of our student body? List enrollment, student/faculty ratio, number of students at each grade level, gender, and civil rights categories (race, ethnic background).
6. What is the nature of our faculty? Compile data on universities attended, degrees held, and honors received.
7. What are our areas of excellence? What areas make our school stand out when compared to others of our size? How many graduates attend college or other post-secondary schools? Do we have any famous graduates? Where do our students attend school?
8. How has our district fared on statewide and other evaluations? How do we fare on the SAT? What do accrediting teams say about us? Have we won any awards? Have we been singled out for any special recognition?

Brochures

Each LEF should have a brochure that contains some of the information gathered for the fact sheet. Lant (1990) calls for a précis, a document that includes a brief history of the organization, a listing of success stories, an outline of the support received during the past three years (government grants, private funds, etc.), special ongoing programs (minigrants, schoolsite grants, scholarship programs), organizational leadership, fund-raising objectives for the year, and the critical role the LEF plays in the community. This brochure can be printed on inexpensive paper and used as a key information piece in fund-raising efforts. In a sense, a good brochure is a "mini case statement."

Sample Representative Materials

There is essentially nothing new in fund-raising. All documents and ideas are generally tried-and-proven approaches that have been given a new coat of paint. While this may be essentially accurate, the world is full of creative people who are able to create new approaches out of old ideas. For example, one college uses a "blue book" for its annual fund drive. The blue book appears similar to the ones most college graduates are familiar with from their college days. The booklet contains facts about the school.

At any rate, the development director should collect materials used by other school districts or even colleges and universities. This file should contain sample proposals, brochures, cover letters, form letters used in soliciting funds, pledge cards, newsletters, reports of other LEF groups, and information on telemarketing. Having such files not only saves time, but it can also prevent directors from reinventing the wheel.

Public-Relations Materials

Almost every public educator has felt disappointed when what was considered a very good story for the local print and broadcast media never appeared in print or got on the air. Also, most educators have felt the sting of journalists who seem to thrive on "bad" news. This is not surprising; reports of problems sell newspapers and increase television ratings. In 1984 a representative of *The New York Times* told a group of aspiring university administrators at a Harvard institute that they should not expect the press to serve as their public relations staffs. That was probably good advice, even though it is a rather sad commentary on the ways our schools are described to the general public.

This means that the task of public relations falls to the school, and in a sense it may fall to the director of the LEF group. Recall that individuals and groups want to fund projects of excellence. If schools can achieve excellence, then ways must be found to publicize that excellence. One of the best publications for this effort is *Going Public: A Public Relations Guide for the Public Schools* written by the New York Alliance for Public Schools. It provides specific information about fact sheets, how to understand the media, a survey of citywide media, a discussion of community and ethnic newspapers.

In telling your story:

1. *First distinguish between hard news and feature stories.* The first is timeless and has major impact. Feature stories should focus on human interest.

2. *Be creative and put your most interesting facts in the first paragraph or two of news releases.* News releases can flow from the curriculum, individual student and faculty accomplishments, alumni achievements, extracurricular activities, student works, athletic programs, and school/community programs. Releases should be positive, written in the third person, use simple language, avoid excessive use of adjectives, be factual and concise. Each release should have the school's name and address, the authorized person to discuss the information,

and the statement that the material is for immediate release. It is also beneficial to inform the press before the event occurs.

3. *Use news advisories or brief statements to alert the press to future events.* These should tell who, what, and where the event is to take place, and whether or not it is open to the public. Provide details about reservations, meals, and other matters.

4. *Be specific with photos.* If you send photos to the media, use black and white 35mm film, limit the number of people in a photo to five, fix a typewritten caption to the back of the picture, and send the picture with cardboard stiffeners.

5. *Tips for releasing your story.* In releasing your story, be sure you have an up-to-date list of names, addresses, and phone numbers of all community contacts. This is your press list. Have a few sets of envelopes preaddressed to your press list handy for last-minute mailings. Mail at least five business days in advance, and call to follow up the day before the event.

6. *Tips for dealing with the media.* The document prepared by the New York Alliance also suggests that you never speak "off the record" or respond to a question with "no comment," since once you have invited the media you no longer have control over what happens. Rather, respond with "I'll get back to you on that" and call back with a response. The publication also suggests that because space is limited "good quality" stories do not always make it in print or on the air. All copies of media releases should be routinely provided to the members of your development board and the board of education.

(New York City Alliance for the Public Schools, n.d., pp. 10–18)

As staffs grow larger, there are a number of organizational patterns that nonprofit groups employ. These are mentioned here in passing because most LEF groups do not now have the luxury of large staffs and are in essence one-person operations. In larger nonprofits, staffs are sometimes organized by placing individuals in an organizational structure according to the source of gifts (foundations, corporations, local support, sponsored constituency such as alumni, government support, and targeted individuals). Some nonprofit organizations are organized according to methods of solicitation (direct mail, telephone solicitation, special events, planned giving, and special gift clubs). Others organize by the purpose of gifts (annual budget, capital expenditure), the organization of volunteers (capital campaigns, local annual campaigns, special project support). Still others are organized by the required management activities (planning, execution, and evaluation). Again, none of these extensive structures is now generally used by LEFs. However, if and when additional staff are added, it will become necessary to consider what organizational plan to utilize.

SUMMARY

Staffing is a critical part of organizing for fund-raising in an LEF, particularly the issue of who will support the salaries and operational expenses. In some cases, private funds can be raised to at least launch the effort.

New programs need appropriate accounting procedures for both ethical and legal (IRS) considerations. Professional accounting help in the initiation of the program may well prevent problems. In addition, all LEFs should develop gift policies to determine how funds will be solicited and how they will be handled internally.

Working with volunteers is an important consideration for the director of the LEF and proper procedures must be developed to insure that this key element of the program operates as smoothly as possible. This process includes the special role that the board plays in fund-raising.

Directors must also understand the role of the superintendent in the fund-raising process and learn to use her/him in major gift solicitations.

In organizing fund-raising, directors should also compile a file of professional fund-raising and public-relations materials for use with grants, individual solicitations, and dealing with the media. As LEFs grow, staffs will grow, which will require careful reconsideration of how to organize professional staff.

5

ANNUAL FUND DRIVES

The primary support for most LEF organizations comes from annual fund drives, often called annual sustaining fund drives. In a number of ways, the annual fund efforts of LEF groups is similar to the annual fund operations of most colleges and universities. One notable difference is that at the university level, faculty are often involved in determining the institution's needs. Recall the basic premise that fund-raising goals should be developed from academic goals. At the public-school level, the tax funds will be used for academic purposes, but LEF groups typically seek private support for minigrants to teachers and principals and for site grants to school districts. Other projects of excellence are funded, but in most cases the faculty is involved in the process only *after* the funds have been raised. It is probable, however, that in the future, school faculties will be involved in assessing the needs of the school in order to create the foundation for fund-raising goals.

Annual giving is what the name implies, an organized effort of the LEF to secure annual ongoing support for a number of school programs. In general, the gifts solicited are of two kinds, those that are restricted to certain purposes, and those that are unrestricted and can be used at the discretion of the board and the director. An example of a restricted gift is that of an individual or company providing funds for a scholarship for a student to attend a college or university for study in a specific area. The local real estate association, for example, could provide funds for a student to study real estate at a specific college. Such gifts are called restricted because the dollars must be used for a specific purpose. Unrestricted gifts provide the most flexibility and are generally considered very valuable. For example, if sufficient unrestricted funds are raised, some of those dollars could support the director's salary and the operating expenses of the office.

Although some LEFs seek specialized gifts for projects and equipment, the annual fund becomes the chief focus. This may be because the public schools organizations have not, for the most part, created sophisticated major and deferred giving programs, while at the university level, annual fund programs are not only designed to obtain operating dollars, but they are also planned as the first step in getting donors onto the giving ladder. If an individual gives to an organization for two successive years, chances are that he/she will be a donor for a longer period of time. Individuals are selected as potential "major donors" from the list of annual contributors. While their annual gifts are important, it is not unreasonable that with proper cultivation individuals will one day give 10, 20, or even 100 times more than they give to annual drives. (Major gift solicitation is discussed in chapter 6.) In addition to the initiation of the major gift process, the annual fund provides an excellent arena to train and develop volunteers and provides excellent opportunities for individuals to "tell the story" of the school district. One of the best ways to recruit new donors and increase the giving of established donors is to have individuals "sing the praises" of the school district. Volunteers who work on the annual fund are likely to do just that!

PLANNING THE ANNUAL FUND

Once the board and the director have developed fund-raising goals, the planning for the campaign should begin. Suppose, for example, that the board decides the goal for the annual drive for the current year will be $100,000, a 20 percent increase over the prior year. (*Note:* Experienced fundraisers will attest to the fact that goals calling for more than a 20 percent increase in funding are difficult to obtain.) Further determinations need to be made with respect to the nature of the funds to be solicited. Will we be seeking program (minigrant) funds? Are we interested in starting an endowment (retain corpus, spend only the earned interest)? Or will we seek special equipment this year? Once the goal has been determined, a good way to start is to create a chart of standards, a technique that professional fundraisers use as a guide to determine in descending order the number of gifts, and the amounts of gift levels needed to attain a specified dollar objective. Recall that the notion of dividing up the donor pool and asking for the average amount needed from each prospective donor is not the way to reach fund-raising goals. The 80/20 rule holds true for most campaigns.

A CHART OF STANDARDS

A chart of standards can be constructed for almost any campaign, and the process is fairly straightforward.* To construct the chart, the director and board should do the following:

1.   Once the overall goal has been set, calculate the top gift as a percentage of that goal. In most cases this gift should fall in the range of 12 percent to 18 percent of the total. Many nonprofits use the midpoint of the range, 15 percent, to determine the total. In a campaign with a goal of $100,000 the midpoint is $15,000, or 15 percent of the total.

2.   Next, compute the amounts needed for the top 10 investments. Do this by the same process used to determine the top investment. Because the top 10 investments should be 50 to 55 percent of the objective, multiply the objective by both 50 and 55 percent. Thus the top 10 gifts should total $50,000 to $55,000. In addition to selecting the dollar amounts in the top 10 gifts, it is necessary to determine the number of gifts at each dollar level. The most common array of gifts follows a pattern that shows one top gift, one gift at the next highest level, one gift at the third highest level, three gifts at the fourth highest level and four gifts at the fifth highest level to provide the top 10 gifts. This chart now shows the amount of the top investment ($15,000 in our example), and a dollar range for the top 10 investments ($50,000). Subtract the top gift from the total amount needed for the top 10 gifts. (In our example, subtract $15,000 from $50,000.) This represents the dollar amounts for the next four rows. Now it is possible to calculate the dollar amounts for the next nine gifts. For example, one gift of $10,000, three of $5,000, and four of $2,500 will complete the totals for the top 10 gifts. Some adjustments to original projections may be necessary, but this formula is a guideline for determining the levels of the major gifts. In general, it is good fund-raising practice to announce a campaign when it has achieved 50 percent of the goal. This means that if at all possible the first 10 gifts should be "lead" gifts that were obtained prior to the announcement of the campaign.

3.   Finally, calculate the dollar amounts of the remaining gifts. To do this, follow the same process as in computing the top 10 gifts. Since the remaining gifts should approximate from 35 to 45 percent of the objective, multiply the campaign objective by both 35 and 45 percent. In our goal of $100,000, the remaining gifts should total about $40,000, which is the midpoint between 35 and 45 percent. Next divide this amount by five because in most cases there are five rows of data. Now select dollar amounts you judge to be in each category. Estimate broadly the number of each gifts needed

---

*Material in this section is adapted from "Conducting a Successful Capital Campaign. CASE Simmer Institute East, Hanover, NH, 1985; and Barnes Associates, *National Fund Raiser,* Vol. xvii, No. 3, January 1991.

in each category by dividing the dollar amount for each row by the total estimate by five. The number five represents the rows of data and $40,000 is the amount needed for the next 100 or more investments. A common pattern for rows five, six, seven, and eight is that if 10 gifts are needed in row six, 15 are needed in row seven, 20 are needed in row eight, and 30 are needed in row nine. Thus if we need $40,000 to complete our campaign after we attain our top 10 gifts, and we divide that amount by five, we discover that we need five rows of $8,000 for our goal. If we divide $8,000 by 10 (most common pattern for row six) we discover that we need 10 gifts at the $800 level. In row seven we divide the total needed by the most commonly used frequency, 15, and this shows that we need 15 gifts at the $533 level. Similarly, we need 20 gifts at the $400 level and 30 gifts at the $262 level to obtain our objective of 40 to 45 percent of the goal. Of course, these figures may need to be adjusted to meet individual campaigns but they offer an excellent starting point.

Tables 5-1 and 5-2 illustrate gift range tables or charts of standards. In Table 5-1, the nonprofit wished to raise $275,000 and elected to raise $150,000 of that from the first 11 rather than the first 10 gifts. The pattern for the remainder shows 14 gifts at the $5,000 level, 20 at the $1,000 level, 30 at the $500 level, 100 at the $100 level, and 200 at the $50 level. This pattern assumes 87 percent of the total from 12 percent of the gifts and adds a ten percent total to allow for those who pledge and do not meet pledges. It assumes a total of 376 gifts.

Table 5-2 illustrates a campaign goal of $6,000,000. In order to reach this goal, the fund needs one gift of $900,000, one of $700,000, one at $500,000, three at $350,000, and four at $225,000, according to the rule of thumb that approximately 50+ percent of goal should come from the top 10 gifts. Note that the remaining amount of $1,950,000 uses a more common pattern for the gift amounts needed to complete the objective. Rows six, seven, eight, nine, and ten have plugged in the common frequency pattern of 10, 15, 20, 30, and 40 as the number of gifts needed to meet the objective.

Using the chart of standards as a guideline, the director and the board are ready to move forward with the campaign. Having set the dollar goals, the task of the board is to complete the planning necessary to meet the funding objective.

Among the first tasks facing the board are to complete the campaign calendar, decide on the various constituencies to be solicited, and determine leadership and volunteer participation. There are no specific time tables for a campaign, but some LEFs conduct campaigns lasting two weeks or less to three months or more. It is not too early to begin planning a yearly campaign in January or February for a solicitation period that begins in September or October.

TABLE 5–1 • **Chart of Standards I** **Objective: $275,000**

Number of Gifts	Amount of Gifts	Total	Cumulative Total
1	25,000	$25,000	$ 25,000
3	15,000	45,000	70,000
8	10,000	80,000	150,000
14	5,000	70,000	220,000
20	1,000	20,000	240,000
30	500	15,000	255,000
100	100	10,000	265,000
200	50	10,000	275,000

Once the calendar for the campaign has been set, the board and director should decide which individuals and which groups and organizations will be solicited. Each targeted group should have a board member as chair of that particular group. Lant (1990) suggests that as a starting point, each target should assume about 10 percent of the goal. If the chart of standards is used, then a plan must be formulated to approach each of the top 10 individuals on a personal basis. If foundations are to receive proposals, then it's necessary to determine which foundations will be approached for what gifts. In general, there need to be chairs for all groups that have been targeted. This list includes (but is not limited to) alumni, faculty, parents, friends, corporations and foundations, civic groups, local businesses, private foundations, the LEF board, and even the school administration and school board members. Each committee chair may use board members and volunteers to assist in solicitation. For example, members of the advisory board are excellent candidates to be used as personal solicitors. In making this determination, it is useful to consider the rule of fives, one leader to every five committee members and one solicitor to every five prospects. If small businesses are to be solicited, a member of the board should be asked to chair the committee that will solicit those in the community. This committee should have five members, some of whom may be on the board and some of whom may come from the volunteer pool. If 30 small businesses are to be solicited, the committee needs six solicitation teams of five members each.

These tasks should be handled in the first week of campaign planning. Additional initial tasks are planning and scheduling a kick-off reception, and further report and planning meetings. Of key importance are identifying range of target solicitation groups and the chairs of the committees to solicit them. If these tasks are not completed early, in the first week, the director and the board may have to deal later with holes in the campaign.

TABLE 5–2 • Chart of Standards II   Objective: $6,000,000

Number of Gifts	Amount of Gifts	Total	Cumulative Total	Percentage of Goal
1	$900,000	$900,000	$900,000	15
1	700,000	700,000	1,600,000	
1	500,000	500,000	2,100,000	
3	350,000	1,050,000	3,150,000	
4	225,000	900,000	4,050,000	52.5
10	60,000	600,000	4,650,000	
15	40,000	600,000	5,250,000	
20	20,000	400,000	5,650,000	
30	10,000	300,000	5,950,000	
40	5,000	200,000	6,150,000	35

HOW WILL WE SOLICIT?

Once the initial plans have been completed, the director and the board chair must decide the specifics of the solicitation process. Most people are familiar with the usual processes used by nonprofits, especially mail approaches and telemarketing. Although these are acceptable ways to raise money, it is important to plan for all the techniques that will be used in the campaign.

Remember the importance of relationship fund-raising. In the context of an annual campaign, "sort out" all individuals, companies, and foundations who will receive a personal visit from a member of the board, the director, and perhaps the superintendent of schools. This is not a random process and it must be done carefully. Each prospect who is seen individually should receive an individual proposal that includes information about the campaign and how the funds are being utilized. Remember the most effective solicitation is a peer (who has made a personal commitment) soliciting someone of equal financial status. In many cases, a team approach is most effective. For example, if the chairperson of the board is a bank director she/he should be involved in solicitation of other bank officials. The peer should arrange the visit and perhaps include the superintendent of schools, a principal, and the director of the LEF. Teams should include no more than three individuals, and the meeting should be held in the offices of the prospective donor. Prior to the meeting, the team should confer on the details of the meeting, including the roles of each team member. In the example noted here, the volunteer peer is perhaps the best person to make the actual request, the superintendent represents the school district and supplies factual information, and the director of the LEF should be the "technical expert" or the "quarterback" who arranges the calls.

Of course in some cases, the total campaign could be conducted with volunteers using a one-on-one approach. The small business committee, for example, could devise a plan that volunteers make personal calls on each small business member in the community. Each volunteer would solicit five individuals.

Although personal solicitation is the most effective approach to raising funds, factors such as the size of the donor pool and the number of volunteer solicitors may require that some prospective donors be solicited with other approaches. The most common approach to reaching large numbers of individuals is through direct mail. Of course, the use of mail is a speculative rather than a relationship technique and can be expensive, because the return rate on the dollars spent is often low. Nonetheless, if direct mail is to be used, it should be done well. Direct mail techniques are discussed in chapter 6.

Telephone solicitation is widely used for fund-raising and has become increasingly popular in the past decade. It is a somewhat more personal approach than that of direct mail, but in many cases, it has been badly overused by poorly trained volunteers, to the point that some donors are "turned off" by phone solicitations. If an LEF uses telephone solicitation techniques, the group must be well prepared prior to initiating the process. A poorly managed telephone campaign can be detrimental to a school district!

As Vice President for Development for a large university, I was involved with many community agencies in Dallas and throughout the state of Texas. Not surprisingly, my name found its way on to many prospective donor lists. I received so many solicitation calls that I decided to track them over a four-month period. From the period of September to December in one recent year I received an average of five calls per week from nonprofit organizations. Most were legitimate and were for good causes, but I had to choose from among many good organizations those that I wanted to support. In the end, I supported those to which I have either a personal or emotional attachment or both. I learned that the competition for private funding is very rigorous and becoming even more so.

In recent years, some nonprofits have used a strategy called phone-mail that incorporates the best concepts of direct mail with the best telephone solicitation concepts. A number of professional fund-raising firms specialize in this approach. Phone-mail approaches are also discussed in chapter 6.

Regardless of which technique or combination of techniques an LEF uses to raise funds, it is important to remember that in the United States, personal solicitation has about a 70 percent success rate, telephone solicitations have about a 25 percent success rate, and direct-mail solicitations have about a 2 percent success rate. This is a powerful clue to directors and boards who are attempting to decide where and how to focus their campaigns.

STRATEGIES TO ENHANCE FUND-RAISING

A number of particular strategies can enhance giving. Many of these have been used by colleges and universities for years, and for the most part, they have been effective. Of these mentioned here, each can be used in any or all of the methods of solicitation. For example, the gift clubs is an appropriate strategy for direct mail, personal, and telephone solicitation.

Class Gifts

Those who have attended a high-school or college reunion will attest to the powerful appeal that the possibility of renewing old friendships has to individual donors. Most graduates of public high schools identify with a particular class, such as the class of 1952 or the class of 1970. This class loyalty should not be overlooked in designing a campaign. If a subcommittee of the board is concerned with alumni giving, one way to approach graduates is through appeals from certain classes. Each of these members have had some common experiences and each has some loyalty to the school. It is a tremendous advantage for the board chair or the director to announce at the kick-off event that the graduates of the class of 1978 have contributed $2,000 to this year's campaign. Classes may be solicited by any method (phone, mail, personal) and the fact that a "fixed" group of individuals has given is an incentive for other groups to do likewise. Solicitation of donors by graduating class is a type of segmentation of the donor pool. More details on segmentation are in chapter 6.

Reunion Gifts

Some educational institutions use a reunion plan as part of homecoming or alumni day festivities. Reunions are often held every five years. The class of 1992, for example, will hold its first official reunion at the 1997 homecoming. Once a reunion pattern has been established, reunion classes can be tabbed for special gifts. The five-year reunion class may be asked to donate special funds to send the school band to the Rose Bowl Parade or some other important function. Reunion gifts tend to be more significant than general requests for annual funds, and those who make reunion contributions may represent potential major donors. It is important to consider carefully the nature of reunion gifts because most recent graduates are probably in the process of establishing themselves in the world of work or are college or university students. A five-year reunion class would be expected to contribute less than a ten-year or fifteen-year reunion class. Special emphasis should be placed on the "big" reunions, such as the 25th and 50th reunions. Remember that reunion solicitation should be built into annual fund-raising plans.

Challenge Gifts

Challenge gifts are those given prior to a campaign and used, as the name indicates, as a challenge to donors to match or exceed the amount given by an organization or an individual. Challenge gifts frequently are given on conditional terms. For example, Helen Jones, Chairperson of The Second State Bank of Denton, announces, "If our alumni raise $50,000, Second State will contribute an equal amount!" This challenge grant can create excitement and provide a powerful incentive for alumni to become donors. It is also a useful approach to show other donors that the school district has strong alumni support.

Leadership Gifts

Leadership gifts are those given by an individual or group to help launch a campaign. The approach has long been used by successful nonprofit organizations such as the United Way. Leadership gifts are an essential aspect of major capital campaigns. In a chart of standards, gifts that represent the top 50 percent of the goal are the kinds of leadership gifts that most nonprofit groups seek. Leadership gifts are often finalized and "kept quiet" until the kick-off event. It is then possible to state to the gathered volunteers and prospective donors that "with leadership gifts from Dr. Mary Jones and Attorney Helen Blaylock, and others, 54 percent of our goal of $60,000 has been reached. It is up to us to complete the funding objective!"

Gift Clubs

Gift clubs are a way to recognize individual donors and also to recognize a "special" group of donors. Gift clubs are commonly used by athletic fundraisers to seek support from graduates interested in sports. Gift clubs usually are named after something symbolic and meaningful to the school. For example, if the school mascot is an eagle, gift clubs could be called the "Fighting Eagle Club," the "Soaring Eagle Club," and the "Golden Eagle Club."

Each of these "clubs" represents different designated levels of support for athletics (or some other cause). One can become a "Fighting Eagle" for an annual contribution of $50, a "Soaring Eagle" for $100, and a "Golden Eagle" for $500. In many cases donors are first asked to contribute at the lowest level, and in succeeding years attempts are made to move them "up" to the higher level gift club.

An offshoot of gift clubs is the creation of specialized societies or organizations that provide support for various aspects of the school. Many college presidents have some form of fund-raising group that interacts closely with them and in turn receives special "perks," such as regularly scheduled socials, gifts, tickets for concerts and athletic events, and the like. Usually donors involved with the head of the institution are *major* donors, and gift organizations at this level usually require donations of $1,000 or more per year. They are typically "elite" donor groups.

The gift club concept can be structured to become part of the annual campaign by the way the gift club is presented to a potential donor. For example, in many schools groups such as the President's Council offer membership to those who donate a specific amount and agree to some conditions such as "Fifty percent of your donation may go to any project in the school, and 50 percent will be used at the discretion of the board and superintendent for the areas of greatest need." This allows a donor to contribute to an area of interest (athletics, music) and also provides funds for general campaign goals (minigrants, site grants, scholarships).

Named Funds

Some nonprofit groups have successfully used the concept of providing a name that characterizes a solicitation. For example, the annual appeal could be labeled the "excellence" fund or the "loyalty" fund to give donors some notion of the use of gift dollars. In general, named funds exist for very specific reasons (the college scholarship fund) and are restricted in nature or used for very general purposes (excellence fund) that most benefit the school district. The use of a specific fund adds stature and gives definition to more generalized terms such as simply "annual fund."

TRAINING VOLUNTEERS

It is the responsibility of the executive director, along with the members of the board, to provide training for all volunteers in the solicitation of funds. In fact, training the members of the board itself may become the first priority of the director. Most volunteers have never had much instruction in the solicitation of gifts. As a result, they are prone to making mistakes, and at worst can do damage to an organization's image. Others do a less-than-adequate job because of the fear of fund-raising and of their own perceived inadequacies. Thus, at least minimal training of each volunteer is essential. In addition, because volunteers often account for 50 percent or more of a goal, the training itself becomes a type of cultivation of the volunteer solicitor. When a volunteer learns about strengths of the school system that she/he will later verbalize to others, she/he is involved in a process that will help create a closer bond with the school district. Remember, involvement precedes giving and volunteer involvement is one of the best forms of cultivation!

As noted, one of the first things volunteers must learn is that prior to any solicitation, they themselves must first be givers. In all cases, campaign volunteers should be solicited by the board chair, the heads of the various committees, or another volunteer who has made a gift.

Beyond that, each volunteer should have an information packet. It is absolutely essential that the LEF director conduct training sessions wherein the volunteers can go over prepared material, ask questions, and share information with each other. In most cases, the director will schedule several sessions in order to meet the schedules of very busy people. Make no assumptions! A degree in medicine or law is no guarantee that an individual will be a good fund-raiser.

Much of the information volunteers need may be in the fact sheets, brochures, and general public-relations materials suggested in chapter 4. Even if such information is available, volunteers can benefit from additional information about their school district. For example, volunteers may need information about:

1. The mission of the school district.
2. The nature of the community.
3. Budgets, faculty/staff, and history of the district.
4. The case for supporting the school district.
5. The academic objectives and the fund-raising goals of the campaign.
6. Lead gifts and gift clubs, if any.
7. Ways to give (will, cash, securities, etc.).
8. Board leadership and campaign structure.
9. How to process gifts, (pledge cards, etc.)
10. Who and where to call for information that the volunteer may not know.
11. The conduct of the campaign. For example, will the campaign be a single phase (face-to-face solicitation) or several phases (face-to-face, phone, direct mail, phone mail, etc.).

Of even more importance is the need to assist beginning volunteers in actively asking for gifts. It is the asking, more than any other part of fund-raising, that strikes fear into the hearts of volunteers. It is therefore incumbent on the director to alleviate as much fear as possible through training. Knowledge is indeed power, and even a little fund-raising knowledge can lessen the fear factor. In training the volunteer to make an actual "ask," several points are very important.

1.   *The volunteer must know the material* (suggested above) and be able to communicate it. Role-playing sessions among volunteers help with this process.

2.   *The volunteer must understand the whole process.* Cultivation is not holding out a tin cup. Individuals will donate if volunteers are effective communicators and understand that more than one visit to a donor may be necessary. The donor must share the concern of the volunteer. Volunteers should practice establishing rapport and listening and understanding the donor's viewpoint. It is essential that volunteers attempt to view the world as the donor views it. Called empathic responses by clinical psychologists, they are good lead techniques to use with donors. Volunteers should be trained to use such phrases as "It seems to you . . ." or "You feel that the school needs to put more emphasis on academics." The objective is not to *argue* or *persuade* the donor. Rather it is to understand her/him and acknowledge her/his point of view. Of course the volunteer must listen, listen, listen.

After volunteers have learned to establish rapport and have learned the value of listening, they should be prepared to deal with objections commonly expressed by donors. Some examples are:

1.   *Objection:*   Our schools are supported by taxes.

    Responses: You are right. This campaign is seeking funds for projects of excellence that are not supported by taxes.

2.   *Objection:*   I called the school to see if my club could use the gym on weekends and got the run-around from some vice principal.

    Response: I'm sorry your experience was bad. I can understand why you are a little angry. I hope you will not let the system prevent you from helping support important projects that will make our school one of the best in the state. You have two children in high school now don't you?

3. *Objection:* Lone Star High is football crazy!

    Response: I know football is important in Texas, and especially here in Lone Star City. However, this project is for academic excellence.

4. *Objection:* How come the only time I hear from the school is when they want something or want to sell me something?

    Response: The school board is aware of the communication problem. They have authorized the superintendent to develop a newsletter to keep parents and other adults in the community up to date.

5. *Objection:* How well do our kids do when they graduate?

    Response: (Volunteer cites material from fact sheet and case statement.)

6. *Objection:* I'm not sure. tell me again what the money will be used for?

    Response: (Volunteer cites several minigrant projects from last year or outlines the current goals, such as scholarships.

7. *Objection:* I give to my college. It's private and they need the money more than this district does.

    Response: I can understand your support of Ivy University. I also support my alma mater. I think it is great that you contribute to Ivy U. I would hope that you can support us, too.

8. *Objection:* I'm still in college, or I'm between jobs.

    Response: I understand. Like you, some of the younger graduates of our high school are in college and looking for a job I'd still like you to be part of our annual drive. Could you consider (ask for a lesser amount and continue to negotiate down if necessary).

The idea is to hear and acknowledge the objection and then ask different questions and/or suggest alternatives.

More Tips for Training and Dealing with Volunteers

1. If the gift is below expectations, teach some basic negotiating skills. "That is a very generous pledge. You know that a pledge of (cite the dollar amount) would make us number one in the area of computer-assisted instruction?"

2. Never offend the donor. If all else fails, thank the donor and ask if she/he would consider a gift at another time.
3. Stay in scheduled time frames. The longer one delays in closing a gift, the more difficult the task becomes.
4. Remember, interested donors want the best. Show them how their dollars will make the school the best and they will be interested.
5. Sound your C's. A volunteer solicitor must be clear, concise, challenging, and able to demonstrate personal commitment!
6. Cite the gifts of others to raise sights of perspective donor.
7. Make prospects feel both needed and wanted.
8. Know your prospect and suggest an appropriate level of support. (The director, with the assistance of the board, may help with appropriate gift levels).
9. Do not just ask for money. Ask for a better school system. Show how the donor's dollars will improve a product that is already good. Give it a chance to be the very best.
10. Above all, volunteers must be sincere and enthusiastic. If a volunteer is not enthusiastic about the school district, and sincere in the desire to help, it is better that the individual not be part of your campaign effort.

CAMPAIGN CALENDARS

All campaigns must have a beginning and ending date. There is no specified time frame for a campaign, but it may be helpful to outline some of the tasks necessary to complete in preparing an annual fund drive. Remember these guides are suggestions only. Assume that the process begins early in the schoolyear, and that some fund-raising (cultivation, publicity, etc.) activities have been going on since the end of the last campaign. For an initial campaign, a planning period of a semester or longer is not out of order. The following are some things to consider in organizing efforts. The number of meetings may vary, but the director should be prepared for an intense period of activity in the two months preceding the actual solicitation process.

September

1. Select the chair of the campaign (if the chair of the board is not going to serve in this capacity).
2. Determine your solicitation groups. With the help of your board begin to review prospects (foundations, individuals, etc.).

3. Set up fund-raising committees based on your solicitation groups. Assign chairs to these committees from members of the board.
4. Determine the total number of campaign workers needed to solicit prospects (rule of five).
5. Develop your campaign calendar. Include dates of all organizational meetings, the kick-off meeting and all report and planning meetings.
6. Meet with leaders of designated solicitation groups and plan enlistment of other members. (Who will solicit whom? Will advisory board be used? etc.) Begin enlistment of team members.
7. Once kick-off reception date has been established, determine the guest list.
8. As volunteers are enlisted, mail them letters indicating dates of training.
9. Publicize campaign goal. Highlight efforts of the board chair.
10. During the last week of the month, hold a meeting of solicitation group members to determine the status of volunteer solicitors.

October

1. Board committee solicits board gifts. Leadership gift committee (or major donor committee) solicits gifts from leaders. Faculty/staff committee solicits gifts from staff and faculty.
2. Solicit board, leadership, faculty/staff and any other family gifts (i.e., friends of board, past board members).
3. Conduct training meetings for volunteer solicitors.
4. Call all individuals who will attend the kick-off reception.
5. Hold report meeting for all gifts solicited in step one above (board, friends of board, faculty, etc.).
6. Hold kick-off reception. Announce all lead gifts. Be certain all solicitation group chairs (sometimes called team captains) have the necessary material for their solicitation volunteers (brochures, pledge cards, fact sheets, cases, any suggested letters if mail is to be used, procedures for reporting, etc.)
7. If mail is going to be used, on the day after the kick-off reception mail all letters to those who are not to receive a personal visit.
8. Also begin solicitation of all involved in the campaign on the following day. Chairs should solicit first volunteers who are working with their committee.
9. Begin personal solicitation of all prospects who will receive a personal visit.
10. Provide all chairs with weekly updates of progress.

November

1. Hold first general report meeting in first week of November.
2. Hold second report meeting in second week of November.
3. Hold third general report meeting during the third week of November.
4. Hold fourth general report meeting in the fourth week of November.

December

1. If necessary, hold a fifth report meeting.
2. Make final check of outstanding pledge cards.
3. Send thank-you letters to all volunteers. Don't forget your board!
4. Hold victory report meeting
5. Have victory celebration for all volunteers.
6. Begin preparing final report for your board for first meeting in January. Begin formulating academic goals for next campaign.
7. If possible, give the school board a final report. Also notify faculty of your success. Attempt to get appropriate publicity in the local media.
8. Check to be sure no "thank-you's" were missed.

SUMMARY

Most LEF groups use some form of annual fund drive as their chief method of raising funds for their school districts, although some are now involved in major fund-raising and deferred giving as part of their overall solicitation plans. In order to determine the number and kinds of gifts needed to meet educational objectives, the director of the LEF should construct a chart of standards to provide guidelines for the campaign.

Once initial plans have been formulated, the director and the board need to decide on how donors will be approached. Many nonprofits use a one-on-one donor solicitation process for gifts, while others depend on direct mail, telephone, or a combination of the three approaches.

Gift strategies include class gifts, challenge gifts, leadership gifts, gift clubs, and named funds.

Volunteers in solicitation should receive proper training to include information about the school district and about the campaign itself. Volunteers should also receive training on how to ask for gifts and how to deal with possible donor objections.

All effective campaigns are planned well and follow a fairly rigorous calendar that outlines beginning and ending dates for the process.

6

DIRECT-MAIL AND TELEPHONE FUND-RAISING

Remember the note that direct-mail fund-raising generally produces the smallest returns and, because of the costs associated with printing and mailing, the process can become expensive. This does not mean that direct-mail efforts should not be used by LEF groups. In fact, more than 70 percent of approximately one million nonprofit groups in the United States use direct mail as a primary approach to raising funds. While some groups employ direct mail to acquire new donors or perhaps expand the donor base, others may use mail exclusively to raise funds. Indeed, even if direct mail is used only to "keep in touch with donors," it may be cost effective because most professional fund-raisers agree that it is 10 times more costly to acquire a new donor than to have a present donor make repeat gifts. For groups with limited volunteer staffs, mail may be the most pragmatic approach to fund-raising; for some it may be the only approach.

The point, however, is not to debate whether or not schools should use direct mail for fund-raising. Because the average business letter captures only about 45 seconds of a reader's time, the point is that direct mail must be made as effective as possible.

Huntsinger (1989) lists four basic marketing principles to guide direct-mail approaches:

1. Techniques employed to create letters and packages must be determined by the nature of the audience receiving the package.
2. Direct-mail packages that are not personalized are compromised.

3. The only way to determine what will work best for your audience is to engage in extensive and ongoing testing.
4. You must learn the basic principles, but you must break the principles to be successful.

Gayley (1981, p. 43) suggests that before writing any development letter, one should ask three questions: "To whom is it going? What is it about? Who is signing it?" This may seem obvious, but it may not be as simple as it appears on the surface. Writers are most persuasive when they focus on the person who will be reading the letter. Graduates of the school, for example, constitute a quite different audience than a group of corporate executives. In addition, subject matter affects writing style. For example, a letter requesting funds to support a site-based grant for staff training will differ from one requesting support for the football team. If the letter will carry a signature, it must echo the style of the person who will sign the communication (Gayley, 1981, pp. 43–44).

In a real sense, the fund-raising letter is the opportunity to make the school district's case for support and to present what schools do verbally and perhaps visually. It also lets donors know that they do indeed matter. The letter may also be used to personalize printed material that may accompany it (brochures, flyers, etc.).

In initiating letters one should, as much as possible, make an emotional appeal to the donor, and then proceed from the general to the specific, since interest is first created by a generality and then directed toward a specific idea. All letters should be affirmative and brief (Nash, 1991). Lant (1990) presents a unique concept of appealing to donors by characterizing two categories of direct-mail approaches: "electric clause" and "essential services." In the former approach, the fund-raiser writes in "us" and "them" concepts, indicating if funds are not provided, some act or action that prospective donors find objectionable will likely happen. In the "essential services" approach (the one school districts should use), attempts are made to motivate the donor by describing the good work of the nonprofit organization.

PRINCIPLES OF WRITING
EFFECTIVE LETTERS

Appeal to the Donor

As you go from the general to the specific, be sure the specific has appeal to the donor. Tell a story that will captivate the reader's interest. For example, a school district that recently finished in first place nationally in an academic competition. If one were to write a letter about this achievement, he/she should first speak to the general excellence of the school system and then say something like, "We can't be certain that we will win the national title every year but we fully intend to compete with the best academic high schools in the country. With your help we will bring back more national championships in the years ahead."

See with the Eyes of the Donor

Try and see the world through the eyes of the potential donor. What do alumni want to know about their alma mater as we approach a new century? What is appealing to each of them? For example, "While the old high school has a new face, the south wing of the building is still there. All of the windows look out over the rolling hills and in autumn the leaves are as beautiful now as they were in the 1970s." As in all approaches sell excellence, appeal to donor loyalty, and above all, stress what we did and do well.

Make It Personal

This task is not as easy as it may seem. Some computer-generated letters are made to appear personal with the use of one's name near the top of the page. They generally read something like, "We have reserved a special prize for you, Mr. Joseph P. Public." Actually, although most recipients are aware of being one of thousands, most probably give the letter the average 45 seconds upon seeing their names in bold print. Attempts at personalization are common among marketing firms.

The salutation of a letter can help personalize the piece. "Dear Alumni," or "Dear Friends of Madison High," are not as effective as the use of a personal name or a nickname. Anyone using first names or nicknames for personalization purposes should be certain that the donor's name or nickname is spelled correctly.

"Hook" the Reader

The opening sentence and the opening paragraph are very important aspects of the fund-raising letter. If the first sentence comes across as dull or boring, then the reader probably will never read the rest of the message. Use as strong a statement as possible in the initial draft and then review it. Take a critical eye to what is written and ask if this sentence and this paragraph is really worth reading. If *you* are not satisfied with what it says, you can be assured the reader will not be either. The opening paragraph is designed to "hook" readers and encourage them to read further.

Goldman (1985) suggests doing everything possible to establish a personal relationship with the reader. Although this is difficult to do with the printed word, Goldman contends that the writer must visualize writing to a single individual. He advocates the use of "you" and "me" words in the present tense. For example, "I am writing to you today because I want to try and convey to you some of the excitement that is now taking place at your alma mater."

Nash (1991) outlines five ways to initiate a letter:

1. *A series of short questions to interest the reader:* Have you heard? Is it true? Are we number one?

2. *Seasonal tie-in:* If you mention Christmas, Thanksgiving, or July 4th, you may get reader attention if the letter is received just prior to the holiday.

3. *Surprise statement:* By the time the envelope is opened, prospects may have figured out that this is a request for funds. One way to get interest is to state something prospects would never expect in a fund-raising letter. For example, "We are aware of the controversy surrounding the new law that allows moose hunting in Maine. For the most part, we do not favor the killing of these animals, even though there is some evidence to suggest that we need to thin the herds to prevent winter starvation. We are also concerned about the parasite that seems to cause a rare brain disease in moose.

We did not write to you, however, to discuss moose. Rather, I am writing to you because I want you to know that I share your pride in what your alma mater has been able to accomplish."

4. *Strong quote:* Sometimes a strong quote can be used.

> I know that try as I may, I will not have the funding to go on to college. While I had excellent preparation for advanced study at Carver High, the plant that employed my father closed in early November. I will be able to get some financial aid from the college I picked, and I can get a part-time job in the college bookstore, but I don't think it will be enough.

> Dear Joe,
> I'm writing to tell you that it *wasn't* enough. Even though a financial aid package would have taken care of about 70 percent of the expenses of this student, and the part-time job would have covered incidental expenses, this student did not enroll in college last fall. We on the Board of Directors of our Local Education Fund are determined to do all that we can to assist bright,

deserving students to complete their degrees. She made excellent grades in our demanding college preparatory curriculum, and we intend to insure that others like her are not denied an opportunity for an education.

5. *Familiar memory:* Most prospects carry with them a store of memories that they react to strongly. A memory that many have in common tied to an appeal may produce an excellent lead. For example,

> Remember the sock hops that we used to have after home basketball games on Friday night? Remember the old jukebox that we used to play records? Well the jukebox was recently "discovered" in a storage facility that our school uses. Some of us have decided to restore it and part of the funds we are seeking this year are to be used to create a special room in the high school to house this old friend and some other important trophies, pictures, uniforms, and even some of our band instruments. I'm writing to ask you to take a walk with me down memory lane at Carver High. Won't you join me in helping all of us relive those precious moments each time we visit the high school.
>
> (Adapted from Nash, 1991)

Make the Case

The middle paragraphs should make the case for support in the same personal "you" relationship (Goldman, 1985, p. 13). As in the opening paragraph, write with the individual in mind. Again the tone should be positive. As in all fund-raising, the letter should involve the donor and get her/him to participate. Remember that individuals give because they wish to belong and because they have developed a sincere belief in what a group is doing. Therefore, the letter should not dwell on things the school district will not be able to do, but instead on what it can do! This section is a good place to use the material from the case for support.

Ask for Action

The final paragraph should suggest action and ask the donor to send a contribution today (Goldman, 1985, p. 13). Give explicit directions. "Won't you please join me in contributing $100 to the minigrant program? To date, donors have made contributions ranging from $25.00 to $100.00. It looks as if we will meet our goal for the third year in a row if people like you continue to help."

Use the Envelope

Do not neglect the envelope. If the prospect does not open the envelope, then it really does not matter how appealing the message is. Nash

(1991, p. 15) offers what he calls 10 "sure-fire ways" to get your envelope opened:

- Offer something free.
- Consider a self-adhesive envelope.
- Offer the prospect a benefit.
- Use a larger envelope to include four-color graphics.
- Use glassine (window) on back of the envelope to show the benefit inside.
- Personalize.
- Use teaser copy.
- Begin the message on envelope.
- Put response date in copy visible through window.
- Indicate what is inside: "Your eagle pin is enclosed."

Most individuals agree that the most important area is the personalization of the approach. If your donor pool is small, type or even hand write addresses on the envelopes. As much as possible, make it look as if it is indeed a personal correspondence between two friends. If the letter cannot have a personal look, at least attempt to make it look important.

Goldman (1985, pp. 2–3) has developed useful suggestions to consider with respect to envelopes:

- *If teaser copy is printed on an angle; it adds attention value.*
- *News headlines can create attention.*
- *Questions can stimulate interest. "Did you overlook this?"*
- *Use an interesting fact to pave the way. "We've been challenged."*
- *Send an appeal indicating it is coming from the superintendent.*
- *The return rate can be increased by 2 percent by reproducing the name of the letter-signer in the upper left-hand corner of the envelope.*
- *If you select an envelope larger than a #9 or #10, print "First Class Mail" on it.*
- *Try a window envelope for some appeals.*
- *The seven-and-one-half by ten-and-one-half monarch size seems to work best for big donors.*
- *Whenever possible, use a postage stamp.*
- *Don't economize too much on envelope stock.*
- *Include a business reply envelope. It should be large (#9 or larger), and contain a message with a case for a contribution. It should have a wallet flap design to allow donors to pen short message. Use a postage-paid envelope, but encourage donors to provide a stamp. The envelope should be attractive.*

Tailor the Appeal to the Group

Consider segmenting direct mail (Royce, 1988). The concept of segmentation involves writing different (specific) letters to different groups. Obviously this consumes more time, but segmentation does allow tailoring fundraising strategies to different audiences and allows the director to track results. Segmentation may be done in many ways (year graduated, local versus out of state, etc.). Successful segmentation practices include a division of the donor pool by frequency of giving, recency of giving, and level of giving. Specific appeals are then directed at different groups. Those in the top level of givers could receive more attractive and expensive letters than those who have never donated. (Examples of fund-raising letters are in Appendix O.)

More Tips for Direct Mail

1. *Credit cards and electronic transfers.* A number of colleges and universities are now using electronic fund transfers (EFTs) and credit cards to pay pledges. This can reduce budgets and can also eliminate repeat solicitations.

2. *Include matching gifts.* Many companies have a policy of matching or sometimes extending the gifts of their employees. Thus a gift of $50 from an individual can mean $100 or more for your LEF. The Council for Advancement and Support of Education has a brochure entitled "Double Your Dollars" that lists companies with matching gift programs; write to CASE at Suite 400, Dupont Circle, Washington, DC 20036-1261.

3. *Change formats.* Individuals tend to get used to mail with a certain look, color, and so forth. It is advisable to change the appearance of your letter from time to time.

4. *The P.S. is overused, but do not ignore it completely.* Some donors may only read the P.S. if the letter appears too long or dull to read in full.

5. *Consider the length.* Some fund-raisers feel that individuals will not read long letters, while others indicate that longer copy actually attracts more readers. In general, shorter copy with quotes and endorsements seems most effective. However, a good rule of thumb could be that one should write letters long enough to get the job done. One thing is certain—letters that are either long or short will not be read by anyone if they are dull!

6. *Know your donor base.* Copy should reflect the donor base as you understand it. Which individuals and groups are you soliciting? How will you convey copy in ways that will help them decide to make a contribution or pledge? The vocabulary should reflect that of the least learned of your potential donors.

7. Send a follow-up letter. In general, funding will be increased if monies are available for at least one follow-up letter.

8. Highlight key points. When appropriate, use underlining and check marks to call attention to important points.

9. Mail letters at the end of the month. Many individuals write checks during the first week of the month because household bills are sent monthly. Thus letters mailed during the last week of the month may arrive during normal bill-paying times.

10. Use a theme. If readers are to be approached more than once (segmentation, multiple mailings, follow-up telephone calls), try and find new ways to state your message. Always tailor the message to meet the needs and interests of your segmented donor pool (Carter, 1978).

11. Remember the five elements. In considering a direct-mail approach, plan to have five basic elements: the letter, reply card, postage-paid reply envelope, brochure (or other enclosure), a jacket or carrier envelope.

12. Color can get attention. In general, the color red has the highest attention-getting value and the color yellow is next. Bright colors tend to attract more attention than softer pastel ones. Also consider a mix of colors since all copy cannot always use a single color.

13. Gunning's principles of clear writing. Robert Gunning's (1968) book entitled The Technique of Clear Writing should become a part of every fundraiser's professional file. The book should be read in its entirety, but the principles he suggests are worth mentioning here. Gunning notes that sentences should be short, that writing should be simple, not complex, and that familiar words are preferable to long complicated ones. Unnecessary words should be eliminated. In addition, he suggests that the writer use action verbs, write in the ways that he/she talks, use terms that can be pictured and tied to experience. Also writing should be varied and the content should be used to express, not impress the reader (Gunning, 1968).

PHONATHONS

For many colleges and universities, the phonathon has become the primary means of conducting annual solicitations. Nonprofit groups outside of education have also increasingly turned to the use of telephones to solicit funds. In addition, telemarketing by commercial companies is so extensive that most people can be assured of several telephone calls each week that offer a wide range of goods and services. In fact the sheer number of these calls serves as a reminder that if phonathons are to be used in fund-raising campaigns, then they must be used well.

Form an institutional standpoint, phonathons have a number of advantages. Perhaps the most important is that those who speak for an institution are likely to become donors either immediately or at some later date. In addition, colleges and universities that use phonathons can be certain that those who call will learn a great deal about the institution! As such the use of student volunteers, or even of paid student callers, serves the key purpose of alerting future graduates to the importance of giving to their school. In addition, phonathons, for the most part, are fun and callers generally enjoy the process. Best of all, they can be cost effective and productive. What colleges and universities have found effective can also be used by LEF groups to solicit funds.

As noted, if phones are to be used, then the process must be done well. Poor use of phone techniques can actually damage an institution. One of the first things to consider is that the phone call to a prospective donor must not be similar to a "junk-mail" letter in that it disappoints the reader. A "junk phone call" will have the same result. The Pacific Group, a professional firm in Long Beach, California, has an excellent publication entitled, *An Introduction to Fund Raising by Telephone*. They make 10 suggestions that can help those soliciting funds to avoid the "junk phone call" problem:

1. *Know who you are talking to. Know names and how to pronounce them. Know their relationship to your organization.*
2. *Speak evenly and clearly.*
3. *Use simple words.*
4. *Talk to a person, never read a script. (Have a script, but never read it.)*
5. *Know why you are calling. Don't waste prospect's time.*
6. *Involve prospects in the conversation.*
7. *Establish rapport.*
8. *Be considerate.*
9. *Be polite.*
10. *Listen.*

(Pacific Group, 1986, pp. 8–9)

Preparations for Phonathons

To eliminate any appearance of "a junk phone call," the organization must do several things to plan the event. Among the planning considerations are issues related to the actual donor base, the location of the event, the method, if any, of alerting potential donors that a call is forthcoming, and training the callers.

Among the most important (and also the most difficult) tasks in phonathons is obtaining accurate lists of prospective donors. If you have used direct-mail approaches or have a computerized list of prior donors, your task is somewhat easier. In many communities, the local phone book becomes the database, but if a district has to seek information from directory assistance to get accurate telephone numbers for its donor base, the process can become more expensive. However, because most phone approaches for LEF groups involve surrounding areas and local calls, developing a list may prove somewhat easier than the task faced by colleges and universities who want to call alumni in distant cities and other states. In most cases schools have accurate phone numbers for the parents of their children, and the telephone book does provide good data for any calls that will be made locally. Of course, the key questions are: what part of the donor base will be solicited by mail? what part, if any, will be solicited by phone? and what segment will receive individual face-to-face calls? Some directors of LEF groups use the telephone primarily as a back up to face-to-face and direct-mail approaches, although some groups do use telephone approaches more extensively for at least part of their campaign.

Who Should Call?

College and universities have used both students and alumni as callers, and have experimented with both volunteers and paid callers. Each approach has advantages and disadvantages. Groups with small budgets tend to use volunteers because it is less expensive. As noted earlier, however, individuals who are willing to actually call for the school are more likely to pledge!

Of course, the use of volunteers also has a down side. The dollars pledged through phonathons is directly related to the number of callers, and the director who relies solely on volunteer help is, in a sense, at the mercy of the volunteer. In many cases, time constraints limit the training volunteers obtain, and this in turn can lead to poor performances. In addition, the normal activities of volunteers often preclude them from making calls at designated times. Illnesses, other meetings, and work schedules can affect the number of callers available for work. Of course, fewer callers means fewer pledges and reduced total funds.

Such disadvantages have caused some nonprofit organizations to pay callers for phonathons. The most obvious advantage of using paid individuals is greater control over those who are "employed," allowing the "firing" of individuals who do not perform well, and also for more extensive training of callers.

Of course, paying callers increases the expenses. If the callers must be paid out of donated dollars, reaching fund-raising goals can be more expensive. Also the use of paid callers takes away the possibility of "cultivating the callers" through the telephone process. In addition, the hiring and screening of paid callers is difficult and often tiring. Even on large university campuses, developing a skilled staff of paid volunteers is difficult. Class schedules, unwillingness to work on certain evenings because of exams, and the desire to have weekends free make recruiting and training callers seemingly endless.

One approach (volunteers) is not necessarily superior to the other (paid callers). The director of one large capital campaign *hired* callers because it needed calling assistance at least 12 hours each day and it was not possible to staff such an effort with volunteers. On the other hand, student volunteers with a sincere interest in the same institution did excellent work in smaller, more focused campaigns. For LEF groups planning to do some solicitation by telephone, use volunteers as the initial approach to eliminate the expense of paying callers. As a unit develops and becomes more sophisticated with fund-raising, the plan may call for employing some callers or using a combination of volunteers and employed workers.

The Calling Site

In order to conduct a phonathon, one must have a site for calling, ideally, a room designated only for phonathons. Obviously, this is a luxury that few LEF groups have, but if a director should be fortunate enough to have a designated phone room, then a major problem of logistics is solved! It is not uncommon for colleges and universities to designate a room for phonathons, and to have callers working phones during normal business hours and at night in order to reach the widest possible donor base. In some cases, a room or space in a building is designated temporarily for phonathons, and phones, desks, and materials are placed there for a specific period of time. For example, some schools conduct phonathons for several weeks or a month, and then do not use phone techniques for another year. In this case, renting phones and placing them temporarily in a room may be a good alternative to permanently designating one room.

In local school districts, particularly those just starting fund-raising, perhaps the best approach is to attempt to obtain space in a building in the community. For example, if a banker is on the LEF board, then she/he may allow use of the phones in the bank (after business hours) for calling. In other communities, one may be able to obtain phones from the telephone company, from a business or corporation, or from a post-secondary school. Of course, when such facilities are used, the site must be ready for the next workday, and problems with moving materials, cleaning up, and security must be considered. In addition, phones in commercial establishments are sometimes scattered in several rooms, making supervision of callers somewhat difficult.

In spite of the difficulties and risks, the possible benefits may justify the use of telephones. The Pacific Group points out that direct mail to a nondonor constituency will produce a 1 percent to 2 percent response and an average gift of $15 to $25. On the other hand, they note that a telephone outreach program to nondonors projects a baseline performance of $25 per contact with a pledge rate of 28 percent and an average pledge of $90 (The Pacific Group, p. 10).

Regardless of whether one decides to use paid or volunteer callers, the individuals should be recruited at least a month before the calling begins in order to allow time for training. An individual should make 30 to 40 calls in a two-hour block of time, but this goal is not always met. Call rates of paid callers are generally better than rates of volunteers. On the average, however, a completed call rate of 20 to 30 completed calls per two-hour block should be acceptable. For example, 20 callers could call 800 people in 40 calling hours.

It is also advisable to alert prospective donors about one week in advance of the actual phonathon, perhaps through a card or letter. This gives the caller a starting point in donor solicitation. In recent years, a more sophisticated approach called "phone/mail" (phone/mail is a registered service mark of the IDC Company) has successfully combined direct mail and the telephone. This approach is discussed later in this chapter.

Training Callers

The most important part of any phonathon is training callers. Some people contend that the number of pledges and the number of dollars raised correlate highly with how well the callers are prepared.

Training is not a one-act play. It should not take place one-half hour prior to a caller making his/her first request for a gift. Rather, training for calling, like other aspects of fund-raising, involves time, effort, and possibly expense.

The Pacific Group notes that training has three objectives. It should motivate callers, introduce callers to the principles and techniques of fund-raising, and provide ample opportunities to practice what they have been taught prior to making a call. They recommend a training period of two to three hours that would cover the following concepts:

- *Introduction to fund-raising;*
- *Fund-raising at the client organization;*
- *The role of telemarketing within the overall development effort;*
- *Techniques of fund-raising by phone;*
- *Goals and expected results;*

- *Callers' responsibilities to the client and program;*
- *Prospects to be called and their relationship to the client;*
- *Lead letter and purpose;*
- *Establishing rapport on the telephone;*
- *Controlling the conversation;*
- *Negotiating an appropriate gift;*
- *Managing objections;*
- *Confirming the pledge;*
- *Follow-up collection and cultivation activities planned.*

(The Pacific Group, p. 22)

It is important that callers be supervised throughout the process; hence, the director or the individual who supervises the process must be available for duty during many evening hours. This is stated here so that LEF directors do not simply compile a donor list, recruit a few callers, and then "put them to work."

Each caller should receive individual attention to determine that each is doing an adequate job. If not, *paid* volunteers can be "fired," but the situation becomes more sensitive with *adult nonpaid volunteers*. When a caller is deemed so poor that ill-will is being created among the donor base, the director or the supervisor may have to channel that person's efforts into helping the cause in some noncalling capacity.

Six hours of training is optimal for most callers. Use a range of materials and generally follow the Pacific Group's suggestions with your own modifications. The initial session might introduce basic concepts such as why individuals give money, the importance of alumni and the support they can provide, and the hope of establishing lifelong relationships with donors. It is important to allow each individual to make a few practice calls at the initial session.

Two additional two-hour sessions might concentrate heavily on roleplaying. A good goal is that each prospective caller make four practice phone calls in each two-hour session. In other words, each caller will have gone through at least eight practice calls prior to making his/her first live call. These supervised practice sessions aim to teach each caller to become a more effective communicator, using a range of listening activities and our calling materials and scripts. (Appendix Q contains some listening activities.) After each roleplay, the supervisor and the group itself provide feedback on each caller's progress. The focus in these sessions is to have each caller feel good about what he/she is doing. Do not ignore errors and do make suggestions, and operate from the assumption that the callers themselves probably are insecure about the process. Build confidence and help them with difficult situations that may occur. Offer opening lines, review message (case), and the reason for calling. Ask them to suggest a specific amount, generally an increase over the amount given during the previous campaign. From prior experience, provide answers to questions and comments that donors use. ("I didn't know about the campaign." "Can I put something in the mail?" "Send me something to read." "I gave last year." "I thought my taxes paid for schools.")

In each phonathon, there are details to cover, and at some point, each caller must become familiar with the materials and the forms used. This may be done at any time during the training, but prior to an individual making his/her first call. Each caller must be familiar with the prospect cards (name, address, giving history, phone number, other information). They should also have a copy of any written instructions (a referral sheet, fact sheets) that will be helpful during the call. Each caller should be thoroughly familiar with the pledge form, including the distribution of carbon copies in order that effective tracking can take place.

On the first evening of actual calling, the fund-raisers should appear at the site at least one-half hour in advance of the first call to review the paperwork and cover last-minute details. They may also want to make a few "practice" calls to friends or relatives as a warm-up activity.

As calling progresses, match up new callers with experienced ones by seating them near each other so the experienced caller can serve as a "phonathon mentor." If possible, advise or counsel each caller periodically (at least once a week if possible). Again, focus on what the caller is doing well and what improvements are needed. It is also advisable to hold sessions to discuss and deal with specific problems at regular intervals throughout the life of the calling session.

Also challenges to groups, prizes (bonuses to paid callers), refreshments, and celebrations are good motivating tools for callers who will be working over a period of time. (An example of a calling script is in Appendix P.)

THE COMBINATION PHONE AND DIRECT-MAIL APPROACH

As noted, a specialized approach using mail and phone have been employed by some nonprofit organizations as an attempt to expand donor bases and increase donations. Of course, most programs that use telemarketing techniques do use direct mail to alert potential donors that they will be receiving a call, but "phone/mail" as practiced by professional fund-raising groups is an attempt to do everything possible to personalize the process. In fact, William P. Freyd, currently chairman and founder of the Institutional Development Council in Bloomfield, New Jersey, is generally given credit for developing the "phone/mail" process in a campaign for Yale University in 1977 (Freyd, 1985).

As in all campaigns, the first step is to identify the prospective donor and her/his relationship with the institution. The prospect is then evaluated to figure the amount of the "ask," determined through zip codes, prior giving records, and other pertinent facts.

After these two basic steps have been completed, the prospective donor is contacted through two letters that are individually addressed, word processed, and hand stamped. The letter is made to look as much as possible like a personal piece of mail. The first generally goes out over the signature of the chief executive officer of the school. In LEF groups this could be the superintendent of schools or perhaps the chairperson of the LEF board. It should be an important individual. The first letter informs the prospective donor to expect a second letter within a few days (the letter should tell who will write the second letter). The first letter also indicates the importance of the second letter and makes statements such as "It is important for you to read the letter from an institution we all know and love." It is, in effect, a personal introduction to the sender of the second letter.

The second letter in this process is generally long (as much as three pages) and it gives the case for support of the institution. It generally carries the signature of an important person (the foundation director), and is printed or typed on personal rather than institutional stationery. The first paragraph of the second letter notes that the prospective donor will receive a phone call within a few days to make a donation larger than had been requested in the past (Freyd states that this is effective). After that, the letter continues to provide reasons an individual should consider giving. Of most importance is the final component of the letter, solicitation of the gift. The total amount is based on the prospect evaluation, but the gift is broken down by quarters. For example, on the "low" end of the giving scale, $30 per quarter may be suggested for a total of $120 over twelve months.

Within five days after the second letter, the phone call is made. A donor may make a pledge, not make a pledge, ask to be called back, or indicate a possibility of a gift. In the latter two cases, a new letter is sent and a second call made within 30 days.

The actual conversation is important. The dialog is based on questions related to the second letter. "How do you feel about what we are doing?" "What do you think about the suggested giving levels that were sent to you in the letter?" Time is also taken to talk with the individual about his/her feelings about the institution. Freyd reports that pledge gifts from this process average from $200 on the low end and up to $800 on the high end. (*Note:* Phone/mail is registered service mark of Institutional Development Council.)

This process suggested by IDC, or a similar one can be very effective and also very cost effective. However, institutions who use professional firms need to understand that although the results are generally higher, the cost of a managed campaign is higher than an ordinary phonathon. J. Barry McGannon, S.J., who is Vice President for Development at St. Louis University and an advocate of the process, reports that callers contacted 7,000 alumni and parents. Of that number 6,300 made decisions and 2,800 made pledges totaling $772,000. Nearly half of those who pledged had never made a pledge to St. Louis University before.

Most LEF groups are not yet large enough to have a professional to manage a direct mail/telephone campaign. In the years ahead, the use of mail combined with telephone calls may well become a common technique of LEF groups.

More Tips for Phonathons

Whether or not your school district uses a combined phone and direct-mail approach, get as much informative material as possible into the hands of prospective donors prior to making a call (Ryan, 1991).

Use phones for reasons other than solicitation of money, for example, to thank donors for a gift. Phones may also be used to inform graduates about such events and organizations as homecoming and alumni associations (Dodds, 1991).

Use graduating seniors as callers. This will encourage them to become donors in the future (Wahlstrom, 1991).

Send videos about your school system to major donors and groups prior to the call. If your school has the capability of developing a good video to highlight achievements or successes in the minigrant and site-grant programs, send it in advance of any phone (or personal) solicitation.

Take advantage of all reunions and other special events in your calling (Haskins, 1989).

Use recent converts to your program as callers (Haskins, 1989).

Train callers to create a sense of urgency and excitement in their discussion with donors over the phone.

Have a theme for your phone calls. For example, "The school district of Long Beach has a dream. It takes a dream to excel."

The telephone is, without doubt, the most powerful, the most widely used, and the least understood medium of communication in the United States today (Pacific Group, p. 7).

The size of your prospect pool may determine whether or not a group elects to use telephone techniques. If there are more than 1,000 prospects, then the management of a campaign becomes more difficult.

SUMMARY

Although direct-mail and telephone fund-raising techniques do not produce as high a rate of return as do personal solicitations, they are nevertheless important tools for all nonprofit groups. It is important that they be done well because poor usage of these approaches can harm the image of the nonprofits.

Fund-raising letters should be specific, as personal as possible, and written as if they were being seen through the eyes of the donor. Common techniques include interesting questions, surprise statements, strong quotes, and familiar memories. These should be in the initial paragraph. Paragraph two should make the case for support, and the final paragraph should ask a donation. Envelopes are also important in direct-mail approaches.

Phonathons are now used by most nonprofit groups and will be used increasingly by LEF groups in the future. Preparation for phonathons and careful planning prior to calling donors are very important. Other critical decisions include who should do the calling, volunteers or paid callers, the calling site, the training of callers, and the preparation of an appropriate script. Some nonprofit organizations now hire professional firms to manage their fund-raising efforts that combine the best aspects of direct mail and telephoning.

7

PERSONAL SOLICITATION

Although telephone and direct mail are effective approaches to fund-raising, there is no substitute for personal solicitation of prospects. Certainly each "top" prospect on the list should receive a personal call, and most such prospects should receive an individual proposal. This concept has not been lost on most LEF organizations; personal solicitation of prospects by organized volunteers, along with direct mail and special events, are the most common fund-raising techniques.

Most nonprofit fund-raisers will agree that face-to-face solicitation produces the largest gifts. Face-to-face solicitation often involves the very successful volunteers in the organization, thus increasing the probability of their support (again, the rock in the pond theory). Face-to-face solicitation is, of course, easier if top prospects are clustered in a relatively small area, because it will be more expensive if they are scattered among states. Fortunately for most LEF groups, nearly all of their prospects will be in geographical proximity to the school district, thus allowing for personal solicitation of most prospects.

As noted earlier, individuals, not private foundations and corporations, contribute the majority of charitable dollars. What motivates individuals to give/ Brackley (1980) notes that in every fund-raising campaign, one or more of the following factors are at work:

- *Individuals, corporations, and foundations have money to give.*
- *The right person or persons ask them, at the right time, in the right circumstances.*
- *People have a sincere desire to help one another.*

- *People wish to belong or be identified with a group or organization they admire.*
- *Recognition of how vital their gifts can be satisfies a need for a sense of personal power in people.*
- *People have received benefits—often personal enjoyment such as from a symphony orchestra—from the services of the organization and wish, in turn, to support it.*
- *People give because they "get something" out of giving.*
- *People may need to give; that is, altruism may not be an opportunity but a "love or perish" necessity for some people.*

(Brackley, 1980, p. 26)

Brackley further notes that individuals give for acceptance, altruism, appreciation, approval, the pleasure of "being asked," a belief in a cause, community support, gratitude, group support, guilt feelings, immortality, the belief that a major gift will "keep the institution off my back," and for power and influence. In addition, individuals may give for a return on an investment, salvation, sympathy, or simply for the fun of giving (Brackley, pp. 26–31).

Gunnin (1991) offers a similar list of why individuals give—religious beliefs, guilt, recognition, self-preservation and fear, tax rewards, obligation, and peer pressure are among the reasons. He also notes that when individuals do not give, it is because the fund-raiser failed to conduct sufficient research on the prospect, ask for a definite amount, ask for enough, present alternative methods of giving, get the right person to ask, include the spouse in the solicitation visit, or follow up.

Effective application of awareness of donor motivation requires common sense in the approach to donors and a true understanding of individuals, their interests, ambitions, and needs (Brackley, 1980). Lord (1985) reminds us of a crucial point in personal solicitation—people give to people. They do not give to an institution or even to a cause. They give to the individual who asks them. A foundation, corporation, or committee never makes a decision. Individuals make decisions. Individuals submit proposals. Individuals read proposals. When a volunteer and a prospect are together, the volunteer's personal influence counts more than anything else (Lord, 1985, pp. 75–80). Good fund-raisers believe in themselves, believe in what they are doing, and overcome the fears of rejection, embarrassment, failure, retribution, and losing (Gunnin, 1991).

David Dunlop, director of capital projects for Cornell University, is one of the leading individuals in the United States in the area of major gift solicitation. He classifies gifts to an institution into three areas: regular gifts, special gifts, and ultimate gifts. Regular gifts are those made repeatedly and at regular intervals. To compare this with other types of giving, Dunlop assigns a unit value of 1 to a regular gift (regular gift = 1x). Special gifts are those an individual makes to help meet an institution's special need. They are usually made to an organization that an individual also supports with regular gifts. These gifts are usually 5 to 10 times larger than the regular gift (special gift = 5x to 10x). Ultimate gifts are those that exercise an individual's full giving capacity. They are typically 1,000 to 10,000 times larger than the regular gift to the same institution (ultimate gift = 1,000x to 10,000x). The emphasis shifts dramatically in preparing a prospect for a regular gift, a special gift, or the ultimate gift. In seeking regular gifts, the fund-raising process is very speculative and little time is spent cultivating the prospect. In fact, most of the time in speculative (regular) fund-raising is devoted to asking (direct mail, phonathons). In seeking special gifts, however, the fund-raiser may spend up to 50 percent of his/her time in cultivation and the other 50 percent in the actual asking process. In seeking ultimate gifts, the fund-raiser spends virtually 98 percent of his or her time nurturing the prospect. For many donors, this requires years or the better part of a lifetime (Dunlop, 1991).

Major gift fund-raising has not been developed into a pure science; in fact, many aspects of fund-raising are creative. In general, most directors of LEF groups have not participated in major donor solicitation, although many are considering it for future campaigns. It is probably safe to assume that the majority of fund-raising by LEF groups around the country is speculative in, although face-to-face solicitation by individual volunteers is a common technique. Because most LEF directors feel solicitations will become part of their work in the future, it may be useful to outline the process that other nonprofit groups use. There are, of course other models, but Dunlop's concepts will serve well for purposes of illustration.

Dunlop notes that all major donors to an institution move through a common experience. Prior to giving, each donor must become *aware* of the nonprofit group, gain an understanding of it, take an interest in it, become involved with it in some way, and develop a sense of commitment, which they express by giving (Dunlop, 1991). In an LEF organization, this process could resemble the following hypothetical situation.

Mrs. Solberg has donated to the Cape Independence Educational Foundation for the past three years. Her son Mark was involved in several seminars and experiences provided by the minigrants to teachers and she was pleased with the results. In fact, her giving increased from $10 the first year to $100 the third year. The director of the Cape Independence Educational Foundation has noted Mrs. Solberg's giving habits and has concluded that Mrs. Solberg is a candidate for a special and perhaps even an ultimate gift. She knows that Mrs. Solberg has an interest in the school district, has knowledge of the minigrants to teachers program, and has shown interest in what is taking place at Cape Independence Regional High School.

The director decides that Mrs. Solberg should become more involved with the school, and after conferring with some members of the foundation, has discovered Mrs. Solberg's keen interest in music. In fact, her son Mark was a member of the school band. With this in mind, the LEF director approaches the band director about having Mrs. Solberg act as the master of ceremonies at the Spring Music Banquet. The band director then calls Mrs. Solberg and asks if she will agree to perform this very special function. Because the Spring Music Banquet is a very big event in the district, Mrs. Solberg is delighted and honored to be asked. At this point, the directors of the LEF and the band have succeeded in getting Mrs. Solberg to participate in an activity with the school. She is now involved, and the director of the foundation must record this event and plan ways to further involve Mrs. Solberg with the school. Mrs. Solberg is not asked at this point for an additional gift, but is a prospect for a special gift in the next two years. In effect, they have laid the groundwork for Mrs. Solberg to become a major donor. She is aware, is knowledgeable about the school, is interested, and has become involved. As a major donor she needs only to have a sense of commitment to the school district and at some point to make an expression of that commitment.

In working with Mrs. Solberg for an additional expression of commitment, a number of key concepts must be kept in mind. The cultivation of Mrs. Solberg is not a one-act play. Having her chair the banquet is only the initial step in a series that must be planned, recorded, carried out, and followed up in the months and years ahead. The director must be certain that the quality, quantity, frequency, and continuity of all initiatives is ongoing and well managed. In fact, one can almost be certain that other groups (church, woman's club) have identified Mrs. Solberg as a potential major donor and are working to get her involved with and committed to their groups. Dunlop notes that one must enter the lives of potential major donors every few weeks if a major gift is to come to that organization.

Newcomers to fund-raising often ask if the process just described is "manipulative." No ethical fund-raiser attempts to "manipulate" anyone into giving away resources. Well over 80 percent of any given constituency will donate each year to one or more charities. Development professionals are in the business of presenting their "case" so that potential donors will consider their organization for a gift. In this sense, a development professional's task is to establish a positive relationship with a prospective donor, who may or may not make a gift to that organization. Good fund-raisers are not "con artists,' nor are they beggars or manipulators. Most people support good causes. Public education is obviously a "good" cause.

In many cases, Mrs. Solberg would be assigned what Dunlop (1991) has called *a prime,* who is often a volunteer who knows her well. It is the responsibility of the prime to be able to put his/her finger on the prospective donor's relationship to the organization. In some cases, the prime could be a member of the organization (in our example, it could be the band director). With some donors, assigned secondaries help guide the initiatives with the prospective giver. Very often, however, primes and secondaries are individuals outside the organization who are peers of the prospective donor.

In the example here, the director of the LEF is what Dunlop (1991) describes as a "moves manager." A *move* is an initiative taken by the nonprofit group with a prospect. In the case just presented, asking Mrs. Solberg to chair the banquet was a move. There are six steps to each move (Dunlop, 1991). First, the director must review what has already been done. (For example, what impact did the chairing of the banquet have on Mrs.Solberg?) Second, the director may plan a new move or initiative. In some cases he/she will confer with the prime (band director) and any secondaries (peers) about the next step to further involve Mrs. Solberg with the school. For example, would the Solbergs like to serve as chaperons and accompany the band to the fall festival at the state capitol? The plan is discussed and if all agree that this is a good idea, it is the job of the director, as moves manager, to coordinate the move. (Will he provide transportation, lodging? Are there possible negative happenings that will "sour" Mrs. Solberg to the band or the school? Who will ask Mrs. Solberg? When? How?). Each detail must be worked out in advance. Fourth, execute the moves management process. In this case, the band director (prime) and the director of the foundation (secondary, and moves manager) will call on Mrs. Solberg at home and ask her to chaperone. After the meeting, the director, prime, and secondaries should (1) review what's been done; (Was he pleased? Will she do it?); (2) plan next move; (3) execute the move; (4) record what took place; and (5) evaluate what took place. The director should maintain a separate file for each major donor to record all moves. Each director will probably make files to meet individual needs, but for purposes of illustration Appendix R includes some forms.

GENERAL GUIDELINES TO SOLICITATION

A number of fund-raising principles used by experienced professionals have been noted in this book. However, they are important enough to mention again in connection with face-to-face approaches to the process.

All volunteers are potential donors. Choose with care the individuals that you ask to do actual solicitation for your LEF. Each selection should receive special consideration by the director and the members of the board.

It is of the utmost importance that volunteers make their own contributions prior to soliciting others for gifts. This point cannot be overemphasized.

In the actual solicitation process, consider the team approach. In the example of the cultivation of Mrs. Solberg, the foundation director and the band director performed as a team in working with her. In most cases, the use of two volunteers or of one volunteer and the LEF director is the best way to approach donors. Volunteers should never solicit alone!

In some instances, a single solicitation visit by a volunteer may not be sufficient. Although some volunteers may balk at multiple visits, it may be necessary. (A step-by-step process is suggested later in this chapter.)

Remember the rule of fives. One team captain for every five volunteers, and no more than five prospective donors for each volunteer solicitor.

Volunteers new to fund-raising sometimes make the mistake of "leaving the material with the prospect for consideration." This approach seldom results in a gift. In addition, when gifts are given, they tend to be smaller than one would expect from a personal one-on-one "live" meeting.

Some volunteers are uncomfortable seeking gifts beyond the range that they have given. They should probably not be assigned such clients. For example, a retired social worker who usually contributes $10 each year may feel uncomfortable asking the president of a local bank for $10,000. The concept of matching individuals with peers who have similar giving capability is worthy of consideration.

Some donors want to know about tax advantages of a gift. It is helpful and useful for volunteers to know basic facts about your LEF (i.e., "Yes, we are a 501(c)3 agency. Yes, your gift is indeed tax deductible.") In fact, basic tax information should be part of training each volunteer. Repeatedly remind volunteers that they are seeking investments, not charity.

SUCCESSFUL STEPS TO SOLICITATION

Solicitation, like so many aspects of fund-raising, is indeed an ongoing process. It is, therefore, difficult to reduce personal solicitation to a formula wherein the director or a volunteer can assure that a gift will be realized if step two follows step one and step four follows step three, and so forth. However, at the risk of oversimplification, a general outline of solicitation presented in a step-by-step approach for illustration purposes may be useful.

Step 1: Getting Started

Probably the weakest part of LEF approaches to funding is the relative lack of information about prospective donors. There is a tendency to believe that a great deal is known about donors, but for the most part this is not so. Colleges and universities often hire people full-time to research individuals, corporations, and foundations as a vital part of their development efforts. Most LEF groups do not enjoy the luxury of such a professional on staff. When possible, the director may spend some time in donor research, and there are some suggestions to this end later in this chapter.

However, the first consideration is to prepare as well as possible prior to making visits to prospects. Of course, the stakes are much higher with major donors, and for a select few, more planning may be necessary.

The director will assess who will be the best person to influence each prospective major donor. He or she may want to know, for example, what major boards the prospect sits on, and who if anybody on this board serves with her/him. In general, the best research comes from informal fact-gathering. A planning session with the members of the board that includes a review of major donor prospects is a helpful exercise in determining the amount of the "ask," the timing, and the plan for approaching the donor for a pledge and a commitment. Of key importance at this juncture is to get an answer to the question, "Who is the right person to make this call?" This is true even in the instances of the LEF approaching a foundation or a corporation. Remember, the objectives that a foundation lists do not always match donors' patterns of giving.

Step 2: Organizing for the First Visit

When research is complete on the prospective donor, it is time to decide which team will approach the prospect. Will the LEF director be included? What will be the amount of the ask? Anticipate any objections, and how to deal with them. What alternatives are there? Who says what at the meeting? Who will make the actual ask?

The meeting should be rehearsed, if at all possible. Role-playing is a helpful tool for preparing the team for the solicitation meeting.

Make initial contact by phone. Never send a letter. The call should come from the individual who knows the prospect best. If this is a volunteer, she/he should make the initial call. Using the caller's own words, the caller should state something like, "We would like to have this meeting to talk about some of the excellent things going on in the Mesa School District." At this point the caller may need to deflect attempts to delay by the prospect's saying, "Send me some material" or something to that effect. The caller should stay with it: "This is a new and exciting program. I just gave to it myself. We really want your input."

The next step is to get a specific date for an appointment. Meet the individual in her/his office. This is in effect a business call.

Once in the donor's office, the immediate task is to establish rapport with her/him. Say things like, "We appreciate the time," "We see you as a key person in our project," "We know you have been very interested in our vocational technical program." This also establishes a common ground for discussion. It is important that the donor knows who all the people present are, the purpose of the visit, which other individuals are involved, what is to be accomplished, and most important, why this particular prospect is needed on the project. Of course, the amount of the "ask" is very important.

If the initial call does not close a gift (and in some cases it may be beneficial not to close after one meeting), the team should return to the office, review the meeting, and send a follow-up note to the individual. "Bob Jones and I will be calling on you again in about a month." Experience with such meetings is that one can expect a "yes" or "no" decision within three to six weeks.

Step 3: Making a Second Visit

The need for a second visit means that either the "ask" was not made on the first call, or this is a follow-up on the initial visit, after sending the prospect a note. The goal is to get the individual to make as large a gift as possible. If the donor seems to be wavering, the task is to close the gap between what is possible and what is impossible. It is very important to have the individual speak from a personal vantage point. When individuals begin to use the pronouns *we* and *us* instead of *I* and *you,* progress is being made. At the second meeting be certain to drive home the point that "We need you and 12 others like you to make this year's campaign a success." A magic moment in this type of solicitation is when a prospect asks, "How may I help you?" If you hear this, the major part of your work has been done.

There are other considerations to keep in mind in closing a gift. First, always ask for a specific amount, and allow time for the donor to respond. In other words, use silence to advantage. Objections can be dealt with by using empathic responses and providing alternatives (i.e., "Have you thought of a gift other than from cash income?"). Donald E. Craig, suggests six closing techniques:

1. *Assume you already have the gift.* Act as if you already have the gift even though you are still expecting to receive it.
2. *Tell a story.* The story should have a close relationship to the needs of your current prospect. In the story, a prospect overcame a problem and made a major gift to Mesa Community School System. Bring up names and make the story entertaining.

3. *Reversing. Have* the prospect ask you a "yes" or "no" question and reverse it into a question of your own. For example,

PROSPECT: Will my gift help the math program?
SOLICITOR: Would you like your gift to go for a minigrant for one of the teachers in our math department?

4. *Close on major objections.* When an individual offers a series of objections, you should,

    a. Hear it out completely.
    b. Restate and put greater emphasis on the objection.
    c. Ask prospect if she/he would donate were it not for that objection.
    d. If no, deal with any minor objections in turn.
    e. If yes, go through last objection and close.

5. *If all else fails, use techniques of last resort.* "Mr. Jones, I believe the Mesa School District is among the top five in the state. All it needs to be number 1 is more support. Is there anything I did wrong to keep you from making a gift?"

If the prospect brings up an objection say: "How slow of me," or "I don't know how I forgot to clear that up for you!" Deal with the objection and then close.

6. *Ask for a reconsideration.* As you start to leave, your final shot may be, "Won't you reconsider?" If no, you may find you are dealing with what Dunlop (1991) describes as the inert fifth, or that one-fifth of the population who will give nothing to anyone under any circumstances. Fortunately, there are fewer of these individuals than there are in the other four-fifths of our population!

(Adapted from Craig, 1987)

GIFT VEHICLES

Major donors may want to make gifts in a variety of ways. Most LEF groups receive gifts of cash, but public-school foundations may need to be aware of other primary gift vehicles.

1. *Outright gifts.* Any asset of value may be presented as a gift to an LEF. The organization may accept or reject the gift. (This is where gift policy is useful.) Gifts of cash, real estate, cash value of an insurance policy, tangible property, stocks, bonds, and so forth may be given for restricted or unrestricted purposes.

   2. *Life income gifts.* A gift may be given to an LEF and the donor retains
a life income from the gift. Vehicles such as a charitable gift annuity, unitrust,
annuity pool, or pooled income funds are available. In most cases, a percentage of the value of the asset is tax deductible. (Planned and deferred
gifts are discussed in more detail later in this chapter.)
   3. *Testamentary gifts.* Gifts may be made to an organization through a
will. Amounts of money or assets may be specified as donations.
   4. *Pledges.* Most groups make provisions for pledges to be made over a
period of time. For most LEF groups pledges that would extend over a period of a calendar year could prove cumbersome because of the necessity to
use pledge reminders and other accounting procedures.

TYPES OF GIFTS FROM A MAJOR DONOR

Although not all gifts to an organization are in cash, cash or checks are the
most common way of transferring an asset. Others are:

   1. *Real estate.* Appreciated property is contributed, the fair market value
is available for tax deductions and no tax is required for capital gains. However, gifts of real estate can involve considerable time and effort by an LEF
board in order for them to become cash assets. In addition, state laws may
prohibit school districts from assuming responsibility for a gift that will
require maintenance or repair with tax dollars. Local boards must make
careful decisions about gifts of real estate. Some groups may not wish to
accept them.
   2. *Securities.* Appreciated securities may be transferred with the same
tax advantages as any other asset. Some nonprofit groups set up accounts
with brokerage firms to handle transfers from individuals. Usually, nonprofit groups sell the stock immediately to insure the preservation of the
gift's value.
   3. *Tangible property.* Tangible property is another asset that may be acceptable as a gift. An asset of value that can be transferred into another
more useful asset may benefit an LEF.
   4. *Insurance.* An LEF can be named the beneficiary of a life insurance
policy. In addition, an individual can take out a policy and name the LEF as
both owner and beneficiary. This allows the donor to deduct the premiums
as a contribution. Life insurance companies are business for profit, so LEF
organizations need to carefully study the numerous programs that are being developed.

5. *Gifts-in-kind.* Pieces of equipment and other useful items (computers, televisions, science equipment, etc.) may be donated. Most nonprofit organizations have a procedure for accepting such gifts (see Appendix S for a sample gift-in-kind form). Remember that the responsibility for affixing the value of a gift-in-kind rests with the donor, although some nonprofit groups have some gifts of this nature professionally appraised. Second, there will always be some gifts you do not want!

RESEARCHING DONORS

Some colleges and universities have specialized staff who spend the majority of their time researching prospective individuals, corporations, and foundations to identify potential donors for fund-raisers. Such help is generally not available to an LEF group, but there are sources that may be useful to the director of the LEF and the board of directors.

To identify donors and gather information about them, the director should seek the help of board members, former board members, donors, and friends of the board. The faculty and staff of the school district may be able to provide names and data on prospective donors. In addition, parents, grandparents, graduates, and friends of the school district may provide valuable assistance.

A primary reference source for donors is the city telephone directory. If available, rosters of boards in the city, lists of social and civic clubs, and the list developed by the United Way can be extremely valuable. If the community has a chamber of commerce and will make its membership list available, this may be one of the most valuable sources that you will need.

Facts about individuals may be gathered through interviews, surveys, reference study, and in-depth investigations. In general, LEF groups seek basic personal and business information. Of particular interest will be the prospect's relationship to the school district, particularly her/his interests (athletics, music, academics, etc.). For LEF directors and their boards, perhaps the best approach is through interviews with those closest to the school district (school board members as well as the LEF board, booster clubs, etc.). If this is done carefully, then the chances of matching prospects with the "right" solicitors are very much enhanced.

Large nonprofit organizations use a large number of external materials to research major publications. Most of these involve some costs and may be beyond the budgets of new organizations. However, many of them are available at local and regional libraries. The most common ones for individual research are:

1. *The Who's Who series.* The books include *Who's Who in America, Who's Who Regional* (4 volumes), *Who's Who in Finance and Industry, Who's Who in American History, Who's Who of American Women, Who's Who of Emerging Leaders in America, Who's Who in the World, Who's Who in the World Jewry,* and a *Master Index of Biography.* These excellent sources are available from Marquis Who's Who Inc., 200 East Ohio Street, Chicago, IL 60611.

2. *Standard and Poors Register of Corporations, Directors, and Executives.* This is a set of three volumes and supplements. The Register provides information on corporations, biographical data on officers and directors. In Volume III is "corporate family" information that makes it possible for one to determine "who owns whom." (Standard and Poors Corporation, 25 Broadway, New York, NY, 10004.)

3. *Dunn & Bradstreet Million Dollar Directory.* The publication provides financial information, officers and directors of most major businesses. (Dunn & Bradstreet, 99 Church Street, New York, NY 10007.)

4. *Dunn & Bradstreet Reference Book of Corporate Management.* The publication provides information of officers and directors in 2,400 companies. (Dunn & Bradstreet, 99 Church Street, New York, NY, 10007.)

5. *Biographical Dictionaries Master Index.* This set has three hardboard volumes, with two supplementary paperbound indices. It is a guide to listings in more than 50 current *Who's Who* volumes and other works of collective biography. (Gale Research Company, Book Tower, Detroit, MI, 48226; Dennis LaBeau and Gary C. Tarbert, editors.)

6. *Harris Michigan Industrial Directory.* This publication has information on 15,000 firms and over 32,000 executives. It is arranged alphabetically, geographically, by product, by SIC, and statistically. Also available are similar directories for more than 30 states or geographical areas. (Harris Publishing Company, 2057 Auroa Road, Twinsburg, OH 44087.)

7. *Rand McNally International Bankers Directory.* This publication is compiled annually and contains up-to-date information on 15,000 U.S. Banks and 35,000 branches by state and city. It includes county, full legal title, address, zip code, telephone number, routing number in fractional form, officers and titles, branch locations with officers of condition, and principal correspondent banks. Also contained is a list of 4,700 foreign banks with principal officers, addresses, cable numbers, phone deposits, resources, and capital. A supplement to every edition keeps it current. (Rand McNally and Company, Attn: Bank Publications Division, P.O. Box 7600, Chicago, IL 60680.)

In addition to these standard works, the director of an LEF may wish to consult local, regional, and national newspaper indices (i.e., *The New York Times, Wall Street Journal*), and the *Reader's Guide to Periodical Literature/ Business Guide.*

WHAT IS PLANNED GIVING?

Planned giving is a term that describes gifts of money, securities, or other property made by a donor or donors for future considerations. LEF groups have not been as active in the solicitation of planned gifts as have colleges and universities, but some LEFs do encourage planned giving. For example, the Temple Education Foundation in Temple, Texas, publishes and distributes a brochure entitled, *Where There's A Will, There's A Way* that explains the fundamentals of planned giving and how individuals may make planned gifts to the public schools of their community. The Bartlesville Public School Foundation and the Weatherford Public School Foundation in Oklahoma have similar programs. It is probably a safe assumption that most LEF groups will pay increasing attention to planned giving as their programs mature. Planned giving is, of course, a special type of personal solicitation.

Planned giving offers a number of benefits to LEF groups. Perhaps the most important is in the area of building endowments. Virtually no major college or university in the United States operates without a significant endowment. Perhaps the best way to understand endowments is to think of them as a type of savings account that earns interest over a period of months or years (Lant, 1990). Individuals with these savings accounts spend only the dollars earned from interest and allow the principle, or corpus, to remain untouched. For example, if Mrs. Henry has $100,000 in her savings account (endowment), and the Second State Bank pays her an annual interest rate of 5 percent a year, Mrs. Henry would spend only $5,000, allowing the $100,000 to remain untouched.

The benefit of this to LEF groups could be very important. Suppose, for example, that the goal of an LEF is $50,000 each year. If the group had an unrestricted endowment of $100,000 invested or "saved" at 5 percent, then it would have at least $5,000 as a start for the annual campaign, thus reducing the amount that would need to be raised to $45,000.

Other benefits of planned giving programs is that they are generally cost effective, they can result in significantly larger gifts, and they can help uncover a whole new pool of prospects. Note that some approaches to planned gifts can become quite complicated, and although it is beneficial for LEF directors to know and understand planned giving vehicles, actually setting up deferred gifts and the relevant documents should be handled by a donor's accountant and attorney. For obvious reasons, the director should not be suggesting the specifics of what should go in an individual's will and should not be suggesting tax consequences, as an attorney would. This would not only be harmful, but it would raise questions of ethics and conflicts of interest. Planned giving can benefit the donor as well as the institution, because planned giving is a way to preserve assets for children and grandchildren, possibly increase retirement income, dispose of liquid assets, and diversify individual investment portfolios.

Common Planned Giving Vehicles

As noted, some planned giving vehicles can become complicated, and a complete explanation of all the possibilities of planned giving are beyond the scope of this book. Most colleges and universities now hire planned giving specialists who work with donors and their accountants and attorneys, but most LEF groups do not have this luxury. However, for the purpose of illustration, the following vehicles provide a basic introduction to these techniques.

Wills and Bequests
Virtually all individuals are familiar with wills. These documents specify what is to be done with what an individual owns at the time of his/her death. It would be possible, for example, for an individual to give all that he/she owns to an LEF group through a will. Individuals may choose to give specific amounts of cash, property, stocks, real estate, or even works of art. The major benefit of such gifts to a nonprofit organization is that it can reduce or even eliminate the estate taxes that would ordinarily be paid by the heirs of the deceased.

Charitable Gift Annuities
A charitable annuity is an arrangement between a donor and a nonprofit group wherein the donor gives either cash or property to the organization in exchange for an income for the rest of the donor's life. Donors who make such arrangements are entitled to an income tax deduction for the value of the gift portion of whatever property is transferred. To be eligible for the tax deduction, however, the gift must be irrevocable (the donor cannot cancel the gift at some later date). Of course, the nonprofit group assumes the responsibility of making annuity payments back to the donor. When the individual dies, the assets become the property of the nonprofit organization. These payments are arranged for varying periods of years or for a lifetime and are "fixed" payments. The payments are at least equal to 5 percent of the initial fair-market value of the assets.

Charitable Remainder Unitrusts
A charitable remainder unitrust is a separate trust that pays at least 5 percent of the value of the trust, but the difference between this and a fixed annuity is that this trust is valued *annually*. Thus what an individual receives will vary as the value of the trust changes. Because the evaluation

is annual, additional gifts may be added to this trust. Again, at the end of the beneficiary's life, the trust income and any other accumulated income will become the property of the nonprofit group. The donor may claim an income tax deduction based on the factors of age of the beneficiary, term of years of the trust, and the payout rate of the trust.

Charitable Lead Trust

In this vehicle, a donor provides a gift to a nonprofit group that the non-profit can use for a specified period of time. What is left after that period of time reverts to the donor or to someone else the donor chooses to name. There are three types of *lead trust:* the *grantor,* or a lead trust that must last less than 10 years and the donor receives whatever remains; the *non grantor,* which lasts a specified number of years, after which someone other than the donor receives whatever is left; and the *testamentary* that takes effect on the donor's death, lasts a number of years, and then goes to a person or persons designated by the donor. How would an LEF use such a gift? Suppose, for example, that the LEF needs "seed" money to get started and to pay the salary of the director. If a charitable lead trust is obtained, the LEF could use its funds to help pay the expenses while the organization was establishing itself.

Gifts of Property

Individuals can make gifts of a wide range of properties (*real estate, land, equipment,* etc.) to a nonprofit group and claim income tax deductions for these gifts. The definition of property is wide ranging—land, houses, auto-mobiles, stock, money, art, music collections, libraries, mineral and oil rights—in effect almost anything an individual owns. An individual may even give his/her home to a nonprofit group and still retain the right to live in the dwelling (a real estate gift with retained life estate). Tax deductions depend on such factors as how long the property was owned, its current value, and whether the nonprofit group can use the gift for tax exemptions. Be careful in accepting such gifts; some people simply wish to "unload" all kinds of property that is of no use to a particular nonprofit group.

Pooled Income Funds

This vehicle offers some individuals an opportunity to make a gift to an institution at a time when they may not have the resources for a large major gift. (However, it will work for those with substantial resources as well.) In the pooled-income approach, individuals make a gift to a nonprofit group and the funds are comingled (pooled) with gifts of other donors. Each do-nor is assigned certain units of ownership and the income earned by the fund is distributed to the donors based on the units or shares owned.

Donors may claim a tax deduction on the earnings history of the fund and the age of the life beneficiary. However, all income received is "ordinary" income and as such is 100 percent taxable. Of course, the ultimate beneficiary is the designated nonprofit organization.

Life Insurance

Nonprofit groups may be named as beneficiaries to life insurance policies. Individuals may give life insurance policies to nonprofit organizations and gain income tax deductions. The donor deducts all premiums or the cash value of the policy as charitable contributions for income tax purposes. Again, be careful with insurance programs designed by organizations with profit motives.

The brief introductions listed here are meant only to outline the essentials of some vehicles for deferred giving. There are other approaches that are complicated and require special training and knowledge, however, it behooves an LEF director to understand the essentials of deferred giving.

It is useful if an LEF group has an attorney as a member of the board, especially one skilled in estate planning and tax laws. With her/his help it is possible to do periodic mailings to a wide range of individuals who may be willing to consider a deferred gift to the LEF group. Planned giving booklets (some are commercially available) and articles in newsletters and reports about planned giving can create interest in individuals who may not otherwise think of your group as a potential beneficiary. Many nonprofit groups sponsor seminars about planned giving and estate planning for prospective donors. These should certainly be considered in the overall plans for an LEF group. Again, remember that these are best done when the director has the specialized assistance of an attorney, an accountant, or both.

SUMMARY

The most effective way to raise funds is through direct face-to-face solicitation of potential donors. Even solicitation of private foundations is likely to be enhanced through a face-to-face appeal. Solicitation of major donors is a process that requires donor awareness, understanding, interest, involvement, commitment, and an expression of that commitment (Dunlop, 1991). Guidelines to successful solicitation include the concepts that all person-to-person solicitors must themselves be donors, that solicitation of major gifts is better when a team approach is used, and may take place over months and even years. In most cases, multiple visits are perhaps necessary for even smaller gifts. Each personal solicitation visit requires careful planning prior to the actual call. Solicitors seek outright gifts, life income gifts, testamentary gifts, and pledges. Gifts may include, in addition to cash, real estate, securities, tangible properties, insurance, and gifts-in-kind. At least preliminary research should be done on all major donors.

Planned giving offers excellent potential for LEF groups, especially in the area of endowments, and approaches to receiving them should be part of LEF group planning. Some of the kinds of gifts noted above may be given to an LEF as a planned gift. These include gift annuities and trusts, wills, pooled-income funds, gifts of property, charitable remainder trusts, charitable lead trusts, and gifts of insurance.

8

RAISING FUNDS FROM FOUNDATIONS

Most LEF groups consider seeking funds from private foundations to help support their educational activities. And well they should, since the number of such agencies exceeds 22,000 and their total assets are worth in excess of $37 billion! In recent years, grants from these foundations have totaled more than $5 billion! However, LEF directors should also understand that the majority of funds in these foundations are controlled by fewer than a dozen organizations. They tend to be concentrated and as a result give in specific geographical regions. This does not mean, however, that an LEF director working in Ohio will not be able to have a grant funded by a large New York foundation. It does mean that the chances for receiving funding are considerably enhanced if the foundation has its offices in a geographical area in relative proximity to the LEF group. For example, a school district in Ohio may have a better chance of funding from a foundation in Cleveland than they would from a foundation in New York City.

LEF directors must also understand that foundations are not the quintessential "bell cow" that will meet needs that taxes do not support. In spite of large grants from foundations, they still contribute only 5 to 6 percent of the amount of private dollars given each year.

The fact that more and more groups are seeking funding from private foundations means that the competition for funding continues to increase. Each foundation must spend 5 percent of its market value or net income each year, but this does not mean an unlimited supply of dollars. In addition, selecting a list of foundations from a source book and sending a large number of proposals is likely to result in a lot of "skinny letters," letters foundations use to tell you they are not interested in what you have proposed, but they wish you well in obtaining funds—elsewhere, of course.

Raising funds from foundations follows principles outlined in this book. Most important of all is the fact that a relationship with the staff of a foundation is as important as the proposal itself. Again, people give to people.

On the plus side for LEF groups is that a trend of supporting public schools seems to be emerging. In the past, colleges and universities received the lion's share of foundation funding of education, but in an attempt to enhance the public education, many foundations now give serious consideration to requests (for excellence!) from public schools. There has never been a better time for public schools to explore the possibilities of foundation funding!

KINDS OF FOUNDATIONS

A foundation* is a nongovernmental, nonprofit organization, with funds managed by its own trustees or directors. It is established to maintain or aid social, educational, charitable, religious, or other activities serving the common welfare (Broce, 1987). Young (1989) notes four types of foundations:

(a) *those set up by a family,*
(b) *those designated to serve a specific community or geographical area,*
(c) *those set up by a corporation,*
(d) *those established to foster a certain interest.*

Each of these specializes its funding in one or more of the following ways: by restricting their giving to a geographical area, by defining specific areas of interest, and by defining the funding they will give. Also, utilize the calendar year as a fiscal year, and some meet only once a year to make decisions on requests (Young, 1989, p. 87).

It is useful to consider foundations in the context of their purpose. For example, the general-purpose foundations ordinarily have large endowments, specific objectives, and professional staffs. There are in excess of 1,600 of these in the United States and they are the philanthropic leaders.

Some foundations, however, could be called "special-purpose foundations" because their objectives are more narrowly defined and restricted.

---

*See Appendix T for a sample foundation worksheet.

There are fewer of these and one must meet their criteria to gain their support. For example, one foundation has been a generous benefactor of educational purposes, however, their guidelines specifically rule out funding of public educational institutions. Even a relationship between the fund-raiser and a member of their board was not sufficient to have them bend their rules. The proposal, though it was one of their major areas of interest, was turned down because the agency was state assisted!

LEF groups can profit from company-sponsored foundations, especially if the company is in or near their community. These company foundations are nonprofit entities that are separate from the companies. They are usually governed by company directors, and generally do not have the large endowment base of some private foundations. A key fact for LEF directors to remember is that these groups tend to make gifts in localities where the company has operations or to centers that benefit employees. Also, these foundations like to make grants that enhance the image of the company and/or its chief executive officer. For example, a large grant to an LEF group by the local utility company, with an opportunity for the chief executive officer to appear in the local paper, could be an important aspect of the funding process!

Community foundations are those designed to sponsor needs and projects within a particular community. Each receives and distributes capital gifts. Although there are approximately 200 of these foundations in the United States, they are not generally good potential sources of support outside rather restricted geographical boundaries.

Independent foundations, on the other hand, offer good potential for LEF groups because they are generally initiated by individuals who are still living. There are more than 15,000 of these in the United States today, and their influence continues to grow. They often reflect the interests of the founder, and the directors tend to be that person's business associates or family members. They are located in almost all geographic areas and tend to be sensitive to those in need of new support. In addition, they are more flexible than most foundations (Broce, 1987).

A good starting point for LEF directors may be a general perspective of the large contributors in private and corporate giving. Though the figures change from year to year, the Taft Group (1990) listed the top 20 companies in terms of contributions as IBM Corporation, American Telephone and Telegraph, General Motors Corporation, Hewlett-Packard Company, Exxon, RJR Nabisco, General Electric, Merck & Company, Ford Motor, DuPont, Procter and Gamble, 3M Company, Sears and Roebuck, Kraft General Foods, Chevron, Digital Equipment, Amoco, US West, Eastman Kodak, and Anheuser-Busch. The top 10 contributors to education were IBM, Procter and Gamble,

General Electric, American Telephone and Telegraph, DuPont, (E.I.) de Nemours & Company, Shell Oil, Ford Motor, Eastman Kodak Company and Boeing Company. Sears, American Telephone, and General Electric have been major contributors to social services; IBM, Dayton Hudson, and Ford Motor are among the leaders in giving to the arts and humanities, and Burroughs-Wellcome, McDonnell Douglas, and Hoffman-La Rouche are leaders in giving to science.

In terms of contributions, the leaders in annual giving are the Ford Foundation, John D. and Catherine T. MacArthur Foundation, W. K. Kellog, Robert Wood Johnson Foundation, Lilly Endowment, Rockefeller Foundation, Andrew W. Mellon Foundation, Kresge Foundation, Arnold and Mable Beckmann Foundation, Duke Endowment, Carnegie Corporation, Lucille P. Markey Charitable Trust, W. M. Keck Foundation, Richard King Mellon Foundation, Gannett Foundation, Moody Foundation, and Starr Foundation (data taken from Taft Group, 1990).

Each of these has been noted to alert the LEF director to those organizations that are typically among the leaders in corporate giving. However, the author suggests that the LEF director pinpoint his community and draw concentric rings around it in terms of 100 miles distances. She/he should then concentrate on all the private and corporate foundations that have locations or operations within one hundred miles of the LEF's school district. Once the foundations in this area have been identified, they should be researched (researching is detailed later in this chapter) and studied for possible grant applications. Once this is completed, the LEF director may wish to turn his/her attention to organizations located 200 miles from the school district and repeat the same process. He/she may want to go 300 or 400 miles away, but in general those groups closest to the school district represent the best chances to obtain funding. A target of 20 to 50 groups of corporate and private foundations constitutes a very good starting point. A general form for outlining essential details of a foundation is in Appendix T.

RESEARCHING FOUNDATIONS

The identification of a number of foundations is only the initial step in the process of preparing a proposal. Do your homework. If the foundation located prints in their guidelines that they will not support publicly assisted institutions, then a proposal to them is probably a wasted effort. Find out as much as possible about the foundation prior to writing a proposal.

Lant (1990) notes nine key elements to the identification of a foundation as a potential source of support:

1. *If the prospect has guidelines, do they exclude groups like yours?*
2. *Are you in the right geographical location for consideration?*
3. *Has the prospect given to you before?*
4. *If so, did it indicate a receptivity for funding again?*
5. *If not, were you told about possible interest?*
6. *Can you approach this prospect without a contact?*
7. *Why do you think so?*
8. *If not, do you know someone who will help craft the approach?*
9. *Is there a specific reason why you think the source might be interested in you?*

(Lant, 1990, p. 93)

This exercise may seem unimportant, but it is not. Neophyte fund-raisers, like eager new faculty, sometimes seem almost unable to understand why every private foundation in the world would not jump at the opportunity to fund what they perceive is an absolutely brilliant idea or a pressing need. University professors, for example, have frequently called fund-raisers with requests such as, "I need a graduate assistant to help do research for my new book. Wouldn't the "X" Foundation be interested in providing me the funds to hire one?" The first impulse is to shout "Absolutely not," but it is better to try to explain that the professor has no needs. If he/she wants funding, then present foundations opportunities to solve problems not meet individual needs!

If one can develop affirmative responses to the questions posed by Lant, then each grant writer or LEF director should engage in introspection and careful thinking. Remember, your proposal will be judged along with hundreds of others. The readers in foundations will want an understanding of who you are, what you do and are able to do, and how your nonprofit group stands out from others seeking funds from this foundation. You must first, then, be able to identify and use those factors that make your school district unique (and of course, excellent!). What are the goals and objectives of your school? What are you attempting to do? In many cases the data gathered from recent accreditation visits (by regional and state accrediting agencies) provide useful information in this area. How good is your staff? How diverse is it? What makes it different and better than that of the neighboring school district? Do they have special talents? Special experiences? What facilities are available that will be useful in meeting the objectives of your proposal?

For example, if you are proposing an adult education grant to teach computer literacy to parents in your district, are computers available? Do you have faculty expertise in this area? Do you have an appropriate room to teach adults? Whom do you serve? What is the nature of the clientele? Will your project be for gifted people? for minorities? for at-risk children? How far will your project reach? Will it serve many, or only a few? (*Note:*

Although not always listed in annual reports, many foundations like to get the "best bang for their bucks." Thus projects that will help many as opposed to only a few individuals often receive favorable consideration, particularly when the funding is requested for initiating projects).

In this planning stage of identifying prospects, it is also important to keep in mind what your specific task will be. Most foundations frown on contributions to operating budgets, many do not like to fund travel, and most do not want to continue funding any idea for a long number of years. In general, foundations like to support projects or programs. Some will consider a new building, or the renovation of an old one, scholarships, or perhaps an endowment fund.

Fortunately for the newly appointed LEF director (and the experienced one as well), a wide range of sources is available to help match your ideas with those of the foundations. The more common ones are listed here:

The Foundation Directory

Available from The Foundation Center, 79 Fifth Avenue, New York, NY 10003. This is perhaps the best known source. This directory contains information on foundations with assets of $1 million or more, with grants of $100,000 or more. More than 3,100 foundations are included in this book. It has basic but essential information: Name, address, giving interests, financial data, officers and directors, and grant application information. It is indexed by state and city locations, personnel, and fields of interests. (*Note:* The Foundation Center, responsible for publishing this directory, is an independent national service organization established by foundations to provide information on private giving. Information is disseminated through public-service programs, publications, and a national network of library reference collections that are available free to the public. Since 1981 the Center has continued to expand via an Associates Program, a network of 90 collections of funding information. Since it was started more than 50 organizations have been designated as Foundation Center Affiliates. Collections have been established in a variety of host organizations including public and university libraries. Chances are an organization near you is affiliated with the Foundation Center through the Affiliates Program.)

Foundations Grants Index

This is another excellent source also published by the Foundation Center. It is issued six times a year and contains a list of 2000 or more foundation grants of $5,000 or more. The index is referenced in three ways: by foundation name and geographical location, by names of grant recipients, and by key subjects such as *school, university, college, medical education, scholarships,* and so forth. It is easy to use and provides a wealth of information.

Comsearch Printouts

The Foundation Center also provides what they have labeled *Comsearch Printouts,* available in paper and microfiche. Printouts include information from The Foundation Grants Index by subject heading. Nine major headings include *communications, education, health, humanities, population groups, physical and life sciences, social sciences,* and *welfare.* It is also available in geographic categories.

The Taft Foundation Reporter

Available from the Taft Corporation, this publication provides extensive information on major foundations, including application procedures and biographical sketches of trustees of more than 500 of the largest and most important foundations. For an additional fee, one can order two newsletters, *Foundation Giving Watch,* and *Foundation Updates.*

National Data Book

Also available from the Foundation Center, this publication has information on every active United States Foundation, all 24,859 of them, with total assets of $74 billion or more and awarding grants worth $5 billion. This, too, has information on addresses of foundations, those in a particular city or region, assets and giving levels by state and region, and which foundations issue annual reports. It also has information on the number and size of small foundations in a wide range of communities.

State Foundation Directories

Organizations in most states have published state foundation directories. (North Dakota and West Virginia are the only states where information is not available at the time of this writing.) State directories are published by groups ranging from community foundations to public libraries. A local or regional foundation in your state will be able to provide LEF directors information on ordering. These directories are valuable tools for narrowing down initial searches.

Annual Register of Grant Support

Available from Marquis Academic Media, this publication provides details of grant support programs of government agencies, and public and private foundations (Marquis Who's Who Inc., 200 East Ohio St., Chicago, IL 60601.)

Foundation Annual Reports

The Foundation Directory and other similar publications list foundations that publish annual reports. Some large foundations send out reports each year.

Corporate Annual Reports

These may be requested directly from the company. These are a must for any corporations that are close to your school district.

America's Newest Foundations

Available from the Taft Group; contains information on 545 "new" foundations.

APPROACHING FOUNDATIONS

Once the LEF director has conducted an initial review of some foundations that may be legitimate prospects for a proposal, the next step in seeking a grant may be taken. Goldman (1985) suggests a general mailing to selected constituents asking them about their relationships with foundations and with foundation trustees and officers. He sends a letter with about 900 offices of foundations to a constituency of 5,000 individuals, asking each to use a key for marking a list in the categories, "I know a little; I know fairly well; I know very well." Each is also asked to place a checkmark after the statement, "I would be willing to help the school in its approach." Goldman indicates that one of his mailings brought 120 responses, and with the information received, a cross-referenced file was developed under the names of each foundation official and each of the constituents who knew this official.

The file then enabled the school to use the constituents in a number of ways. Some were asked to set up appointments at foundations, some were asked to attend meetings with foundation officials and school development professionals, and still others were asked to make a phone call or write a follow-up letter (Goldman, 1985).

Lant (1990) suggests a similar process with the additional step that the director of nonprofit groups compile lists of foundation directors and members of corporate boards. Once compiled, these lists are presented to board members at a specific meeting that Lant labels a "facilitation session." In the meeting, each board member is asked to describe his/her relationship to foundation boards and corporate boards and to indicate if each is willing to help make a contact, attend a meeting, make a phone call, write a letter, or perform other useful functions. Both Lant and Goldman are suggesting a process that enables an LEF director to meet personally with one or more foundation officials. Such meetings may start the formation of a personal relationship between the LEF director and the foundation official. If this takes place, the LEF director has a tremendous start on obtaining a grant (other factors being equal) from that foundation.

Broce (1987) suggests an additional approach that LEF directors may find useful. He advocates sending a letter to all foundations that are legitimate prospects for a proposal from your school district. This letter may come from the LEF director or the board chair and should briefly describe your institution and why the foundation information is being sought. The letter should ask for information concerning grant policies, mutual interests, and preferred methods of solicitation. In addition, the letter should specifically ask if your school district and its related activities fall within the institution's range of support. The letter should also note that the director is available for an interview at the convenience of the foundation if such a visit is required or desirable. All of this should be written on a single page! (Broce, 1987). The Funding Information Center (no date) suggests these questions:

1. Do you have an application and printed guidelines?
2. Do you have an annual report?
3. When does the board meet? *Note:* If "no deadline," ask when grant applications are reviewed.
4. When will a decision be made/announced? Do you notify either way? If an applicant has not received a grant, do you send a rejection letter?
5. Is there anything about our request/project that the board doesn't like? The proper time to ask is during an initial review.

Through the methods suggested here, an LEF director may want to forward an initial letter of inquiry of not more than two pages to introduce your institution, tell what you are trying to do and why, provide a description of the project for which support is being sought to include cost, timetable, and institutional and other donor investments. In addition, the letter should ask if this is an area in which the foundation may be interested in investing. Of course, if the LEF director is able to secure a personal visit, this letter may not be necessary. Letters of inquiry are recommended if a personal visit is not made. Obviously there is little to be gained by spending hours on a proposal and then sending it to a foundation that has absolutely no interest in your institution or what you are attempting to accomplish (Broce, 1987).

Such letters of inquiry may be sent to several foundations at the same time; it is possible that one foundation will not be able to provide total support, but may be willing to join others to support your endeavor.

WRITING THE PROPOSAL

There is no lack of helpful material on proposal writing. In fact, it is the one aspect of fund-raising that seems to attract the most interest, and hence the greatest number of articles outlining essential elements of writing proposals.

Goldman (1985, pp. 12–14) has developed a series of tips for proposal writers that have been adapted for this book. They represent some solid ideas for grants writers ass they develop proposals.

1. *Proposals should be as brief as possible, usually no more than five pages. Additional information may be added in appendices.*
2. *Proposals may include: a brief description of your school district, evidence of the specific need, details about how the need will be met, duration of the project, evaluation process, staff capabilities, total cost of the project, amount requested from the foundation, list of other supporters, and future funding potential. Stated another way, include the who, what, when, where, why, and how of your project.*
3. *Say the important things first. In the first few paragraphs, detail the purpose of your project, and the link between it and the foundation's field of interest.*
4. *Put the amount you're asking for in a prominent place.*
5. *If you have other funding sources, say so.*
6. *Foundations are pleased if they feel you will not be coming back to them with repeated grants requests. If you are asking for a one-time request, say so.*
7. *Write clearly and precisely. Use the active voice. Use simple words. Use concrete examples and facts to support your case. Avoid jargon and focus on the human elements involved. Project optimism and confidence.*
8. *Your cover letter should be addressed to the person specified in the Foundation Directory.*
9. *Proposals should be single spaced, and typed on one side of the page only.*
10. *People do sometimes judge a proposal by its physical appearance. Packaging your proposal is important. Shun gimmicks, and be sure the materials you use are not overly expensive, thus giving the impression that the institution squanders money.*

The Proposal and Accompanying Materials

As noted, proposal formats vary, but most contain the elements listed here. A complete grant packet to a foundation may include the following information:

    I. *A Cover Letter.* This letter should come from the director or chair of the LEF group. It should contain information on the funds requested, the importance of the request, and the specific reasons this request is being sent to this particular foundation. (Appendix U contains an example of a cover letter.)

    II. *Summary Sheet.* Each proposal should have a summary sheet that identifies the applicant, and outlines the specific grant request. The summary should also contain material on the needs, objectives, and the methods for reaching these objectives.

    III. *The Proposal.* The proposal should begin with an introduction that includes the name of the applicant, the program, the funding request, description of the applicant's purpose, programs, and clients.

        Broce (1987) suggests including in the introduction a statement of why the institution is seeking the support of this foundation. Lefferts (1978) suggests that the geographic area to be served, the persons to be served, and the significance of the program be included in the introduction to the proposal. Kirtz (1980, p. 8) suggests additional examples of what might be included:

- when, how, and why the organization was started
- a statement of purpose, goals, and philosophy
- significant events in your history
- prior and current activities
- accomplishments and impact
- size and characteristics of your constituency or clientele
- assistance asked of you and given to other organizations
- referring agencies (if you provide direct services)
- your funding sources and their positive comments on your work
- the results of internal or external evaluations of your work
- quotes from letters of support from clients, other agencies, experts in the field, public figures
- invitations you've received to provide testimony on legislation
- important agency publications

Statement of Need

In this section include specific documentation of the problem, the limitations of existing programs, and some indication of the demand for the program (Lefferts, 1978). In a sense, it can indicate "What is wrong here?" and "Why does it matter?" The problem should be related to the purposes and goals of the institution, and be supported if possible by statistical evidence and statements from authorities. It should also be stated in terms of clients or beneficiaries and be free from jargon, assumptions, and boring material (Kirtz, 1980). This section must be compelling!

Program Objectives

A clear presentation of the program's objectives will provide a base for later evaluations. This section, though brief, may include goals (these are broad) and specific objectives that can be numbered and measured. Kirtz (1980), for example, notes that if writers use words like *to provide* or *to create*, they are writing about methods, not objectives, which are written in terms of *to increase, to decrease,* and *to reduce.* In essence, program objectives should tell who is going to do what, when, how much, and how it will be measured (Kirtz, 1980, p. 20).

Action Plans

Once you have listed your objectives, the next step is to develop an action plan or the methodology that will be used to meet them. In this plan, describe past approaches to the problem, your new approach, and the reasons that your approach is superior. Clearly describe the sequence of activities and outline the reasons for selecting those activities. Other important inclusions in this section could be a description of volunteer and professional staffing, and a justification that the activities listed can be completed in reasonable length of time (Kirtz, 1980).

Evaluation

Evaluation sections of proposals are often poorly prepared or at least individuals seem to spend the least amount of time dealing with them. Evaluation of what is proposed, however, is critical to many foundations. In a sense, your evaluation provides answers to the questions, "How will you know that your objectives have been met?" Will you use pre-test/post-test approaches? Will you use opinion data (client satisfaction) or perhaps simple counting (i.e., 300 disadvantaged students will benefit from this program). In some instances, you may suggest an outside evaluation, or the approval of an agency (State Department of Education). If you will produce a final report that includes evaluations, this should be noted here.

Future Funding

Most foundations are interested in how the proposed project will be funded next year (or beyond the scope of the grant). Remember, few foundations support an institution forever. They tend to like projects with specific beginning and ending dates that have measurable objectives that lend themselves to evaluation. If there are ongoing funding needs, note that in this section, and if the school district will assume future costs of the project, note this fact also.

Conclusion

In this section the specific request is identified. In addition, it contains expressions of community or professional support, shows the impact the grant will have on the school district, and emphasizes how the grant reflects the foundations values and ideas. This section, too, must be compelling!

Attachments

Some of the following may be attached:

- an itemized project budget
- an agency budget
- a list of board members
- any pertinent information not previously included
- brief biography of board chair or LEF director
- articles, clippings, letters of support from key people
- charts, brochures, pictures

There are, of course, other outlines for developing proposals, but most contain one or more of the elements suggested here. There is, however, one outline that the author has used a number of times with good success. Lant (1990) feels that institutions spend too much time developing proposals, so he outlines a format that with minor modifications can be used to submit proposals for different projects by changing only some parts of the proposal. Lant's book should be read in its entirety, but his suggested outline for proposals (Lant, 1990, pp. 24–30) is worth noting. A proposal writer will need:

A synopsis of summary: Describe in about 150 words the program. It presents the need and includes a one-figure cost, an indication of evaluation, a description of how the program connects with the agency's overall goals, and a specific indication of who will benefit.

A problem statement: This is a narrative of 250 to 500 words that deals with local, regional, and national dimensions of the problem.

A history of your organization: A brief narrative, 100 to 150 words, highlights the character and development of your organization.

Successes of your school: Use bullet points about what the school does well, awards, testimonials, and so on.

A description of ongoing programs: Each one, such as minigrants and scholarships, should be described in 25 words or less.

Past supporters: Name supporters over the past three years.

The people: Provide biographical data on the board chair and executive director.

Fund-raising objectives: These should be your goals.

Critical role: Relate why the school district is important.

Line item budget: Include costs for staff, space, equipment, telephone, travel, and so forth.

Appendices: You may want to include your 501(c)(3) letter, a list of your board members, current operating budget, other public relations materials.

If one has followed the guidelines suggested here, there is a good chance that a good proposal will evolve. It is wise, of course, to have others read what has been written. Few proposals are the result of a single draft or of the sole thinking of one writer. Good proposals require a team effort. Perhaps there is no greater feeling to a fund-raiser than that of securing funding for a project that will benefit the school district, and more important, the teachers and children who are the very soul of the district. (Appendix U has an example of a modified proposal.)

As a final word on proposal writing, it may be useful to heed the words of Michael Radcock (1990), who surveyed a group of foundation directors for descriptions of what they perceived as the most common errors in the proposals they receive. They are:

1. Failure to conform to the grantor's guidelines and/or to confer with grantor prior to submitting the proposal.
2. Apparent distortion of an agency's objectives just to attract funding.
3. Carelessness in preparation of the proposal.
4. Unrealistic funding requests
5. Inappropriate response to a rejection.
6. Failure to report progress on funded grants.
7. Inappropriate recognition for grant support (expensive plaques).

SUMMARY

Raising funds from private foundations can be a worthwhile activity for LEF directors, even though funding from these sources may not be the chief source of support for their school districts. Foundations may be classified as general purpose, special purpose, company sponsored, community sponsored, or independent. There is a wide range of both private and corporate foundations that are generous supporters of education as well as other causes.

The LEF director must research foundations that may be willing to support his or her school district, and there are excellent sources to help in this process of identification.

The development of proposals requires careful planning and involves steps to contact foundations, determine their degree of interest in your school district, and secure specialized guidelines they may have. Most proposal packets contain a cover letter, a summary sheet, and the proposal itself. The elements in a proposal generally include an introduction, a statement of need, objectives, an action plan, an evaluation plan, and a summary and conclusion. Many also contain an appendix of material that supports and enhances the proposal.

9

RAISING FUNDS WITH SPECIAL EVENTS

WHY SPECIAL EVENTS?

It is safe to assume that the majority of nonprofit groups in the United States utilizes some form of special event or events to raise funds. In fact, most Americans probably think of special events when they think of ways to raise money. Many of them have been involved with fund-raising through this vehicle as members of church groups, school groups, and local civic organizations.

There are a number of good reasons for special-event fund-raising. Lant (1990) notes that it is a good way to raise unrestricted revenue, boost the image of a particular group, attract new friends and donors, help with cultivation of individuals; and the event itself may be a special way of saying "thank you" to donors and volunteer workers (Lant, 1990). Special events are also a good way to attract media attention.

There is, however, a down side to special-event fund-raising. It seems that no other fund-raising activity causes as much staff and volunteer burnout as does a special event. In most cases they are extremely labor intensive, and require that the chair of the event pay very close attention to a wide range of details. In one case, three students who had been hired as coordinators of special events resigned their positions within the period of a single month, citing the pressures associated with special-event fund-raising. This does not mean that LEF groups should not attempt to raise funds with special events. Rather, the LEF director must be certain to understand why he/she is conducting a special event, and what the expectations for it should be. In general, special events are not the best ways to raise money when one subtracts the hours spent and the cost of putting on these events from the number of dollars raised. On the other hand, if a major objective of the LEF director and the board is publicity, then a well-organized, imaginative fund-raiser is an excellent public-relations vehicle.

ORGANIZING FOR THE SPECIAL EVENT

It is useful to prepare a plan or an outline of the necessary elements to consider in the development of a special event. An outline suggested by Lant (1990) is a useful guide that an LEF director can modify for personal use:

1. *Name the event.* What will it be called? Is there a theme?
2. *Select a date.* When will you hold the event? Lant (1990) suggests that each organization hold two special events a year and that they be repeated each year on the same date so that individuals will expect them. The Easter Seal Society, for example, begins planning for special events six months prior to the actual event in order to accomplish planning, site selection, mailing, and other special considerations in ample time to have the event run smoothly.
3. *Draw up your budget.* How much do you anticipate making after you deduct expenses from your gross income?
4. *List major expenses.* What will you have to purchase? How much will be donated? Will you need to rent a room? Pay for mailings? Will you have a caterer if a meal is planned? Do you have sound equipment or must you rent it? Will you pay for advertising, entertainment? Will you be presenting gifts (plaques, trophies)? Will you need to have funds "in advance" to meet the expenses?
5. *Estimate volunteer resources.* Who will chair the event? How many subcommittees will you need? What other events will need to be managed by volunteers (ticket sales, ushers)? Lant (1990) says that each special event needs a strong chair, a facility committee to select and manage a site, a program committee to develop the agenda for the event, a publicity committee, a ticket committee, a hospitality committee, a mailing committee, and of course a clean-up committee. It is possible to combine the duties of the mailing committee and the telephone committee. One special event required the presence of at least 20,000 individuals. Needless to relate, a massive effort was needed to attract that many people, and phones were used extensively to meet the objective of "filling up the facility," which in this case was an outdoor stadium.

6. *Appoint committees.* This is a very important question, especially for LEF directors who may constitute the entire staff. It is important in terms of the objective of the special event. Remember that if raising money is your major objective, then special events are not very efficient. An LEF director who spends the majority of her/his time in one or two special events each year will soon discover that precious little time remains for major donor programs, annual campaigns, or proposal writing. Therefore, key committees should be appointed.

7. *List additional sponsors if any.* Will you ask local business for support? Will you seek cash contributions? What impact, if any, will seeking this support have on your annual campaign? Will you prepare a proposal to a local foundation seeking support for your efforts?

Of course, many of these details can be assigned to committees, and if you are fortunate enough to have a strong chair for the event, then the task becomes simpler. It is obvious that in order to stage a successful event, one needs a large and diverse number of dedicated people. If you are not able to do a special event with "class" and "community appeal," it is perhaps better not to do it at all. Some events have more appeal than others, and you may have to study your community to determine what kind of event will have the most appeal. Of course, it is good to have as much as possible donated; this will increase profits from an event (Young, 1989). The experience of conducting special events where the expenses exceeded the profits teaches some valuable lessons:

1. Careful advanced planning is essential for a good special event.
2. Large numbers of dedicated volunteers are necessary.
3. Special events are usually not cost effective.
4. Well-organized special events are excellent public-relations vehicles.
5. The amount of time an LEF director wants to spend on special events impacts her/his work in other areas of fund-raising.
6. Some special events are lots of fun!

KINDS OF SPECIAL EVENTS

An LEF director and the board may consider a number of special events. Most of these are familiar to adults who are actively involved in the community.

Film Nights

The LEF director can rent popular films in advance and hold a film night, either at one of the buildings in the school district or in another building in the community. Volunteers can make cookies, popcorn, and other snacks to be sold at the event (Young, 1989).

Auctions

If you can obtain a large range of donated materials, you may want to conduct an auction. This requires a site, good publicity, and a good auctioneer. A great variety of things are auctioned. For example, Lant (1990) suggests a travel auction where everything auctioned is related to travel (airline tickets, luggage, beach clothing, time share arrangements in a pleasant climate, ski trips, etc.). Food concessions can also be part of the auction. A popular type of auction in recent years is auctioning "celebrities" (important people in your community) to perform certain tasks if they are "sold" at auction. For example, the town mayor or the star of a nearby professional athletic team would probably command a good auction bid, if the winner could have lunch or dinner with the celebrity. Variations of this include "celebrity waiters," who wait tables and turn all tips back to the nonprofit group, or events that require an important person to spend time in a makeshift or real jail until he/she is ransomed.

Dances and Concerts

If you are fortunate enough to be able to secure good entertainment for a special dance, ball, or concert, and the entertainment is donated, this type of event can make a handsome profit (Young, 1989).

Other popular special events include art shows, celebrity golf tournaments, bowling tournaments, picnics, exhibition athletic contests, stage shows, and in some states where it is legal, raffles of everything from candy to a house built by the students in one of the vocational shops of the school district.

As a final note, the LEF director who initiates a special event must be certain to properly thank all who have been involved in helping to plan and conduct the event.

SUMMARY

Fund-raising through special events is one of the more common approaches to fund-raising by LEFs. Special events can raise money and are a good way to obtain publicity and recruit new donors and volunteers, and to say "thank you" to others. They are, however, time consuming, and may not always be cost effective. If an LEF director wishes to use special events to raise funds, careful planning with a large and dedicated staff of volunteers is probably necessary. A strong chairperson and a well thought-out committee structure will help.

Special events include auctions, meals, musical events, film nights, athletic contents, and in some states, raffles. Although they are work intensive, good events generate good will and can be fun to do.

CONCLUSION

One can hypothesize that in the 1990s and beyond the budget crunches that face most states and most school districts will not disappear. Public education to many U.S. taxpayers seems akin to a bottomless pit or a huge sinkhole that swallows tax dollars. In addition, the results produced from these expenditures seems to fall short of the public's perception of what schools should be doing. Almost daily, the media points out one problem after another and the total of these endless negative reports on education has alarmed parents, business and industry leaders, and legislators. In fact, the quality of public education was very much a topic in the 1992 presidential campaign and both George Bush and Bill Clinton offered solutions and promises related to public schools that each hoped would find acceptance with the electorate.

In fact, however, much of what is taking place in U.S. public education is as good or better than what is taking place in other countries with which it is most often compared. The United States is a place where all are educated; our public schools deal with students who would never be enrolled in countries that educate only the elite.

There is, of course, room for improvement in U.S. schools. To deny this is myopic and foolish. Most professional educators and in fact most citizens agree that there is work to do to insure excellence in our public schools. There is, however, less than complete agreement on what should be done to improve public education.

Legislators in most states and at the national level are fond of saying that money alone will not solve the problems in the public schools. Perhaps not, but lack of money, or funding at a level that allows schools to be only mediocre will not solve the problems either. In fact, few school systems in the United States enjoy a level of funding that allows them to become excellent in all that they do. Most receive sufficient funds to allow them to be average or mediocre. One would be naive to believe that future funding patterns will change dramatically. Therefore, excellence in U.S. public education will take place only when communities and school districts engage in new and creative approaches to finding resources to support programs and projects that are of the best quality.

In recent years, one approach to finding new and different sources of revenue for public education is the growing movement to create and operate private foundations whose major role is to raise additional revenues for public schools. These foundations are not being formed to supplement budget shortfalls or supplement programs that taxes either can not or will not support. Rather, they are focused organizations that use privately raised funds in a variety of ways to promote and foster excellence in public education. This excellence ranges from simple, small, grant programs that help teachers and schools purchase teaching materials and supplies to sophisticated efforts that promote racial harmony and innovative approaches to school governance. In most cases, local organizations arise from grass-roots efforts by concerned citizens who seek new and better ways to improve the education of children. In so doing they seek to create a better relationship among parents, educators, business and industry, and government. The local education foundation, in effect, sees public education as the business of all. They do not, nor should they, seek to replace tax dollars as the primary source of funding for schools. What they have done and are continuing to do, however, is to issue a challenge to educators—create programs and activities of excellence and together we will find ways to promote and support that excellence.

The idea has caught on and it is growing. From Maine to California, public foundations seem to come into existence almost weekly. It is a new and exciting concept that seems to be one that almost all can support, a rarity in public education.

Private foundations, however, are not to be taken lightly. They are and must be much more than a booster club. They are educational advocates, constructive critics, and a talent pool dedicated to the cause of improving public schools. To be effective requires planning, good organization, good community leadership, and a professional approach to raising funds to support endeavors of excellence. The ideas in this book are a step in that direction.

Appendix A

ARTICLES OF INCORPORATION
OF
LAFAYETTE PUBLIC EDUCATION FUND, INC.

STATE OF LOUISIANA
PARISH OF LAFAYETTE

BE IT KNOWN, that on the 27th day of February the several subscribers hereto, each of the full age of majority, availing themselves of the provisions of the Louisiana Nonprofit Corporation Law (Title 12, Chapter 2, Louisiana Revised Statutes of 1950 as revised and codified by Act 105 of 1968, and as amended), do hereby organize themselves, their successors and assigns, into a corporation in pursuance of that law, under and in accordance with the following Articles of Incorporation:

ARTICLE I

The name of the corporation is LAFAYETTE PUBLIC EDUCATION FUND, INC.

ARTICLE II

The objects and purposes for which this corporation is organized and the nature of the business to be carried on by it is stated and declared to be as follows:

1. The Lafayette Public Education Fund shall be an independent, community-based organization formed for the purpose of promoting excellence in education and in furtherance of that goal shall:

159

    a. Develop supportive community and private relationships with the Lafayette Parish public school system;

    b. Provide limited private sector support to launch initiatives for creative educational improvements; and,

    c. Develop strategies to stimulate optimism and inspiration among educators, parents, and students.

2. To do all other things necessary or appropriate to accomplish the stated objectives and purposes of the corporation.

ARTICLE III

The duration of this corporation shall be in perpetuity or such maximum period that may be authorized by the laws of Louisiana.

ARTICLE IV

This is a nonprofit corporation.

ARTICLE V

Anything contained herein notwithstanding, the corporation is organized exclusively for charitable, educational, and scientific purposes including for such purposes the making of grants or distributions to those organizations, persons or other entities who or which may serve the objects and purpose for which this corporation is organized.

Proposed Budget

Year 1

INCOME:

Fund-raising	$35,000	
Total Income		$35,000

EXPENSES:

Programs		$13,000
Staffing (part-time)		$5,000
Administrative (other)		$5,000
Contingencies		$2,000
Total Expenses		$25,000

Accumulated Reserve	$10,000

Year 2

INCOME:

Fund-raising	$75,000	
Total Income		$75,000

EXPENSES:

Programs	$36,000	
Staffing	$14,000	
Administrative (other)	$5,000	
Contingencies	$5,000	
Total Expenses		$60,000

Accumulated Reserve (Years 1 and 2)	$25,000

Year 3

INCOME:

Fund-raising	$125,000	
Total Income		$125,000

EXPENSES:

Programs	$47,000	
Staffing	$25,000	
Administrative (other)	$7,500	
Contingencies	$5,000	
Total Expenses		$85,000

Accumulated Reserve (3 Years)	$65,000

Appendix B

BYLAWS
OF
LAFAYETTE PUBLIC EDUCATION FUND, INC.

SECTION I

Paragraph 1. Designation of Members; Term of Office.   The members of the Fund ("Members") shall consist of those persons who shall at any given time be serving as members of the Board of Directors of the Fund and such other persons or entities meeting such qualifications for membership as the Board of Directors shall from time to time establish.

Paragraph 2. Annual Meeting.   The annual meeting of Members shall take place at such time as the Board of Directors or the President shall determine on the same date and at the same place as the annual organization meeting of the Board of Directors.

Paragraph 3. Special Meetings.   A special meeting of Members may be called at any time by the President or by five or more Directors. Special meetings shall be held at the principal office of the Fund or, in the case of a special meeting called by the President, at such place within or without the State of Louisiana as the President shall determine.

Paragraph 4. Regular Meetings.   Regular meetings of the Board of Directors shall be held at least quarterly, on such dates and at such times as the Board of Directors of the President shall determine. Regular meetings shall be held at the principal offices of the Fund or at such other place in Lafayette as the Board of Directors or the President shall determine. The purposes of regular meetings of the Board of Directors shall be to consider and act upon any matters which are proper subjects for action by the Board of Directors.

Paragraph 5. Special Meetings.   The President or any four other members of the Board of Directors may call a special meeting of the Board of Directors, to be held at any time at the principal offices of the Fund or, in the case of a meeting called by the President, at such other place in Louisiana as the President shall determine. Any special meeting may also be held through use of telephone or other communications equipment if all persons participating can hear each other. A special meeting may be held for any purpose which would be a proper purpose of a regular meeting.

Paragraph 6. Notice of Meetings.   Not less than five days before the date fixed for an annual organization or regular meeting, or two days in the case of a special meeting, written notice stating the date, time, place, and, in the case of a special meeting, the purpose of such meeting shall be given by and at the direction of the President or of the other person or persons calling the same. The notice shall be given by mail addressed to the members of the Board of Directors at their respective addresses as they appear on the records of the Fund.

Paragraph 7. Quorum.   A majority of the Directors then in office shall constitute a quorum for the transaction of business at any meeting of the Board of Directors. At each meeting of the Board of Directors, all questions and business shall be determined by a majority vote of those present and voting.

Paragraph 8. Waiver of Notice.   Notice of the time, place, and purposes of any meeting of the Board of Directors may be waived in writing either before or after the holding of the meeting. The attendance of any Director at any meeting (or participation in a meeting held through the use of telephone or other communications equipment) without protesting, prior to or at the commencement of the meeting, the lack of proper notice shall be deemed to be a waiver by the Director of notice of the meeting.

Paragraph 9. Action without a Meeting.   Any action which may be authorized or taken at a meeting of the Board of Directors may be authorized or taken without a meeting with the affirmative vote and approval of, and in a writing or writings signed by, at least two-thirds of the Directors, which writing or writings shall be filed with or entered upon the records of the Fund.

Vacancies of the Board of Directors caused by death, resignation, removal from office, or failure to continue to meet the qualifications for Directors, or any other cause other than the expiration of a term shall be filled by majority vote of the Directors then in office for the unexpired portion of the three-year term.

Any Director may at any time be removed from office for any cause deemed sufficient by the Board of Directors, by the affirmative vote of a majority of all Directors acting at a meeting of the Board of Directors.

No Director shall receive, directly or indirectly, any compensation for services as a Director. The Board of Directors may authorize reimbursement of reasonable expenses incurred by Directors in connection with carrying out the activities of the Fund.

SECTION II

Paragraph 1. Annual Organization Meeting. The annual organization meeting of the Board of Directors shall take place at such time and on such date during the month of February of each year at the principal offices of the Fund or at such other time, date, or place in Louisiana as the Board of Directors or the President shall determine. The purpose of the annual organization meeting shall be to elect the President and the other officers of the Fund, and to transact such other business as may properly come before the meeting.

SECTION III

Committees

Paragraph 1. Committees of the Board of Directors. The committees of the Board of Directors shall include an Executive Committee and may include such other committees as the Board of Directors may from time to time hereafter establish. Initially, the committee shall include an Organization Committee, a Finance Committee, a Program Committee, and a Communications Committee. The Executive Committee shall consist solely of members of the Board of Directors. Each other committee shall be chaired by a member of the Board of Directors that may include committee members who are not members of the Board of Directors. Each such committee shall serve at the pleasure of the Board of Directors and shall have such authority and shall perform such duties as the Board of Directors shall from time to time hereafter determine.

Paragraph 2. Executive Committee. The Executive Committee shall consist of the President, Vice President, or Vice Presidents, if any, the Secretary, the Treasurer, and two other members of the Board of Directors designated by the President. The President shall be the Chairman of the Executive Committee. The President or any two other members of the Executive Committee may call a meeting of the Executive Committee. The President or other persons calling the meeting shall give or cause to be given written notice to each member of the Executive Committee of the date, time, place, and purpose of the meeting at least two days before the scheduled meeting. Three members of the Executive Committee shall constitute a quorum for the transaction of business at any meeting thereof. The Executive Committee shall sit only in the intervals between meetings of the Board of Directors and shall, except to the extent otherwise provided herein or determined by the Board of Directors, have all authority of the Board of Directors other than the authority to fill vacancies in the Board of Directors. Subject to the aforesaid exceptions, any person dealing with the Fund shall be entitled to rely upon any act or authorization of an act by the Executive Committee to the same extent as an act or authorization of the Board of Directors. The Executive Committee shall keep full and complete records of all meetings and actions, which shall be reported to and open to inspection by the Board of Directors. At each meeting of the Executive Committee, all questions and business shall be determined by a majority vote of those present, or without a meeting by a writing or writings signed by all of its members.

Paragraph 3. Waiver of Notice.   Notice of the time, date, and purpose of any meeting of the Executive Committee may be waived in writing either before or after the holding of the meeting. The attendance of any Executive Committee member (or participation in a meeting held through the use of a telephone or other communications equipment) without protesting prior to or at the commencement of the meeting, the lack of proper notice shall be deemed to be a waiver by the Executive Committee member of notice of the meeting.

SECTION IV

Officers

Paragraph 1. Election and Designation of Officers.   The Board of Directors shall elect a President, a Secretary, and a Treasurer from among its members; may select an Executive Director who shall not be a member of the Board of Directors; and may elect such other officers as the Board of Directors may deem necessary or desirable, including one or more Vice Presidents (where order of election may be designated).

Paragraph 2. Term of Office; Vacancies.   The Officers of the Fund shall hold office until the next annual organization meeting of the Board of Directors and until their successors are elected, except in case of an officer's resignation, removal from office, or death. The Board of Directors may remove any officer at any time with or without cause by a majority vote of the Directors then in office. Any vacancy in any office may be filled by the Board of Directors.

Paragraph 3. President.   The President shall, subject to direction of the Board of Directors, have general supervision over the affairs of the Fund. He may execute all authorized deeds, mortgages, contracts, and other obligations in the name of the Fund and shall have such other authority and shall perform such other duties as may be determined by the Board of Directors. If an Executive Director is not selected, the President shall perform the duties of the Executive Director as outlined in Paragraph 7.

Paragraph 4. Vice Presidents.   A Vice President first elected shall have all the authority and perform all of the duties of the President in the absence of the President or when circumstances prevent the President from acting; the Vice President second elected shall have all such authority and perform all such duties in the absence of both the President and the Vice President first elected or when circumstances prevent both the President and the Vice President first elected from acting; and each

Vice President shall have such other authority and perform such other duties as may be determined by the Board of Directors.

Paragraph 5. Secretary. The Secretary shall keep the minutes of meetings of the Members, of the Board of Directors, and of the Executive Committee. The Secretary shall keep such books as may be required by the Board of Directors, shall give notices of the meetings of the Members and Board of Directors required by law, or by these bylaws, or otherwise, and shall have such authority and shall perform such other duties as may be determined by the Board of Directors.

Paragraph 6. Treasurer. The Treasurer shall cause to be kept, under the Treasurer's supervision, accurate financial accounts and shall hold the same open for inspection and examination by the Directors, shall prepare or cause to be prepared a full report concerning the finances of the Fund to be presented at each annual organization meeting of the Board of Directors, and shall have such authority and shall perform such other duties as may be determined by the Board of Directors.

Paragraph 7. Executive Director. The Executive Director shall be the chief executive officer of the Fund and, subject to the direction of the Board of Directors, shall have general supervision over the daily operations of the Fund. The Executive director shall also prepare or cause to be prepared the annual administrative budget of the Fund and shall have such other authority and perform such other duties as may be determined by the Board of Directors.

Paragraph 8. Other Officers. The other officers, if any, whom the Board of Directors may elect shall, respectively, have such authority and perform such duties as may be determined by the Board of Directors.

Paragraph 9. Delegation of Authority and Duties. The Board of Directors is authorized to delegate the authority and duties of any officer to any other officer and generally to control the action of the officers and to require the performance of duties in addition to those mentioned herein.

SECTION V

Indemnification

The Fund shall indemnify its Officers, Directors, and employees in accordance with and to the full extent allowed by R.S. 12:227.

SECTION VI

Amendments

The Bylaws of the Fund may be amended, or new bylaws may be adopted, by the Members at a meeting held for that purpose, by the affirmative vote of a majority of the Members present at a meeting at which a quorum of the Members is present, provided that notice of the general nature or subject matter of the alteration or amendment shall have been given in the notice of the meeting, or without a meeting, by the written consent of at least two-thirds of the Members.

Appendix C

SAMPLE LETTER FROM BOARD CHAIR TO TEACHERS

LAFAYETTE PUBLIC EDUCATION FUND
P.O. Drawer 51307, Lafayette, LA 70505-1307

March 1, 1994

Dear Principals of Lafayette Parish:

As President of the Lafayette Public Education Fund, I would like to invite you to review the Spring Mini-Grants for Teachers packet, which is attached. At least $10,000 in grants will be awarded in May of this school year, for implementation in the next school year.

To date, projects totaling more than $15,000 have added to the learning experience of more than 8,000 Lafayette Parish students in 25 of our schools. Perhaps we will count your students this year.

We hope you are all now familiar with LPEF's Mini-Grants for Teachers, and will support the grants with enthusiasm. If you feel you need more information, or have questions, please call our Executive Director for LPEF, or the Grants Committee Chairperson.

This will be the third grants cycle, and the program is flourishing, with over $200,000 in pledges and contributions to our endowment fund which will provide the revenues for these grants in the future. Your support and

Continued

the participation of your faculty is vital to the success of the LPEF. We are to assist you in providing resources for quality education, and look forward to receiving a number of applications from your teachers.

Please be sure to dispose of any prior year's application forms. All applications should read "Spring Mini-Grants for Teachers."

Please notify all of your faculty of this opportunity, and we hope to receive their outstanding ideas for learning in this spring's competition. Good luck and thank you for your assistance!

Sincerely,

President

Attachment

Appendix **D**

CRITERIA FOR JUDGMENT
OF PROPOSALS

LAFAYETTE PUBLIC EDUCATION FUND
P.O. Drawer 51307, Lafayette, LA 70505-1307

Application Rating Sheet*
Spring Minigrants for Teachers

Reviewer's Name: _____ Application No.: _____

Please evaluate each category by the criteria listed below. The following
numerical scores should be assigned in each category:

   4 = Excellent   3 = Good   2 = Fair   1 = Poor

CRITERIA:

- Goal   Is the goal of the project clearly defined?   _____

- Achievability Can the project be accomplished through
                the proposed plan? Are the objectives
                clearly stated? Are they realistic and
                worthwhile? Are the procedures to be
                followed clearly described? Are the
                methods, needed materials, resource per-
                sonnel, and project data specified?   _____

*NOTE: This page will not be in all application packets. This is for your records in the
principal and librarian packets.

Continued

- Creativity   Is the project innovative and/or stimulating
                   for students?   _____

- Student   Are students involved in the project as
  Involvement   directly as possible? Does the project have
                   promise of benefitting students in the school
                   in which it is conducted or Lafayette Parish
                   Public Schools in general?   _____

- Evaluation   Are the plans for evaluating the project
  Procedure   suited to the nature of the project?   _____

- Budget   Is the budget request reasonable and suffi-
                   ciently detailed?   _____

- Educational   Does the project enhance the learning expe-
  Value   rience of the students in an educationally
                   sound fashion?   _____

                              TOTAL (Maximum points)   28   _____

Comments:_____

_____

Appendix E

SUBMISSION INFORMATION

LAFAYETTE PUBLIC EDUCATION FUND

P.O. Drawer 51307, Lafayette, LA 70505-1307

Thank you for your interest in the Mini-Grant Program. Mini-grants are designed to reward the creative initiative of teachers and to invest private-sector monies in classroom projects that increase learning opportunities.

The Mini-Grant Program is made possible through the resources of the Lafayette Public Education Fund, a 501(c)(3) nonprofit corporation, whose activities are guided by a community board comprised of members of the business community, educators, and other community leaders. Its mission is to enhance the quality of public education by channeling available funds directly to the classroom for worthwhile projects to enable children to achieve their pull potential.

The information you include in the attached application form will provide the Mini-Grant Review Panel with the data it needs to make a judgment regarding the funding of your project.

Applications will be reviewed on a competitive basis, and a limited number of grants of up to $300 for an individual teacher and $600 for a team of teachers will be awarded. The deadline for **receipt** of this application is **Monday, May 6 at 4 P.M.**

Continued

If hand delivered, the application should be brought to: The Greater Lafayette Chamber of Commerce, 804 E. St. Mary Boulevard, Lafayette, LA.

To mail the application, address it to: Lafayette Public Education Fund, P.O. Drawer 51307, Lafayette, LA 70505-1307.

Grant recipients will be notified by phone **Tuesday, May 21.** The Awards Conference will be held **Friday, May 24.** Each project selected will be for implementation and completion during the school year. Grants must be expended within the schoolyear designated, or the grant returned to the Lafayette Public Education Fund. A written evaluation and statement of expenditures must be submitted when the project has been completed.

For further information contact: LPEF Executive Director or the LPEF Grants Committee.

Appendix F

GENERAL SPECIFICATIONS SHEET

LAFAYETTE PUBLIC EDUCATION FUND
P.O. Drawer 51307, Lafayette, LA 70505-1307

- **Who is eligible?** Any Lafayette Parish public school classroom or special education teacher, librarian, or guidance counselor directly involved in the instruction of children.

- **May I submit more than one application?** There is no limit to the number of applications per school nor per teacher; however, applications to the LPEF Mini-Grants Program may not be submitted simultaneously to other mini-grant programs.

- **How do I apply?** Fill out the LPEF Grant Application packet that includes the following parts, and return the correct number of copies of each part for panel review:

Statement of Support	one original
Summary Information Sheet	one original
Project Description (2 pages)	twelve copies
Funding Request Sheet	twelve copies

One additional typed page of information may be included, if necessary. Only official LPEF application forms will be accepted. *Note:* Application forms may be photocopied.

Continued

Please place the originals and all copies of the application in a large manila envelope labeled with the teacher's name and school.

- **What is the timetable?**

Friday	March 1	Distribution of grants information to schools
Monday	May 6	Deadline for receipt of applications to LPEF
Tuesday	May 21	Notification of successful grant recipients
Friday	May 24	Awards Conference—presentation of checks
Friday	May 31	Deadline for return of letter of agreement
	Next May	Completion of project; return evaluation and expense report

Grant monies **may not** be used to supplement the regular salaries of any school personnel employed by the Lafayette Parish School Board. Outside resource persons participating in the project may be eligible for honorariums or incurred expenses.

Grants are not limited to instructional schooltime implementation; however, grants must bear a direct relationship to the learning process for which the grant is developed.

Appendix G

SELECTION CRITERIA

LAFAYETTE PUBLIC EDUCATION FUND
P.O. Drawer 51307, Lafayette, LA 70505-1307

The Mini-Grant Review Panel includes: 1 retired principal; 1 retired teacher; 1 LPEF Board member; 1 USL representative; 5 business representatives; and 2 community representatives. The Executive Director of LPEF will coordinate the grants process, but will not serve as a voting member of the grants review panel.

Based upon panel review, one of three actions will be taken:

1. Approve application for funding,
2. Return application with suggestions for revision and resubmission, or
3. Grant will not be funded.

The LPEF grants program and the Acadiana Arts Council's Arts Grants for Teachers are similar in design. Arts related grants should be submitted to the Arts Council for primary funding. The two agencies cooperate in referring applications to the appropriate review panel. For more information, please call.

Continued

The grants review panel will evaluate each application using the following criteria:

- Is the goal of the proposed project clearly defined?
- Is the process clearly outlined? Is the project realistic and worthwhile?
- Are students involved in the project as directly as possible? Is the project designed to maximize student participation?
- Are the methods, needed materials, resource personnel, a tentative schedule, and completion date of the project specified?
- Are the plans for evaluating the project detailed and suited to the nature of project?
- Is the budget request reasonable and sufficiently detailed?
- Does the project have demonstrated educational value? Does it benefit either students in the school or the Lafayette Parish School system, or both?

Appendix H

PRINCIPAL'S STATEMENT
OF SUPPORT

LAFAYETTE PUBLIC EDUCATION FUND
P.O. Drawer 51307, Lafayette, LA 70505-1307

I have studied the following proposal and believe it is a valuable and appropriate undertaking for this school and the target audience. I affirm that it is my responsibility as teacher/administrator to oversee and assist in the successful completion of this project as described in the attached proposal, if funds are awarded.

I understand that grant monies are to be expended within the designated schoolyear as submitted in this application. I will do everything necessary to see that the full benefits of this project will be considered an integral part of the education mission of this school.

I understand that if my teaching assignment for the schoolyear is different from my present assignment, I will inform the LPEF immediately for approval to implement the project.

I will also cooperate and assist in the evaluation process so this project can be referred to for application in other settings within this school (and other schools) in the future.

Continued

By affixing my signature, I agree to these terms and certify the following:

1. This proposal has been developed according to the guidelines for the Lafayette Public Education Fund.
2. I grant to the Lafayette Parish School Board the right to use this proposal and the results in this project, if funded, for public information or to help other educators.

_____   _____
Teacher   Principal

_____   _____
Date   School

Appendix I

ADDITIONAL FORMS USED IN MINIGRANT PROCESS

LAFAYETTE PUBLIC EDUCATION FUND
P.O. Drawer 51307, Lafayette, LA 70505-1307

Spring Grant Cycle Summary Information Sheet

Date Submitted: _____

> (For Office Use Only)
> Date Received: _____
> By: _____
> Application Complete: _____

Individual Grant: _____   Team Grant: _____

Team Leader: _____   Address: _____

Grade/Position: _____   School: _____

Additional Teachers: _____   _____

_____   _____

Project Title: _____

Continued

Funding Requested from LPEF: _____

Summary of Proposal (Use only the space given)

_____   _____
Teacher   Principal

LAFAYETTE PUBLIC EDUCATION FUND

P.O. Drawer 51307, Lafayette, LA 70505-1307

Spring Grant Cycle Project Description

Applicant's Name: _____   School: _____

Project Title: _____

1. Describe your project. Describe WHAT this project will be, WHO will do it, WHAT resources and/or materials will be required, and WHERE project activities will take place.

2. What is the goal of your project? What objectives will you use to meet this goal and how do they enhance the curricula?

3. Why do you think there is a special need for this project? Please specify what needs or opportunities the project will address.

Continued

4. Approximately how many pupils will be affected by this project? Explain this number.

5. Give a general schedule of events from planning to project completion.

6. How will you evaluate whether the project objectives have been achieved and your goals accomplished?

7. What are the plans/possibilities for continuation of this project beyond the grant completion? How will this project infouence your classroom instruction and your school? If it is to continue after the grant expiration, how will it be funded, if applicable?

(Include 12 copies of the description with the proposal.)

LAFAYETTE PUBLIC EDUCATION FUND

P.O. Drawer 51307, Lafayette, LA 70505-1307

Spring Cycle Funding Request Sheet

Applicant's Name: _____   School: _____

Project Title: _____

Detail your budget request. Include specific information such as types of materials and equipment needed, sources of supply, and approximate cost. List all anticipated costs, including all revenue sources, such as matching funds, in-kind donations, and so on.

1. Request to LPEF

Cost Item Description	*Supplier*	*Dollar Amount*

Total LPEF Funding Request: _____

2. Other Revenue Sources Included in Project Cost

Cost Item Description	*Supplier/Funding Source*	*Dollar Amount*

Total Other Sources: _____

Total Budget for Project: _____

Appendix J

EVALUATION FORMS

LAFAYETTE PUBLIC EDUCATION FUND
P.O. Drawer 51307, Lafayette, LA 70505-1307

Grants Implementation for the Schoolyear

Name of School: _____

Project Name/Description: _____

Date(s) and duration of project: _____

Actual time involved in project (include preparation and volunteer time):

_____

Name of Project Teacher(s): _____

_____

Total Project Expenses: Number of Student Participants: _____

1. Were there any changes from the original grant proposal as submitted? If so, please explain.

Continued

2. In evaluating the project, what worked well and what improvements could be made?

3. Are you or your school planning a similar program for next year? If so, please explain.

4. Please add any comments or criticisms concerning this grant or the grants process.

Thank you for participating in the LPEF Grants Program. Please apply again soon! Complete this and the following form and return them at the completion of this project to: Lafayette Public Education Fund, P.O. Drawer 51307, Lafayette, LA 70505-1307.

LAFAYETTE PUBLIC EDUCATION FUND
P.O. Drawer 51307, Lafayette, LA 70505-1307

Expense Report

Project Title: _____

Length and Dates of Project: _____

Specifically, how was the grant award used? _____

_____

_____

Expenses	*Cost*
Personnel	_____
Supplies/Materials	_____
Equipment Rental/Purchase	_____
Travel	_____
Publicity/Promotion	_____
Printing	_____
Postage & Telephone	_____
Other (please specify)	_____
LPEF Subtotal:	_____
Other Funding:	_____
Total Expenditures:	_____

Name of Teacher(s) _____

_____

Date: _____

Appendix K

MINIGRANT APPLICATION FORMS

BRIDGEPORT PUBLIC EDUCATION FUND

280 State Street, Bridgeport, CT 06604

TO: Bridgeport Public School Principals and Parent Organization Presidents

FROM: Bridgeport Public Education Fund

RE: Parent/Community Involvement Grant Applications for the Schoolyear—**Deadline: November 1**

The Bridgeport Public Education Fund is pleased to be able to continue the Parent/Community Involvement Grant Program. This program was developed to encourage schools to develop parent or community projects that will enhance our children's education. Each school team may submit ONE proposal for a project that will strengthen or create a strong parent or community relationship with the school. Enclosed is a copy of "Grants for Parent & Community Involvement" which describes programs previously funded under this program.

Continued

General Guidelines

1. Proposals must be written by a team. (The team should include the principal, teachers, parents, the Adopt-A-School liaison or other appropriate individuals or community groups.)
2. Grants will be awarded for amounts up to $1,000 per school.
3. Funds may be used for projects that would not normally be part of the school budget.
4. Grants may be used to compensate experts hired to work with staff or parents but may not be used to compensate school personnel for work done during the regular schoolday.
5. It is hoped that the projects will take place before school ends in June.

Application deadline is November 1

Please call if you have any questions regarding the application process or deadline.

Good luck to you; we look forward to reviewing your projects.

BRIDGEPORT PUBLIC EDUCATION FUND
280 State Street, Bridgeport, CT 06604

Parent/Community Involvement Grant Program

INSTRUCTIONS: We ask that you use only the space provided. Do not attach any supplementary materials and please type your information.

1. Describe the special need or problem identified by your team and how your project will address this need.

_____

_____

_____

_____

_____

_____

_____

_____

2. What method will your team use to implement your project and how will you evaluate the results?

_____

_____

_____

_____

_____

_____

_____

_____

Continued

Parent/Community Involvement Grant Program – Page 2

3. Detail your budget request. It should not exceed $1,000.

Materials/Equipment/Services   Amount

_____ $_____

_____ $_____

_____ $_____

_____ $_____

_____ $_____

_____ $_____

TOTAL $_____

4. Personal Information

School Name _____

School Address _____

Number of Students _____   School Phone _____

Team Members (name & position) _____

_____

_____

Project Title _____   Budget Request _____

_____   _____
DATE   PRINCIPAL'S SIGNATURE

Please send applications to: Director, Bridgeport Public Education Fund, 280 State Street, Bridgeport, CT 06604

Deadine for submission of applications is **November 1**

BRIDGEPORT PUBLIC EDUCATION FUND
280 State Street, Bridgeport, CT 06604

TO: Bridgeport Public School Teachers, Administrators, and Supervisors

FROM: Director, Bridgeport Public Education Fund

RE: Mini-Grant Application for the Schoolyear—
Deadline: March 15

The Bridgeport Public Education Fund is delighted to offer, for the eighth year, the Mini-Grant Program. This Mini-Grant Program was developed to allow you to apply for outside funding for a specific classroom project that will nourish students' curiosity and motivation to learn. The Fund is specifically looking for project ideas that are creative and, if successful, can be replicated in other classrooms throughout the system. We invite you to explore creative ideas in the area of electricity or energy education that will be funded through a special grant to the Mini-Grant Program from United Illuminating. The third edition of "Mini-Grants for Teachers" is available for reference in your school or directly from the Fund office. Attached is the application form. Only this form will be accepted for evaluation. PLEASE TYPE and please do not include supplementary materials.

General Guidelines

- You may apply for up to $500 for your project.
- Low-priority items are software, fieldtrips and consumables.
- Funds may not be used for stipends for public school personnel.
- You will have the opportunity to discuss your project with a member of the Allocations Committee.
- Application deadline is **March 15.**
- Please call if you wish to discuss the application process.

Good luck to all of you; we look forward to reading your proposals.

BRIDGEPORT PUBLIC EDUCATION FUND

280 State Street, Bridgeport, CT 06604

Teachers, Administrators, and Supervisors Grant Program

INSTRUCTIONS: We ask that you use only the space provided. Do not attach any supplementary materials and please type your information.

1. Describe the special need or problem identified by you and how your project will address this need.

   _____

   _____

   _____

   _____

   _____

2. What method will you use to implement your project?

   _____

   _____

   _____

   _____

3. How will you evaluate the results?

   _____

   _____

   _____

   _____

   _____

Teachers, Administrators, and Supervisors Grant Program – Page 2

4. Detail your budget requests. It should not exceed $500.00.

    Materials/Equipment/Services   *Amount*

    _____ $_____

    _____ $_____

    _____ $_____

    _____ $_____

                                                    TOTAL $_____

5. Personal Information

    Name _____

    School Name & Address _____

    Position _____   Number of Students _____

    School Phone _____   Home Phone _____

    Project Title _____

    _____   _____
    DATE   SIGNATURE

Send applications to: Director, Bridgeport Public Education Fund, 280 State
Street, Bridgeport, CT 06604.

Deadline for submission of applications is **March 15**

Appendix L

GRANTS TO PRINCIPALS APPLICATION FORM

ALLEGHENY CONFERENCE EDUCATION FUND

600 Grant Street, Suite 4444, Pittsburgh, PA 15219

Building a schoolwide project

This application is for: _____ Principal's Grant
_____ Parent Involvement Grant

Note: Principals/Teams applying for two grants must submit a separate application for each request:

_____
Principal's Name   Home Address and Zip Code

_____
School Name # of Students in Building School Phone Number

_____
Program Manager, if other than principal Manager's Home Phone No.

_____
Program Manager's Home Address, City, and Zip Code

_____
Project Title   Budget Request

Continued

Grants to Principals Application Form – Page 2

One paragraph summary description:

By affixing my signature, I certify the following:

1. This proposal has been developed with the collaboration and support of the project team.
2. I grant to the ACEF the right to use this proposal and the results of this project, if funded, for public information purposes or to help other educators.

Date _____   _____
                                 Signature of Program Manager

Date _____   _____
                                 Signature of Principal

Forward Proposal by **April 4** to: Project Director, c/o Grants for Principals Program, Allegheny Conference, 600 Grant Street, Suite 4444, Pittsburgh, PA 15219.

Grants to Principals Application Form – Page 3

A. **NEED**

1. What school need, problem, or opportunity does the proposed project address? If applying for a Parent Involvement Grant, please discuss the obstacles to parent/school interaction that exist in your particular school. (The more specific your answer, and the more it applies to just *your* school, the better.)

2. Describe the pregrant process you followed in reaching this conclusion. Who was involved? Be certain to include names and titles of the project team members. Describe the process used to reach consensus.

B. **PROJECT DESCRIPTION**

3. What are your objectives? Include specific desired outcomes.

4. Describe the project activities you wish to undertake. Address *what* you will do, *who* will do it, and *where* project activities will take place. Include a time schedule conforming to the one-year time frame.

Continued

Grants to Principals Application Form – Page 4

C. **EVALUATION**

5. How will you determine whether the project has successfully met your objectives? Describe specific means of evaluation.

6. What will happen to the project at the conclusion of the grant? Will it continue to operate/influence the school? How will it be funded?

D. **HISTORY**

7. If you have implemented other projects in the past two years to address this need, please describe them, the funding, and your evaluation of the results.

E. **BUDGET REQUEST**

8. Detail your budget request. Organize the budget items according to the project activities. Include kinds of materials, services and equipment needed, sources of supply, and cost. Be specific. Payment for services to Pittsburgh Public School employees is prohibited.

Item	*Suppliers*	*Budget Amount*

Total Budget Request: $_____

(Transfer this amount to cover page)

F. Will you be using additional materials, labor, or dollars which will be devoted to this project (i.e., donations, volunteer labor, other grants, school funds)? If so, please describe.

Item	*Suppliers*	*Budget Amount*

Total Other Contributions: $_____

Total Budget to Accomplish Project: $_____

Appendix M

CASE STATEMENT
AND PROPOSALS

The Case for Supporting the Long Horn Educational
Foundation's Annual Campaign for Excellence

Education is truly the key to complete living. It is the mission of the Long Horn Educational Foundation to work closely with the staff and administration of the district to provide a climate of excellence that allows each student to reach his/her full potential. The Long Horn Independent School District is considered one of the best districts in the state of Texas. Its large and diverse staff is truly committed to assisting students to lead productive lives and to become good citizens of Long Horn City, Hereford County, and the state of Texas. The members of our foundation feel that there can be no higher cause than that of helping insure that our school district maintains its outstanding reputation for quality education. At a time when public education is facing severe criticism for poor student performance, the Long Horn Schools continue to be a beacon of light and a model for other districts in this state to follow.

Excellence cannot be achieved without cost. As a state-assisted public school, the Long Horn District has in place a basic curriculum that meets state and national guidelines, and is broad enough to provide a challenge for students who will be college bound and for those who will be seeking employment upon graduation from Long Horn High School. However, one critical difference between public schools that are very good and those that are excellent is that of the degree of public support that those considered excellent enjoy. To maintain our standards of excellence requires community support that enhances the

Continued

Case Statement   *continued*

regular academic curriculum. Specialized mini-course offerings in the sciences, the humanities, in computer programming, in art and music will not be possible unless the district receives the kind of support that allows the faculty to create these unique educational experiences.

The school district has a proven record of performance. More than seventy percent (70%) of the graduates of Long Horn High School were admitted to four-year colleges and universities last year. Students who do not elect to further their educations in four-year schools have little difficulty obtaining further technical or vocational training or obtaining a wide range of entry-level positions. The majority of the 30 percent of those who do not elect to enroll in colleges and universities, attend specialized programs at nearby community colleges, enter the work force, or become members of the armed services. A recent survey by the guidance department of Long Horn High School indicates that more than 90 percent of the graduates of last year's graduating class feels that the education they received in our school district has adequately prepared them for their present activities.

This year we are asking you once again to make an investment in a school district that would make any community proud. The Long Horn City Real Estate Association has noted that the major reason for the city's ability to attract new citizens is the reputation of the school system. Again that reputation has been forged by your generosity and your willingness to contribute the additional funds needed to insure that we remain on the cutting edge of what is new and good in education. This year the Long Horn City Mayor is serving as honorary chair of our campaign. The Mayor is joined by the League of Women Voters and the Civic Group Association in actively supporting our cause. Second State Bank, under the leadership of the former mayor recently announced a challenge grant of $25,000 that will be donated to the district if we reach our goal of $123,000!

Note: Most LEF groups have an annual campaign that seeks to raise unrestricted dollars for specialized academic programs such as the minigrants to teachers and the minigrants to principles programs. However, at some point, the school district and the LEF group may decide to focus the annual campaign on a project or projects that are either in addition to the minigrant program or are simply a project that the school district both needs and wants. The Educational Foundation of Williamston, MI, has developed more than 250 public-school foundations in 25 states since 1982. The following program proposals are examples of projects that were actually used in school districts across the country. Projects similar to these could be included as part of a written case statement provided to volunteers and other prospective donors. They are used with the permission of Educational Foundation Consultants.

Program Proposal

PROJECT: CREATION STATION

Introduction

_____Public Schools has continued to provide current, viable, and innovative experiences with enabling technologies. Various components of desktop media creation, hardware, software, and training exist throughout the district, but *all* are not present in any one location. As part of the middle school technology enhancement program, funds are being used to effectively incorporate these components for use by students to empower them at a critical point in their development.

Proposal Request

The development of computer-based tools for video production, publication, and artistic creation has blurred traditional curricular divisions. Applications in journalism, writing, fine arts, graphic arts, music, and other related areas require the integration of instructional objectives from many subject areas. Four creation stations, two at each middle school, will house a state-of-the-art microcomputer, mass storage, high-resolution display, color ink-jet printer, cassette recorders, and optical retrieval systems, which will provide creative and research opportunities for students in courses, extracurricular activities such as journalism and yearbook, and independent studies.

Benefits to Be Gained

This proposal will provide new instruction opportunities in a multitude of departmental areas. In addition, the community will have an opportunity to utilize this equipment through programs designed to support, distribute, and promote technology in the community. New and enhanced application will include: availability of equipment to support the writing process, new experiences in authoring music, a new tool to produce computer art, an expanded facility to meet the increasing needs of our journalism and yearbook programs in the area of desktop publishing, and a complete production station in one location.

Summary

The strength of the public schools' curriculum is the commitment of its staff to quality instruction aimed at carefully considered objectives. Support programs are in place to develop instruction lessons, implement new curricular objectives, train instructional staff, and provide ongoing support.

Estimated Cost

The estimated cost for this project is $25,000.

Program Proposal

PROJECT: ENHANCED COMMUNICATIONS

Introduction

_____Public Schools has continued to provide current, viable, and innovative experiences with enabling technologies. Communicating about these changes, as well as the day-to-day contacts regarding student progress and other school business, is a high priority. Fulfilling this communication commitment is difficult due to staff scheduling and equipment location. As part of our middle school technology enhancement program, funds are being used to effectively utilize telephone equipment and related technologies to aid in the instruction of students at a critical point in their development.

Proposal Request

Teachers have limited access to telephone services while in the classroom. Improving access to basic telephone equipment and developing a telephone management system is the objective of this proposal. In addition to place-ment of telephone sets and outside lines for critical home/school communi-cation, a messaging and information system would be created using the digitized voice telephone technologies that are currently available. This system would allow voice-mail messaging within the community, auto-mated telephone answering services, community information bulletin board services, and dial-and-deliver messaging.

Benefits to Be Gained

This proposal will provide new community communication opportunities. In addition, the community education will be enhanced through programs designed to support, distribute, and promote technology in the community. Community events, special projects, and even the daily activities of class-rooms will be accessible from any touchtone telephone set.

Summary

The strength of the public schools' curriculum is the commitment of its staff to quality instruction aimed at carefully considered objectives. Support programs are in place to develop instructional lessons, implement new curricular objectives, train instructional staff, and provide ongoing support. Communication with the community provides both important information about educational activities and support for school-based projects.

Estimated Cost

The estimated cost for this project is $7,000.

Program Proposal

PROJECT: VIDEO EDUCATION, A HOME/SCHOOL/ COMMUNITY CONNECTION

Introduction

_____Public Schools has continued to provide current, viable, and innovative experiences with enabling technologies. Videocassette recorders are nearly as widespread as the television itself. Nearly every block supports a video rental outlet. A wide range of educational programming exists. As part of the middle school technology enhancement program, funds are being used to effectively consolidate these components for use by students to empower them at a critical point in their development.

Proposal Request

The development and widespread distribution of video materials has increased the potential for providing independent learning opportunities. By providing access to educational videocassettes and inexpensive playback units where necessary, developing recommended viewing lists for distribution to video outlets, and distributing informational cassettes throughout the community, the middle schools hope to build a foundation for video education and community education.

Benefits to Be Gained

This proposal will provide new instructional opportunities. In addition, the community will have an opportunity to enhance video education through programs designed to support, distribute, and promote technology in the community.

Summary

The strength of the public school's curriculum is the commitment of its staff to quality instruction aimed at carefully considered objectives. Support programs are in place to develop instructional lessons, implement new curricular objectives, train instructional staff, and provide ongoing support.

Estimated Cost

The estimated cost for this project is $25,000.

Program Proposal

PROJECT: COMPUTER INTERFACING

Introduction

_____Public Schools has continued to provide current, viable, and innovative experiences with enabling technologies. New awareness of the world is a hallmark of the adolescent years. Sensors, probes, and interactive devices connected to existing computers provide opportunities for integrated learning approaches that were not possible even a few years ago. As part of our middle school technology enhancement program, funds are being used to effectively utilize these devices to empower and instruct students at a critical point in their development.

Proposal Request

Physical education, health, science, and industrial/technological education offer opportunities for the use of various computer-interfaced devices. These devices provide information about the environment that can be collected by and manipulated on the computer. Likewise, robotic devices offer opportunities to understand the impact of technology on the home and workplace. Funds will be used to build an inventory of devices that can be connected to existing computers and used in nearly all subject-area courses.

Benefits to Be Gained

This proposal will provide new instructional opportunities. In addition, the community education will be enhanced through programs designed to support, distribute, and promote technology in the community.

Summary

The schools' curriculum is the commitment of its staff to quality instruction aimed at carefully considered objectives. Support programs are in place to develop instructional lessons, implement new curricular objectives, train instructional staff, and provide ongoing support.

Estimated Cost

The estimated cost for this project is $10,000.

Program Proposal

PROJECT NAME: "SAFE HOMES" AND "TALKING WITH YOUR KIDS ABOUT ALCOHOL"

Introduction

Adolescent alcohol and other drug abuse is a major social problem that has significant impact on schools. To address this problem, the School District has initiated drug education at all levels plus PASS as prevention and early intervention programs. These programs would be most effective if the information students received through them were strongly reinforced by parents. Students need to receive firm and consistent messages about alcohol and other drug use from both the home and the school.

Proposal Request

It is appropriate to implement two programs in Troy designed for use with parents. The first program is *Safe Homes*. This is a nationally disseminated program that encourages parents to pledge not to allow unchaperoned parties in their homes or allow minors to consume alcohol or other drugs. The second program is *Talking with Your Kids about Alcohol (TWYKAA)*, a well-tested program that will add a parent-education component to the existing school-based programs. A description of TWYKAA and its effectiveness is attached. It was recognized in 1987 and 1988 as one of the top 20 exemplary prevention programs in the country.

Benefits to Be Gained

Both *Safe Homes* and *TWYKAA* are designed to generate a strong parental message that reinforces the drug education students receive in school. Through *Safe Homes*, parents develop a support network that sends a clear message to teenagers about acceptable behavior. *TWYKAA* teaches parents about the variables that determine appropriate alcohol-use levels, how to establish individual family expectations for alcohol use, and how to transmit these expectations without alienating children.

Summary

A combination of family-based alcohol and other drug abuse prevention efforts, such as *Safe Homes* and *TWYKAA*, and programs from the schools, the criminal justice system, and the community has a much higher probability of reducing the levels of adolescent alcohol and other drug use than any one program implemented in isolation.

Continued

Estimated Cost

The estimated cost of initiating *Safe Homes* is $2,000 to cover costs of printing and mailing materials and conducting a "kick-off" meeting. At a cost of $10,000 ($325 per participant), it is possible to train 30 *TWYKAA* facilitators. These facilitators, in turn, would disseminate the program to the entire Troy community. The cost of training includes teaching manuals, numerous transparencies, a program for promoting *TWYKAA* and ongoing support from the Prevention Research Institute in Lexington, Kentucky.

The total cost of initiating both programs is $12,000.

Program Proposal

PROJECT: ARTIST-IN-RESIDENCE

Introduction

For the last three years the Fine Arts Department has arranged for professional artists to come into our schools as enrichment to our ongoing arts programs. All groups require varying fees for their services. We have sponsored a visual artist, JoAnne Westerby ($500); the Lafayette String Quartet ($2,000); the National Shakespeare Co. ($4,400); the Attic Theatre ($3,500); creative dramatics, Beth D'zodin ($2,700); the Warren Symphony ($4,300); and most recently, Michigan Opera Theatre (approximately $10,500). In the past, fees for many of these groups have been subsidized by Oakland Schools. With the imminent retirement of our Oakland Schools' Fine Arts liaison that policy may change, and we must be prepared to be self-supporting.

Proposal Request

$20,000, annually designated as a cultural arts fund for support of these types of programs.

Benefits to Be Gained

The individual program evaluations illustrate and research shows that exposure to the arts at an early age benefits children. The humanizing features as well as the demonstration and participation in art forms that allow alternative communication skills can help our students develop creativity. Exposure to the arts can teach our students how to see and hear as well as read and write.

Summary

A civilization is remembered through its music, dance, drama, architecture, visual arts, and literature. We must do everything possible to be certain our students are arts literate and make a commitment to insure these types of arts residencies continue.

The school district is becoming a statewide leader in arts education due to the continuing commitment and support for the arts. Monies designated for cultural arts residencies reach not only our students, but also the community. The response has been overwhelmingly positive! The monies requested from the Educational Foundation will insure this fledgling program will continue.

Estimated Cost

The estimated cost for this project is $20,000 yearly.

Program Proposal

PROJECT: CAMPING PROGRAM

Introduction

A major concern for middle-school educators is developing programs for the increased number of young people who are considered "at-risk" students. Through grades, attendance, and/or family dynamics, early identification is possible. It is our responsibility to develop programs for early intervention to deal with these students who are not only "at-risk" but potential school dropouts. Camp Tamarack offers a camping program designed to benefit these "at-risk" children. Problem solving in the woods, rope courses that build group cooperation, and trust-building activities are but a few of the activities designed to boost a child's self-esteem and enhance their interpersonal skills. These programs will be facilitated by trained camp staff with support of Troy teachers. For many of these children, the opportunity to go to camp will be a new and positive experience.

Proposal Request

We will identify approximately 100 youngsters from four middle schools to participate in this program. We request that the Foundation for Educational Excellence sponsor a camping experience for "at-risk" middle-school students in the School District at Camp Tamarack.

Benefits to Be Gained

1. Opportunity for these young people to have an outdoor camping experience
2. Opportunity for these young people to go through a designed program to build trust, develop interpersonal skills, and enhance self-worth
3. Opportunity for students to spend time with Troy teachers and adults as positive role-model
4. Early identification and intervention program for "at-risk" students in the School District.
5. Camp Tamarack staff would work with School District personnel to make modifications and implement these modifications of their program so the unique needs of the students will be met.

Continued

Summary

The development of a program of early identification and intervention for "at-risk" students, combined with the development and success of a self-awareness camping program would be a positive step in the reduction of our potential dropout population. Students who feel positive about themselves and have self-worth are more likely to be successful in the classroom and in their relationships with family, students, and adults.

Estimated Cost

The estimated cost for this project is $10,500.

Program Proposal

PROJECT: CAD (COMPUTER-AIDED DESIGN) EQUIPMENT

Introduction

During the 1987–1988 schoolyear, vocational education was in the first year of the curriculum review plan. The dean of career education at Oakland Community College conducted the external audit of the program. He recommended that more computer support in the form of CAD (computer-aided design) be made available to students in the drafting program. Currently, there is one CAD station in the program.

Proposal Request

One CAD lab for the high school consisting of twelve student stations and one teacher station. Each station would consist of an IBM computer and monitor, digitizer, software, and table. The stations are to be serial cabled to a plotter. (See attachment for additional information.)

Benefits to Be Gained

The drafting program will be updated to include traditional on-the-board drawing as well as computer-aided design. Students would be better prepared to (1) seek employment; (2) continue their education in a related field; or (3) become eligible for better jobs (positions) within a company.

In addition, drawings will be down-loaded to Computer Numeric Control (CNC) equipment located in the Machine Manufacturing Technology program at the high school. Students will experience the cycle of developing and producing parts from the planning/drawing stage to the machining stage.

Enable the school district to become involved with partnerships within the business community to train or retrain employees when the equipment isn't used by students.

Summary

The school district is developing a "Tech-Prep" agreement with Oakland Community College in drafting. The agreement will be signed in May. The inclusion of CAD equipment will enhance our program and will become the impetus for a second agreement; specifically, CAD drafting.

Estimated Cost

The estimated cost for this project is $64,915.

Program Proposal

PROJECT: I-NET CABLE PROGRAM

Introduction

The school district has consistently been a front-runner in use of technology. With the advent of cable, new possibilities exist to utilize this communication tool to enhance our present delivery system and provide new opportunities as we enter the twenty-first century. As technology continues to emerge, we must remain current in order to provide our students with optimum opportunities.

Proposal Request

Funding to install I-NET cable capability in all school buildings to create an interactive network. This is the institutional level of hookup (as opposed to residential) with appropriate capacities for a districtwide system in conjunction with the Cable Company.

Benefits to Be Gained

Interactive instruction, staff development, and conferencing both inter- and intra-district; video, data, and information resources availability unlimited; staff efficiencies; monitoring energy maintenance; reduced insurance premiums from video surveillance/sensors; standardization of district publications and communications, administrative efficiencies in scheduling, memos, meetings.

Summary

This project has a districtwide benefit. It also has a long-term impact on our educational delivery system and allows us to move aggressively into the future.

Estimated Cost

The estimated cost for this project is $250,000.

Program Proposal

PROJECT: ADVANCED PLACEMENT PROGRAM

Introduction

Each year seniors have the opportunity to take an advanced placement exam which with past successes can result in the student receiving college/ university credit and can eliminate tuition costs. In some cases, students have a difficult time coming up with the money to take these advanced placement courses.

Proposal Request

This request is for the Foundation for Educational Excellence to support the advanced placement exam program by budgeting money that would pay for or defray the cost of taking advanced placement exams.

Benefits to Be Gained

As indicated, benefits would be that those students that successfully pass the exam would receive college credit on their college or university transcript. Furthermore, they would save the college tuition which, in some cases, in private schools can range up to $4,000.

Summary

We believe this project will assist us in promoting the advanced placement program in the school district. The fact that students would have the advanced placement test costs partially defrayed or paid for will result in not only helping those who are economically having problems, but will encourage more students to participate, which would greatly increase the enrollment in this program.

Estimated Cost

The estimated cost for this project is $33,000 (600 students @ $55.00 per test).

Program Proposal

PROJECT: MACINTOSH LAB

Introduction

The School District Board of Education, administration, and instructional staff have all worked hard to provide students with current, viable, and innovative computer experiences. Thousands of hours have been invested in the planning/development of these experiences and training staff on the effective application of such technologies. With a solid base of curriculum in technology, the district now faces several new frontiers in technology and education.

Proposal Request

The new technologies have provided an opportunity for cost-effective school applications in journalism, writing, fine arts, graphic arts, business, yearbook, and computer-aided design. These applications have become cost effective with the introduction of MC68000 processors, large disk storage, file servers, and laser printing technologies. A single, multidepartmental computer lab of this design would include: eight Macintosh Plus Systems, four Macintosh SE HD20 Systems, three Imagewriter Network printers, one LaserWriter IINT, one 40 MB networking fileserver, and the necessary computer software. The hardware will be installed in one of the district's two high schools.

Benefits to Be Gained

The true strength of this proposal is that it will provide new instructional opportunities in a multitude of departmental areas. In addition, the community will have an opportunity to utilize this equipment through our Adult & Community Education Department which is very interested in providing this access through its programs. New and enhanced applications will include: availability of equipment to support the writing process, new experiences in authoring music, a new tool to produce computer art, an expanded facility to meet the increasing needs of our journalism and yearbook programs in the area of desktop publishing, a lab to teach the concept of networking and business applications, plus a new opportunity to teach both two- and three-dimensional CAD.

Summary

The strength of the computing program is based on the commitment that we have made to carefully plan our technology applications, develop instructional lessons, implement new curricular applications, train instructional staff, and provide ongoing support.

Estimated Cost

The estimated cost for this project is $39,893.30.

Appendix N

GIFT SOLICITATION POLICY

LONG HORN EDUCATIONAL FOUNDATION

The Long Horn Educational Foundation gift solicitation policy is established to meet the following objectives:

1. to coordinate the approach(es) to prospective donors in order to prevent multiple requests to donors at the same time or at closely related times
2. to properly evaluate donor interests and ability to give in order to maximize potential gifts
3. to determine the most appropriate time for solicitation of gifts
4. to assure that all solicitation is in keeping with the priorities and goals of the University as determined by the board of directors of the Long Horn Independent School Board

Solicitation of businesses and individuals will be made in accordance with ethical business and fund-raising practices. Appeals to vendors and businesses with the potential for a future (or present) commercial relationship with the school district will be made in the spirit of philanthropy with no overt or implied promise of business or threat of withdrawal of business. Purchasing and development functions at our school district are, and shall remain, completely separate.

Bequests and Trusts

A bequest through a will is frequently a means of making a substantial gift to the school district. The drafting of a will is, of course, a task for the donor's attorney.

As a matter of general policy, any faculty or staff member contacted concerning a gift to school districts in the form of a bequest should contact the executive director of the foundation at the earliest possible date.

A trust is an arrangement where cash, securities, or other assets are transferred to a trustee to be held and managed for the trust's beneficiary.

Gifts through the establishment of a trust may be in several forms. For example, a testamentary trust may be established and administered as directed by the donor's will or a living trust or life income agreement may be administered in accordance with an agreement between the donor and the foundation. Under one type of trust agreement, the charitable remainder trust, a lifetime income can be provided to the donor and/or members of his or her family with the remainder going to benefit the Longhorn Educational Foundation upon the death of the lifetime income beneficiaries.

Gift Procession

Gifts from the private sector are a vital aspect in the continued growth and development of the Long Horn District. Careful processing by all involved in the solicitation of gifts from private sources can prevent strained relationships with our donors.

For advancement purposes, a *gift* is defined as any transfer of personal or real property made voluntarily.

The following procedures have been established for the orderly processing, acknowledging, and recording of gifts. The process is essential to insure that each donor receives a prompt and appropriate acknowledgment; all gifts are properly receipted and recorded; members of the Long Horn School District, administrators, faculty, foundations, and volunteers are kept fully informed; and a central record is maintained on all gifts. These procedures also have been established to handle more efficiently and expeditiously the flow of gifts to the designated recipient.

1. *Donor's name and address.* If the gift is from an entity other than an individual (i.e., corporation, foundation, association), an individual's name and title must be reported in addition to the firm's name.
2. *Amount of gift.*
3. *Date gift received.*
4. *Account number and name* in which gift is to be deposited. If a new account is to be established for the gift, provide account number and name of account.
5. *Designation.* State the program or activity to be funded.

6. *Purpose.* Indicate the purpose of the gift, such as scholarship, minigrant program, unrestricted, research, and so forth.
7. *Contact person's name and address.* If other than the donor is the contact person, this information is necessary.
8. *Other comments or special instructions.* Such information may be preference(s) of donor.

For each gift, one gift transmittal form is prepared and distributed to the executive director of the foundation, the Long Horn Foundation, and the contact person responsible for soliciting the gift. An acknowledgment and letter of appreciation are sent within three working days of receipt to each donor of $100.00 or more.

Matching Gifts

Numerous businesses and industrial firms offer matching gifts. In these programs, a donor may have her/his gift matched by an employer on a one-to-one, two-to-one, or three-to-one basis. Information or matching gift forms are available in the foundation office.

Gift Recording and Reports

Permanent records of all gifts are maintained in the foundation office. Gift receipts are prepared and filed in numerical sequence and each donor has a permanent donor card, which is filed alphabetically and serves as the central cumulative record of gifts. The correspondence that accompanies each gift is also filed alphabetically by donor's name.

All solicitations of support from private sources shall be cleared through, coordinated, and recorded by the executive directors of the Long Horn Educational Foundation. This includes alumni, parents, individuals (friends, corporations, including corporate and other foundations.

Protection of Donor Interests

No agreement shall be made between the Long Horn Independent School District and any person, agency, company, foundation, or organization which would knowingly jeopardize or compromise the donor's interest.

All information concerning a donor or prospective donor, including information derived from public sources in the course of donor research and donor giving history, shall be kept strictly confidential unless written permission is obtained from the donor to release such information.

Donated Securities

Upon receipt of a gift of donated securities, the executive directors of the Long Horn Educational Foundation shall notify the business manager (for school accounts). As soon as possible, all securities should be placed with a recognized broker with instructions to sell. Proceeds from the sale of such securities shall then be deposited in the appropriate account for management and/or disbursement.

Annual reports of all gifts from the private sector are prepared by the executive director of the foundation. The reports are submitted to the UNT Foundation, school board, and superintendent of schools on a regular basis.

If the acceptance of special gifts or gifts-in-kind is contemplated, or an inquiry concerning a gift of this nature is received, the executive director of the foundation should be contacted immediately. The need for independent appraisals and the tax consequences resulting from gifts-in-kind must be resolved prior to their acceptance. School district personnel should not place a monetary value on gifts-in-kind of equipment, machinery, art, and so forth.

Solicitation of Long Horn Alumni

The executive director of the foundation is charged with the responsibility of maintaining records on all Long Horn alumni.

Appendix O

SAMPLE LETTER

THE LONG HORN FUND
of the
LONG HORN EDUCATIONAL FOUNDATION
and the
LONG HORN INDEPENDENT SCHOOL DISTRICT

Dear Friends and Supporters of Long Horn Schools:

Long Horn Is Number One Again!

The superintendent of schools announced last week that the scores of Long Horn students on the Scholastic Aptitude Tests were among the highest in the state of Texas and were number one in the Dallas–Fort Worth Metroplex! Perhaps you have read reports of declining SAT scores across the United States, but there was no decline in the Long Horn District. In fact our students outperformed the national average by almost 10 points on the verbal section of the test and by almost 15 points on the math section. This is just one more indication of how hard our dedicated teaching staff is working to insure that our school system will remain one of the best in

Texas. A lot of the credit for our success can be given to you, the friends and supporters of Long Horn education. Last year you contributed more than $100,000 for special projects that were dedicated to the goal of excellence in academics. This year we have a goal of $125,000 to ensure that our quest for excellence continues. We are again asking for your generous support because:

> Our school district wants to continue our minigrant program that helps teachers provide special enrichment activities in science, math, English, and history.
>
> Our school district will continue to provide special seminars to help juniors and seniors prepare from the SAT and ACT tests.
>
> Every three dollars that you give generates another dollar from the Bank.
>
> Contributions from parents and friends will provide a powerful argument in our continuing efforts to seek funds from corporations and private foundations.

Last year, Long Horn High graduates and friends rose to the challenge! The number of contributors increased by more than 30%, and the amount increased by almost 40%! No other school district in the Dallas Metroplex can match the generosity and caring of our graduates.

We have a long way to go to reach our goal of $125,000, but donations from the Foundation, and the Computer company have provided a $30,000 head start. Will you please join us and your friends and help us meet and exceed our goals. Please pick up the enclosed envelope and return it now!

Appendix P

SAMPLE PHONE SCRIPT

LONG HORN INDEPENDENT SCHOOL DISTRICT
LONG HORN EDUCATIONAL FOUNDATION

INTRODUCTION:	HELLO! MAY IS SPEAK WITH M.____? HELLO, M. ____, THIS IS (your name) CALLING FOR THE LONG HORN SCHOOL DISTRICT EDUCATIONAL FOUNDATION. HOW ARE YOU THIS EVENING? I AM HERE WITH A GROUP OF PEOPLE CALLING GRADUATES OF LONG HORN HIGH ABOUT OUR ANNUAL FUND DRIVE.
LETTER:	DID YOU RECEIVE THE LETTER FROM FUND DIRECTOR? IT WAS ABOUT MY PHONE CALL TO YOU THIS EVENING.
IF YES:	GREAT, M____. WHAT DO YOU THINK OF THE EFFORT TO HELP OUR SCHOOL DISTRICT? (if positive, go directly to program goal)
IF NO:	M____, THAT IS PERFECTLY ALRIGHT, IT WAS JUST TO LET YOU KNOW I WOULD BE CALLING YOU THIS EVENING.
PROGRAM GOAL:	WE ARE LOOKING TO EVERY GRADUATE TO HELP US MEET OUR UNPRECEDENTED EFFORT TO RAISE $120,000. IN FACT, M____, AS A RESULT OF THIS CAMPAIGN, WE HOPE TO STRENGTHEN LONG HORN'S EMERGING POSITION AS ONE OF THE BEST SCHOOL DISTRICTS IN TEXAS!
FIRST ASK: $50.00 $25.00 These are used for examples only.	SOME ALUMNI ARE CONSIDERING A PLEDGE OF ($50.00–25.00 FOR THIS YEAR. HOW WOULD YOU FEEL ABOUT A PLEDGE ALONG THESE LINES? (if yes, thank and go to confirmation process)

Continued

SECOND ASK: $15.00	I CAN UNDERSTAND THAT, M____, NOT EVERYONE IS COMFORTABLE WITH THAT TYPE OF PLEDGE. BUT LET'S DISCUSS A SPECIFIC PLEDGE AMOUNT THAT MIGHT BE MORE APPROPRIATE FOR YOU. POSSIBLY A PLEDGE OF $15.00 THIS YEAR. HOW WOULD THAT SOUND TO YOU, M____? (if yes, thank and go to confirmation process)
THIRD ASK: $10.00	I CAN APPRECIATE THAT, M____, ONLY A FEW GRADUATES ARE ABLE TO GIVE AN AMOUNT LIKE THAT. COULD YOU CONSIDER A COMMITMENT OF, SAY, $10.00 THIS YEAR? (if yes, thank and go to confirmation process)
FOURTH ASK: $5.00	WELL, I CAN UNDERSTAND THAT, M____. HOWEVER, IT IS IMPORTANT TO OUR EFFORT THAT WE MAKE ALL OF OUR GRADUATES AWARE OF THE NEEDS OF THE CAMPAIGN AS WELL AS TELL THEM ABOUT THE OPPORTUNITIES FOR EXCELLENCE THAT THE DOLLARS WILL PROVIDE. BECAUSE THIS PROGRAM WILL HAVE A DRAMATIC IMPACT ON THE FUTURE OF OUR SCHOOL DISTRICT, HOW DOES A GIFT OF $5.00 SOUND TO YOU? (if yes, thank and go to confirmation process)

GO TO CONFIRMATION PROCESS

CONFIRMATION PROCESS

GIFT REVIEW:	THANK YOU VERY MUCH. WE ARE GRATEFUL FOR YOUR GENEROUS GIFT OF (amount). LET ME GO OVER THIS JUST TO BE CERTAIN I HAVE ALL THE CORRECT INFORMATION. YOUR CURRENT ADDRESS IS: (number, address, city, state, zip).
FIRST INSTALLMENT:	DO YOU THINK YOU COULD SEND YOUR GIFT WITHIN THE NEXT THREE WEEKS? GREAT, THEN WE WILL SEND YOU A RECEIPT AND A NOTE OF CONFIRMATION. IS THIS ALL CORRECT? (Pause, wait for response).
MATCHING GIFT:	AND M____, DO YOU HAPPEN TO KNOW IF THE COMPANY YOU WORK FOR HAS A MATCHING GIFT PROGRAM? WHERE IS IT THAT YOU ARE WORKING? I CAN CHECK MY LIST HERE TO SEE IF IT DOES. (pause and wait for response). (if yes:) ALL YOU NEED TO DO IS TO PICK UP A FORM FROM YOUR PERSONNEL OFFICE AND RETURN IT WITH YOUR GIFT. I'LL NOTE IT ON YOUR PLEDGE CARD AS A REMINDER.
FINAL CLOSING:	I'LL BE SENDING YOU A WRITTEN CONFIRMATION CARD WITH YOUR TOTAL GIFT OF ($total amount) NOTED ON IT. I HAVE MARKED YOUR GIFT TO GO TO THE CAMPAIGN—THE SCHOOL DISTRICTS MINIGRANT PROGRAM. ONCE AGAIN LET ME EXTEND MY SINCERE THANKS FOR YOUR GIFT TO OUR SCHOOL DISTRICT. I WILL MAKE SURE THAT DIRECTOR AND SUPERINTEN DENT ARE INFORMED ABOUT YOUR COMMITMENT. HAVE A NICE EVENING, GOODBYE!

Appendix Q

ACTIVE LISTENING SKILLS PRACTICE

Directions: Use a card or a piece of paper the width of this page. Place it so that it covers the response of the prospect. Read the message. Your job is to show empathy by reflecting the attitude, not necessarily the content, of what the donor has said. Reflection is a powerful clinical tool that helps an individual feel understood and helps clarify his or her thinking. After you have formulated your response, slide the card down to compare your response with that of a fund-raiser.

1. *Prospect:* I support the school district with my taxes.

   Fund-raiser: Um humm, you feel that your tax dollars should cover the activities of the school.

2. *Prospect:* Long Horn High seems to overemphasize the athletic program.

   Fund-raiser: I understand you see more attention being given to sports than to other areas of the school.

3. *Prospect:* I'm never sure how my gift will be used.

   Fund-raiser: You would like a better understanding of how the district will spend your gift dollars.

4. *Prospect:* I made a donation to the Long Horn Band.

   Fund-raiser: You feel that you have made your contribution for this year.

5. *Prospect:* If we're so good, how come more kids don't go to Harvard, and Yale?

   Fund-raiser: I understand. We say we are excellent, but you are wondering why more of our students are not accepted at Ivy League schools.

6. *Prospect:*   My wife and I give to other causes.

   Fund-raiser: I see. You have other areas that are a higher priority.

7. *Prospect:*   I can't afford to give to you and my college.

   Fund-raiser: I can see where this is a problem. You feel that you can't support all causes.

Appendix R

MAJOR DONOR FORMS

File Record

Name of prospect: _____

Prime associate

   1.

   2.

   3.

Manager of prospect: _____

Gift size and type: $_____   _____

Personal time spent in last 30 days:

   1. Office _____

   2. Phone _____

   3. Face-to-face with volunteer or with prospect _____

   4. Call report _____

Six-month Cultivation Plan

Name _____

L–Letter   T–Telephone
V–Visit   C–Campus Visit

Name																											

Potential Donor Contact Request

Potential donor _____

Title/organization _____

UNT connection _____

Address _____

_____ Phone _____ Zip _____

Purpose of visit _____

_____

Person making request _____ Date _____

Person making contact _____ Date _____

Today's date _____ Copies to _____

REPORT/RECOMMENDATIONS

Report _____

_____

_____

_____

Follow-up required (next 30 days) _____

_____

_____

_____

Future follow-up _____

_____

_____

Appendix S

GIFT-IN-KIND FORMS

Noncash Gift

Please follow the procedures below to enable the Office of Institutional Planning and Development to post and acknowledge a noncash gift.

1. Complete sections A and B of this form.
2. Get appropriate signatures as listed in Section C.
3. Send copy of form to the business manager.
4. Send original form, a copy of the appraisal, and any other relevant documentation of the director of the Long Horn Foundation.

* * *

Section A: Donor Identification

Name of donor _____ SS# _____
                                                    (required)

Address _____

City _____ State _____ Zip _____

Phone _____

Organization/Company   IRS Employer
(if applicable to gift)   Identification No.
                                        (required)

_____   _____

Continued

Noncash Gift – Page 2

Address _____

City _____ State _____ Zip _____

Donor's affiliation with organization/company _____

*   *   *

Section B: Gift Information

Description: (Use a second sheet or attachments, if necessary.)

_____

_____

_____

_____

Donor's estimated value: _____

For use by (school) _____

Benefit to Long Horn Independent Schools: _____

_____

_____

Expense to Long Horn Independent Schools: _____

Foundation contact: _____

*   *   *

Section C: Posting Authorization

1. Director of foundation _____

2. President of foundation's board _____

3. Business manager, Long Horn Independent
    School District _____

_____

Appendix T

FOUNDATION WORKSHEET

Outline Report

Name _____ Value score _____

Address _____ Phone _____

Contact _____ Title _____

Grant Information:

Fiscal Year _____

    Assets: _____

    Total amount of grant $_____ Total no. grants _____

    Average grant size: $_____

    Dollar range of grants: $_____ to $_____

    Amount of grants in our field: $_____ % of total: _____

    Number of grants in our field: $_____ % of total: _____

    Funding cycle: _____

    Restrictions: _____

Continued

Granting Pattern

   Subject focus:

   Current special interests: _____

   Geographical area of grants: _____

   Kinds of support given: _____

   _____

   Types of organizations funded: _____

   Sample grants in 19___: Amount:

   _____ $_____

   _____ $_____

   _____ $_____

   _____ $_____

Application Information

   Deadlines: _____

   Preferred initial contact: _____

   Information requested:

   Application procedures:

   Board meeting dates _____
   Funding cycle/time required to consider requests:

Appendix U

SAMPLE PROPOSAL PACKET

Cover Letter

Dear _____ :

For more than two decades, the Long Horn Independent School District has provided a quality education for all children of Hereford County.

The academic reputation of the school district is widely recognized throughout the Dallas–Fort Worth Metroplex and the entire state of Texas. During the past four years, the academic reputation of the district has been enhanced through its innovative Mini-grants to Teachers Program, a concept that involves financial support for teachers who create experiences of academic excellence for children.

The Long Horn Educational Foundation, a private 501(c)(3) organization dedicated solely to the support of Long Horn Schools has led efforts to raise funds for the mini-grants project for the past four years. This year our goal for the program is $123,000. However, student demand for the program indicates that we will need to add 10 more educational excellence activities to the 40 that we now sponsor.

The purpose of this proposal is to request a grant of twenty thousand dollars ($20,000) from the Foundation to assist us to expand our efforts.

Continued

Attached you will find a detailed description of our program. I hope that you will take this opportunity to join the members of the Long Horn Education Foundation, The Long Horn School Board, and a wide range of alumni, parents, and business, industry, and civic groups in helping insure that this district retains its well-deserving reputation for academic excellence.

Sincerely,

Chair
Long Horn Educational Foundation

Superintendent of Schools
Long Horn School System

Summary Statement for Proposal

The subject of this proposal is to request a grant of twenty thousand dollars ($20,000) from the Foundation to enable the Long Horn Education Foundation to expand the Mini-grant to Teachers Program of the Long Horn School District in order that at least 40 percent of the children in the district will be able to enroll in specialized programs of academic excellence during the current schoolyear.

The Long Horn School District has eight campuses, all located in the corporate limits of Long Horn City. All students residing in Hereford County attend Long Horn City Schools. The school system has a tradition of academic excellence as evidenced by the number of students who attend post-secondary schools and colleges and by the number of awards and honors the students and faculty receive each year.

The Mini-grants to Teachers Program has been in operation for four years and has attracted widespread support from alumni, parent, and business and industry. In fact, it is the popularity of this program that prompts our request to your foundation so that more children in the Long Horn City School System will be provided an opportunity to enroll in one or more programs of academic excellence.

A Proposal on Behalf of
the Long Horn School District

Introduction

The Long Horn Educational Foundation, located in Long Horn City and serving all of the children of Hereford County, is seeking a grant of $20,000 from the Foundation for the purpose of expanding our Mini-grant to Teachers Academic Excellence in Education Program. Approval of this request will enable up to 40 percent of the children in the Long Horn School District to enroll in activities that expand and enhance the regular school curriculum. The Foundation has a distinguished history of providing support for public education in Texas. We are confident that this request meets the guidelines of your foundation.

The Long Horn Independent School District has been a leader in providing quality education to children of Long Horn City and Hereford County for over two decades. At the end of the 1993–1994 schoolyear, graduates of our high school will number two thousand individuals. More than 65 percent of these graduates have continued their educations at quality colleges and universities in Texas and throughout the United States.

Although the Long Horn District is a tax-assisted public school system, it is dedicated to the goal of providing a quality education that will allow our graduates to compete favorably with graduates of private schools for entry-level positions in business and industry and for admission to competitive colleges and universities. While we are proud of our college placement record, we are equally pleased with the depth and scope of our vocational programs. More than 70 percent of those who do not elect to attend a four-year college or university enroll in vocational-technical programs throughout the state.

Our motto, "A quality education for all children," is not only an expression of our mission; it is a statement that also serves as a guide for our approach to teaching and learning. The Long Horn Independent School System sees failure in school as a failure of the school. Students who are not working up to their potential are viewed as challenges rather than problems. If a child does fail, our faculty view this as a signal for a change in our approaches to teaching him/her. Since our drop-out rate is less than 4%, we feel that our approach to learning is sound.

The Long Horn Independent School District is accredited by the Texas Education Agency and the Southern States Association. All faculty are fully certified by the Texas Education Agency. More than 65 percent of our professional staff holds master's degrees.

The Long Horn Independent School System is a success story:

- An independent survey conducted by the Long Horn Guidance Department revealed that the cumulative grade point average of all Long Horn High graduates currently attending college is 3.4.
- Five members of the Class of 1992 were National Merit Semifinalists. One was a National Merit finalist.
- Twenty-nine members of last year's graduating class received academic (non-need based) scholarships.
- Seven Long Horn High students won university Scholastic Awards in music, drama, journalism, and debate.
- A teacher in the Long Horn High School Mathematics Department was named "Teacher of the Year in Texas." He also placed third in the national competition for teacher of the year.
- Last year graduates of Long Horn High School, parents, and members of the business community in Long Horn City contributed more than $123,000 to support projects of academic excellence in the school district.

The Problem

The $123,000 raised by the Long Horn Educational Foundation last year supported 40 excellence projects in the Minigrants to Teachers Program. Of this number, 24 projects were in the elementary schools, 12 were in the district's two junior high schools, and 8 were at Long Horn High School.

In the Mini-grants to Teachers Program, a teacher or group of teachers are encouraged to submit proposals for funding support to the Long Horn Educational Foundation. Each program is judged by an independent panel for its creativity and for its potential for further enhancing the regular academic programs of the district. Projects that received support last year included "An Advanced Seminar in Computer Program Planning," "Preparing for College Placement Examinations," and "Guided Tours of Six State Museums." Projects of excellence that are not funded by tax dollars are given priority in determining those that will receive support.

Objectives

It is the objective of this proposal to increase the number of sponsored minigrant proposals in the Long Horn District from the present total of 10 to a total of 50 for the next academic year. A second objective is to provide enrichment programs for a minimum of 40 percent of the student body. Last year 32 percent of the student body was able to enroll in at least one excellence project.

Continued

Method

The Long Horn Educational Foundation is currently involved in its annual campaign to raise funds to support the Minigrants to Teachers Program. A challenge grant from the Gas and Electric Company of $25,000 provides strong motivation for others in the community to support this innovative program. Each member of the Long Horn Educational Foundation and the school board has made a pledge of at least $100.00. Pledges from the alumni, parents, faculty of the school district, and members of business and industry will help us reach our goal of $123,000. A grant from your foundation will enable us to increase the number of excellence activities by 10. The addition of 10 activities will increase the number of students involved by eight percent.

Evaluation

Each teacher application for a minigrant program must submit a detailed request for support. A key aspect of this request will be that of providing a plan for the evaluation of the project. At the termination of the project, each teacher must submit a written report that will indicate how each objective was met. All reports will be evaluated by the chair of the Long Horn Educational Foundation and the member of the foundation board. In addition, the school guidance department will survey all students involved in any of the projects and their parents to determine the degree of satisfaction with each excellence event. The results of the survey will be compiled and forwarded to the members of the foundation board.

Conclusion

The Long Horn Educational Foundation requests a grant of $20,000 from the Foundation to provide support for 10 additional excellence activities in the school district's Minigrants to Teachers Program. At present alumni, parents, and business and industry leaders in Long Horn City and Hereford County support 40 projects through contributions totaling $123,000. Approval of this one-time request would allow the district to expand the offerings to involve more students in a greater variety of activities.

Appendix V

OTHER USEFUL FORMS

Basics of Wills

A will is the final evidence of one's stewardship—the careful management of his or her assets.

A will is the basis of a deferred-gift program. The major portion, by far, of the endowment funds of universities has come from gifts made through wills.

All persons related to our school should be encouraged continually to include the district in their wills—especially board members, retired faculty and staff, and older ex-students.

The primary motive for making a gift by will is that most persons want to be remembered after death, and each of us wants to leave this world having done something to make it a little better. The establishment of a memorial for oneself or a loved one is an incentive for a bequest. there are also tax benefits because a bequest to our school is granted an *unlimited* federal Estate Tax deduction.

Of course, our school district would prefer immediate gifts, but in many cases a person is unwilling or unable to part with a substantial portion of income-producing assets during his or her lifetime. For example, a single person has only a modest estate, and wants to make a proportionate gift, but needs the income to meet regular expenses, and the corpus as a reserve to meet emergencies. A bequest is the answer.

Advantages of Deferred Gifts

1. Gifts of retained income many times make possible a much larger commitment than would be possible as an immediate, outright gift.

2. Compared to a gift by will, a retained-income gift has such advantages as:

   a. irrevocable
   b. certain, even if the estate is depleted
   c. minimal possibility of wills being contested
   d. avoidance of delay and expense of probate procedures
   e. encouragement of additional gifts

3. The availability of a deferred-gift program for potential donors in some cases will be helpful in working out a substantial gift.

Possibilities for a Deferred-Gift Prospect

1. An interest in our school
2. Age 65 or older
3. Single person
4. Married persons with no children
5. Married persons who have provided amply for their children
6. Persons who have a parent for whom they provide financial support
7. Minimum assets of $100,000
8. Assets include highly appreciated but low income-producing property
9. A wealthy person whose principal asset is stock in a closely held business. At death, the business interest will be sold under a buy-and-sell agreement, and liquid funds will then be available. A bequest of a portion of the sale proceeds is the answer.
10. Persons who take pride and joy in working their money and assets often are reluctant to part with a substantial portion of their "stake" during their lifetimes. A bequest is the answer.

In any case the person's desire to make a gift must be present! Once this is determined, the form of the gift (immediate or deferred) can be discussed along with the tax implications and other advantages of the various vehicles for gifts.

Living Trust

THE STATE OF
COUNTY OF

I, _____, of the County of _____, State of _____

do give, grant, transfer, assign, and convey to the Board of _____

_____, as trustees, irrevocably and forever for the use and

benefit of (our school), the following described property: _____

_____

_____1_____

This trust shall be called the _____ Fund.

The _____2_____ of this trust shall be used _____.
If the purpose of this trust becomes impracticable, or if by reason of changed
conditions its further execution becomes unnecessary or unwise in the judgment
of the trustees, such trustees, acting by a majority vote, may designate another
purpose which they may deem more appropriate under the circumstances, and
the purpose so designated shall thereupon become the purpose of this trust.

The trustees shall have the following powers in addition to powers and authority
granted by law:

a. The trustees are empowered to administer this trust in accordance with
   such uniform rules and regulations as they may from time to time adopt
   regardless of whether said rules and regulations contain a specific
   reference to this trust.
b. The trustees shall have full and complete power and authority to
   determine and allocate income and other receipts as well as expenses
   between principal and income.
c. To the extent that any such requirements can be legally waived, the
   trustees shall never be required to give any bond as trustees.
d. The trustees may retain any property or undivided interests in property
   regardless of nonproductivity, risk or lack of diversification.
e. The trustees may hold, manage, control, exchange, lease, sell, alienate,
   mortgage, invest and reinvest the trust estate in any property or undivided
   interest in property, including common trust funds, without being
   limited by any statute or rule of law concerning investments by trustees.
   the trustees are specifically empowered to transfer or sell assets to
   common trust funds in return for cash, other assets or participations in
   such funds.

Continued

The trustees, in the administration of this trust, shall be liable only for their own gross negligence or willful misconduct.

The legislature shall not have power or be in anywise authorized to change the purpose of this trust or any fund or property arising therefrom, or to divert such trust, fund, or property from the purposes herein.

Witness my hand this _____ day of _____, A.D. 19 ____.

_____
Signature

_____

1. Insert the following if realty is being conveyed by this instrument: "To have and to hold the above described premises, together with all and singular the rights and appurtenances thereunto in anywise belonging unto the said grantees, their successors, and assigns forever."
2. Stipulate net income or principal and income.

Contingent Bequests

_____1_____ I give, devise and bequeath to _____

_____ Foundation _____2_____

that portion of my estate which would, except for this provision, pass by intestate

succession.

---

1. Wording such as the following may be inserted: "It has been my fond desire to show my love for _____, as well as my concern for higher education, by leaving a bequest to _____, but the persons named in this will have a greater call on my resources. I recognize, however, the frailty of human life and the possibility of devisees predeceasing me causing all or part of my estate to pass by intestate succession; therefore . . ."
2. If nothing is added here, the bequest would be expended or used wherever in the school the need was the greatest. On the other hand, the bequest could be limited to a particular unit of the university or to a particular purpose.

Continued

Gifts of Personal Property[1]

Gentlemen:[2]

We hereby give, transfer, assign, and convey all of our right, title, and interest in and to the below-described property to (school) _____ 3 _____.
This gift is irrevocable and without reservation.

The property referred to above is as follows:

_____

_____

_____.

Please indicate on your records that this is a gift from:

Name: _____ 4 _____

Address: _____

Sincerely,

---

1. This form is suitable for use when the donated property itself is to be used (book, art objects, etc.) as well as when the donated property is to be used to produce funds for expenditure.
2. See discussion of addressee under Gift Letters.
3. If the donated property itself is to be used, the donor may wish to designate the place of use. If the property is to be used to produce funds for expenditure, see section on Purpose.
4. This allows us to carry the donor's name and address on our records in the exact manner desired.

Library Memorial Gifts[1]

Gentlemen:[2]

Please use my enclosed gift of $_____3_____ for the purchase of a book or

books for the school library in memory of _____4_____.

Please send a memorial card to:

     Name: _____5_____

     Address: _____

               _____

Please indicate on your records that this is a gift from:

     Name: _____6_____

     Address: _____

               _____

                           Sincerely,

---

1. Specially prepared Library Memorial Fund Gift Forms may be used instead of the letter. They are available upon request.
2. See discussion of addressee under Gift Letter.
3. Please make checks payable to Educational Foundation. Books are memorialized at the rate of *one* book for each *$10.00* donated.
4. The following may be inserted at the donor's option: "I prefer that the books purchased be in the field of _____."
5. Usually this is the next-of-kin of the person being memorialized.
6. This allows us to carry the donor's name and address on our gift records in the exact manner desired.

REFERENCES

Allegheny Conference on Community Development. (No date). *Small grants for teachers: A handbook.* Pittsburgh: Public Education Fund Network, 600 Grand Street (Nancy Bunt, Project Director).

Allegheny Conference Education Fund. (1988). *Grants for principals: Building a schoolwide project.* Pittsburgh: Allegheny Conference Education Fund.

Boston Plan for Excellence in the Public Schools. (1990). Annual report. Boston: Boston School Department (12 School Street, Boston, MA 02116).

Biles, F. R. (1987). Working with volunteers in institutional leadership. Presentation at the Williamsburg Development Institute, Williamsburg, VA (June).

Brackley, G. A. (1980). *Tested ways of successful fund-raising.* New York: AMAC Publishing.

Brose, T. C. (1987). Foundation fund-raising. Presentation at the Williamsburg Development Institute. Williamsburg, VA (June).

Cargill & Associates. (1992). Capital campaigns. Class presentation to the University of North Texas Program for Management in Nonprofits, Dallas, TX (April).

Carter, V. L. (1978). The ABC's of raising money by mail. In V. L. Carter (Ed.), *Annual fund ideas.* Washington, DC: Council for Advancement and Support of Education.

Cellis, W. (1991). Schools starting their own foundations. *The New York Times,* October 16 (reprint, no page number).

Chattanooga Educational Foundation. (1989–91). Report of the public education foundation (compiled by Steven Prigohzy). Chattanooga, TN: The Foundation. Available from Public Education Fund, Suite 10, Market Court, Chattanooga, TN 37400.

Council for Advancement and Support of Education (CASE) Workshop. (1985). Writing winning proposals (mimeo). Washington, DC: The Association (Suite 400, Dupont Circle).

Craig, D. (1987). How to close the gift (mimeo). Presentation at CASE Conference on Major Donors, San Diego, CA (December 1).

Denver Public Schools. (1990). *Innovation* (Annual Report). Denver, CO.

Dodds, D. R. (1991). Dialing for members. CASE *Currents,* xvii: 39–40.

Dunlop, D. (1991). Concepts from major gift fund-raising. Presentation at DataTel Executive Development Seminar. Los Colinas, TX (March 13–14).

Funkhouser, P. (1991). Personal communication.

Gary Educational Development Foundation, Inc. (1975–1990). Fifteenth anniversary booklet. Gary, IA.

Gayley, H. (1981). *How to write for development.* Washington, DC: Council for Advancement and Support of Education.

Goldman, L. (1991). Personal communication.

Goldman, R. T. (1985). Attracting foundation grants: Six steps to success. Presentation to CASE Summer Institute on Fund Raising. Hanover, NH (July).

Goldman, R. T. (1985). Direct mail and fund raising. Presentation to CASE Summer Institute on Fund Raising, Hanover, NH (July).

Grand Rapids Public Education Fund. (1981). *Partnership Newsletter,* 1: 7. Grand Rapids, MI.

Gunnin, G. (1991). Major gifts. Presentation at the Seventh Annual Southwest Fund Raising Symposium. Arlington, TX (March).

Gunning, R. (1968). *The technique of clear writing.* New York: McGraw-Hill.

Haskins, S. C. (1989). By hook or crook. CASE *Currents,* 15(4): 29–32.

Huntsinger, J. (1989). *Fund raising letters. A comprehensive study guide to raising money by direct response marketing,* 3d ed. Richman, VA: Emerson.

Kirtz, N. J. (1980). *Program planning and proposal writing.* New York: The Grantsmanship Center.

Lant, J. (1990). *Development today.* Cambridge, MA: JLA Publications.

Lefferts, R. (1982). *Getting a grant.* Englewood Cliffs, NJ: Prentice-Hall.

Lord, J. G. (1985). *The raising of money.* Cleveland, OH: Third Sector Press.

Lynn Business Education Foundation. (1989). A partnership between Lynn schools and Lynn business. Lynn, MA: The Foundation.

Metropolitan Area Committee and New Orleans Public Schools. (No date). STEP. Available from Partners in Education Program, The Metropolitan Area Committee Education Fund, 1148 TNBC Building, 210 Baronne Street, New Orleans, LA.

Muro, J. J. (1992). A survey of private foundations operating in public schools of America. Unpublished manuscript.

Nash, S. H. (1991). Direct mail. Presentation at the Seventh Annual Fund Raising Symposium of the Dallas–Fort Worth Chapter of NSFRE, Arlington, TX.

New York City Alliance for the Public Schools. (n.d.). Going public: Public relations guide for the public schools (33 Washington Place, New York, NY).

Oklahoma State Department of Education. (No date). Oklahoma School Foundations (mimeo). Oklahoma City, OK.

Pacific Telemarketing Group, Inc. (1986). An introduction to fund raising by telephone (200 Pine Avenue, Suite 503, Long Beach, CA 90802).

PEFNet. (No date). *The local education fund: A handbook.* Allegheny Conference on Community Development. Pittsburgh, PA. Now available from Public Education Fund Network, 601 Thirteenth Street, NW, Suite 370 South, Washington, DC.

Pray, F. (Ed.) (1981). *Handbook for educational fund raising.* Washington, DC: Jossey-Bass.

Public Education Coalition. (1990). Annual report. Denver, CO.

Public Schools of Hawaii Foundation. (No date). Education is everybody's business. Honolulu, HI.

Public Education Foundation. (1986–1991). Report to the Public Education Foundation. Chattanooga, TN.

Race, L. (1988). Divide and conquer. CASE *Currents,* XIV: 5, 22, 24, 25.

Radcock, M. (1990). Words to the wise. Foundation executive comments on the most frequent errors made in grant proposals. *NSFRE Journal,* (Winter): 10–23.

Ryan, E. (1991). On the phone again. CASE *Currents,* XVII: 28–30.

Snelling, B. W. (1985). How to enlist and motivate volunteers (mimeo). Presentation at CASE Summer Institute on Fund Raising. Hanover, NH (July).

Taft Group. (1990). *Corporate giving: Who spends most and for what* (5125 MacArthur Boulevard, Washington, DC 20016).

Utley, R., and Waldrop, K. (1991). Special events. Presentation at the Seventh Annual Southwest Fund Raising Symposium. Arlington, TX (March).

Wahlstrom, C. J. (1989). Small miracles. CASE *Currents,* XV: 4, 30–33.

Young, J. (1989). *Fund raising for nonprofit groups.* Bellingham, WA: Self-Counsel Press.

INDEX